D0879361

www.wadsworth.com

www.wadsworth.com is the World Wide Web site for Thomson Wadsworth and is your direct source to dozens of online resources.

At *www.wadsworth.com* you can find out about supplements, demonstration software, and student resources. You can also send e-mail to many of our authors and preview new publications and exciting new technologies.

www.wadsworth.com
Changing the way the world learns®

Founding Principles
of the
United States

Volume I Reader

Steven Bullock
University of Nebraska at Omaha

Carson Holloway
University of Nebraska at Omaha

EDITORS

THOMSON

™

WADSWORTH

Australia • Brazil • Canada • Mexico • Singapore
Spain • United Kingdom • United States

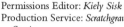

THOMSON

™

WADSWORTH

Founding Principles of the United States, Volume I Reader
Steven Bullock and Carson Holloway

Publisher: *Clark Baxter*
Acquisitions Editor: *Ashley Dodge*
Associate Development Editor: *Julie Yardley*
Editorial Assistant: *Lucinda Bingham*
Technology Project Manager: *Dave Lionetti*
Marketing Manager: *Lori Grebe Cook*
Marketing Assistant: *Teresa Jessen*
Marketing Communications Manager:
  Laurel Anderson
Senior Project Manager, Editorial Production:
  Kimberly Adams
Executive Art Director: *Maria Epes*

Print Buyer: *Rebecca Cross*
Permissions Editor: *Kiely Sisk*
Production Service: *Scratchgravel Publishing
  Services*
Copy Editor: *Mary Anne Shahidi*
Cover Designer: *Lisa Devenish*
Cover Image: *Patrick Henry addressing the Virginia
  Assembly/Art Resource, NY*
Cover Printer: *Malloy Incorporated*
Compositor: *Cadmus Professional Communications*
Printer: *Malloy Incorporated*

For more information about our products,
contact us at:
**Thomson Learning Academic
Resource Center
1-800-423-0563**

For permission to use material from this text
or product, submit a request online at
http://www.thomsonrights.com.

Any additional questions about
permissions can be submitted by email to
thomsonrights@thomson.com.

Library of Congress Control Number:
2005923111

ISBN 0-495-03001-5

**Thomson Higher Education
10 Davis Drive
Belmont, CA 94002-3098
USA**

Asia (including India)
Thomson Learning
5 Shenton Way
#01-01 UIC Building
Singapore 068808

Australia/New Zealand
Thomson Learning Australia
102 Dodds Street
Southbank, Victoria 3006
Australia

Canada
Thomson Nelson
1120 Birchmount Road
Toronto, Ontario M1K 5G4
Canada

UK/Europe/Middle East/Africa
Thomson Learning
High Holborn House
50–51 Bedford Row
London WC1R 4LR
United Kingdom

Latin America
Thomson Learning
Seneca, 53
Colonia Polanco
11560 Mexico
D.F. Mexico

Spain (including Portugal)
Thomson Paraninfo
Calle Magallanes, 25
28015 Madrid, Spain

Brief Contents

PREFACE   xiii

INTRODUCTION TO VOLUME I   xv

Chapter 1   Equality   1

Chapter 2   Virtue   32

Chapter 3   Religion   62

Chapter 4   Education   88

Chapter 5   Republican Government   117

Chapter 6   Limited Government   146

Chapter 7   Economic Liberty   178

INDEX   208

Contents

PREFACE   xiii

INTRODUCTION TO VOLUME I   xv

CHAPTER 1 Equality   1

1 Acts Passed in the Virginia House of Burgesses Pertaining to Slavery   1

2 Thomas Jefferson: The Declaration of Independence (1776)   3

3 Thomas Paine: *Common Sense* (1776)   4

4 Benjamin Franklin: Letter to Sarah Franklin Bache (1784)   5

5 Statement by Massachusetts Yeomen Opposing the Constitution (1788)   6

6 Thomas Jefferson: Letter to John Adams (1813)   8

7 John Adams to Thomas Jefferson (1813)   9

8 James Madison: *Federalist* No. 54 (1788)   10

9 Judith Sargent Murray: On the Equality of the Sexes (1790)   12

10 John C. Calhoun: Speech in the Senate on the Oregon Bill (1848)   14

11 Daniel Webster: Speech to the United States Senate on Slavery (1850)   15

12 Stephen Douglas: Speech on Slavery and the Founding (1858)   19

13 Abraham Lincoln: Speech on Slavery and the Founding (1858)   20

14 Abraham Lincoln: Speech on the Kansas–Nebraska Act (1854)   21

15 Alexis de Tocqueville: *Democracy in America* (1840)   23

16 Elizabeth Cady Stanton: The Seneca Falls Declaration (1848)   26

17 Statement to the People of the State of South Carolina
     by the Colored State Convention (1865)   28

Discussion Questions for Chapter 1   31

CHAPTER 2 Virtue   32

 1 William Penn: Letter to His Children (1682)   32

 2 Benjamin Franklin: *Autobiography* (1771)   34

 3 Samuel Adams: Letter in the *Boston Gazette* (1772)   35

 4 Samuel Langdon: A Government Corrupted by Vice and Recovered
     by Righteousness (1775)   36

 5 Thomas Paine: *The American Crisis* (1780)   39

 6 Benjamin Franklin: Dangers of a Salaried Bureaucracy (1787)   40

 7 George Washington: Inaugural Address (1789)   42

 8 George Washington: Farewell Address (1796)   42

 9 Thomas Jefferson: Letter to His Grandson,
     Thomas Jefferson Randolph (1808)   43

10 Lyman Beecher: *Six Sermons on Intemperance* (1828)   45

11 Abraham Lincoln: Address to the Washington Temperance Society
     in Springfield, Illinois (1842)   47

12 William A. Alcott: *The Young Wife* (1838)   50

13 "Friend of Virtue": "The Just Treatment of Licentious Men.
     Addressed to Christian Mothers, Wives, Sisters, and
     Daughters" (1838)   52

14 Susan B. Anthony: Speech on Social Purity (1875)   53

15 Alexis de Tocqueville: *Democracy in America* (1840)   56

16 William Ellery Channing: On the Elevation of the Laboring Classes
     (1840)   58

Discussion Questions for Chapter 2   61

CHAPTER 3 Religion   62

 1 John Winthrop: Excerpt from "A Model of Christian Charity"
     (1630)   62

 2 John Adams: An Excerpt from His Diary (1756)   64

3 Benjamin Franklin: Reasons Against Satirizing Religion (1757) 65

4 Benjamin Franklin: An Excerpt from His *Autobiography* (1771) 66

5 James Madison: Letter to Thomas Jefferson (1787) 67

6 James Madison: Excerpts from the Memorial and Remonstrance (1785) 67

7 A Bill for Establishing Religious Freedom (1786) 70

8 George Washington: Thanksgiving Proclamation (1789) 72

9 George Washington: An Excerpt from the Farewell Address (1796) 73

10 George Washington: Letter to Hebrew Congregation at Newport (1790) 74

11 Thomas Jefferson: Letter to the Danbury Baptist Association (1802) 75

12 Thomas Jefferson: Letter to Rev. Samuel Miller (1808) 75

13 Mercy Otis Warren: An Excerpt from *History of the Rise, Progress, and Termination of the American Revolution* (1805) 76

14 Justice Joseph Story: An Excerpt from the *Commentaries on the Constitution of the United States* (1833) 79

15 Alexis de Tocqueville: *Democracy in America* (1835) 81

16 Abraham Lincoln: Message to the Voters of the Seventh Congressional District (1846) 83

17 Abraham Lincoln: Farewell Address at Springfield (1861) 84

18 Abraham Lincoln: Proclamation of Thanksgiving (1863) 85

19 Abraham Lincoln: An Excerpt from the Second Inaugural Address (1865) 86

Discussion Questions for Chapter 3 87

CHAPTER 4 Education 88

1 Thomas Shephard: Letter to His Son at Harvard College (1637) 88

2 Regulations at Yale College (1745) 90

3 Benjamin Franklin: *Proposals Relating to the Education of Youth in Pennsylvania* (1749) 93

4 The Alphabet in the New England Primer (1777) 95

5 Thomas Jefferson: *Notes on the State of Virginia* (1781) 96

6 George Washington: Letter to George Chapman (1784) 98

7 Noah Webster: *On the Education of Youth in America* (1788)   99

8 Benjamin Rush: Of the Mode of Education Proper in a Republic (1798)   102

9 Thomas Jefferson: Letter to Nathaniel Burwell (1818)   104

10 Emma Willard: *Improving Female Education* (1819)   105

11 Catharine Beecher: *Suggestions Respecting Improvements in Education* (1829)   108

12 The Massachusetts Compulsory School Attendance Act (1836)   110

13 Horace Mann: *Tenth Annual Report of the Secretary of the Massachusetts State Board of Education* (1846)   111

14 Morrill Act (1862)   113

15 *Harper's Weekly* Editorial: "An Undoubted Right" (1874)   115

Discussion Questions for Chapter 4   115

CHAPTER 5 Republican Government   117

1 An Excerpt from the Declaration and Resolves of the Continental Congress (1774)   117

2 Alexander Hamilton: An Excerpt from "The Farmer Refuted" (1775)   118

3 Jonathan Boucher: An Excerpt from *A View of the Causes and Consequences of the American Revolution* (1775)   119

4 Sam Adams: An Excerpt from a Letter to Noah Webster (1784)   120

5 James Madison: Excerpts from *Federalist* 10 (1787)   121

6 Robert Yates: An Excerpt from *Brutus* 1 (1787)   124

7 Samuel Bryan: An Excerpt from *Centinel* 1 (1787)   127

8 James Madison: An Excerpt from *Federalist* 39 (1788)   128

9 Alexander Hamilton: An Excerpt from *Federalist* 71 (1788)   130

10 James Madison: An Excerpt from *Federalist* 52 (1788)   131

11 Chancellor James Kent: Speech to the New York State Constitutional Convention (1821)   132

12 David Buel: Speech to the New York State Constitutional Convention (1821)   134

13 Alexis de Tocqueville: *Democracy in America* (1835)   136

14 Alexis de Tocqueville: *Democracy in America* (1835)   138

15 Senator William Stewart: Speech in Favor of the Fifteenth Amendment (1869)   140

16 Senator James Dixon: Speech Against the Fifteenth Amendment (1869)   141

17 Senator Willard Warner: Speech on the Fifteenth Amendment (1869)   143

Discussion Questions for Chapter 5   144

CHAPTER 6 Limited Government   146

1 John Locke: An Excerpt from the *Second Treatise of Civil Government* (1690)   146

2 An Excerpt from "An Old Whig No. 2" (1787)   147

3 James Madison: An Excerpt from *Federalist* 44 (1788)   148

4 James Madison: An Excerpt from *Federalist* 39 (1788)   150

5 Robert Yates: An Excerpt from *Brutus* 1 (1787)   151

6 Robert Yates: An Excerpt from *Brutus* 2 (1787)   152

7 Alexander Hamilton: An Excerpt from *Federalist* 84 (1788)   155

8 James Madison: The Virginia Resolutions (1798)   157

9 Rhode Island's Response to the Virginia Resolutions (1799)   158

10 Chief Justice John Marshall: Opinion of the Court in *Marbury* v. *Madison* (1803)   159

11 Chief Justice John Marshall: Opinion of the Court in *McCulloch* v. *Maryland* (1819)   161

12 Chief Justice John Marshall: Opinion of the Court in *Barron* v. *Baltimore* (1833)   165

13 South Carolina Declaration of the Causes of Secession (1860)   167

14 Abraham Lincoln: An Excerpt from the Message to Congress in Special Session (1861)   169

15 Justice David Davis: Opinion of the Court in *Ex Parte Milligan* (1866)   171

16 Chief Justice Salmon P. Chase: Concurring Opinion in *Ex Parte Milligan* (1866)   174

Discussion Questions for Chapter 6   176

CHAPTER 7 Economic Liberty   178

1 Gabriel Thomas: An Account of West Jersey and Pennsylvania (1698)   178

2 John Dickinson: Letter from a Farmer (1767)   179

3 William Manning: Observations on Shays' Rebellion (1799)   181

4 Thomas Jefferson: Notes on the State of Virginia (1784)   183

5 Alexander Hamilton: Report on Manufactures (1791)   184

6 Alexander Hamilton: Remarks on the Constitutionality of the First National Bank of the United States (1791)   185

7 Thomas Jefferson: Views on the First National Bank of the United States (1791)   187

8 Andrew Jackson: Veto Message Regarding the Bank of the United States (1832)   189

9 Daniel Webster: A Reply to Jackson's Veto (1832)   191

10 John Quincy Adams: State of the Union Message (1825)   193

11 Henry Clay: A Defense of the American System (1832)   195

12 John C. Calhoun: Speech Against the Force Bill (1833)   197

13 The Bylaws for the Philadelphia and California Enterprise Association (1849)   200

14 Homestead Act (1862)   202

15 California Anti-Chinese Immigration Law (1862)   204

Discussion Questions for Chapter 7   206

INDEX   208

Preface

By the time of the American Revolution, the Founding Fathers of the United States had already begun the task of forming a new nation that would be, to them, a beacon for others to follow. Even before the battles of Lexington and Concord, Enlightenment thought had permeated most of Western society and was beginning to influence the manner in which individuals perceived the world. The musings of Locke, Montesquieu, and Voltaire held tremendous sway over the intellectuals of Europe, though the rigid hierarchical and monarchical structures of most of those societies did not lend themselves to the adoption of Enlightenment ideals.

However, the American Founding Fathers, most of whom were intellectual descendants of Enlightenment thought in Europe, were not saddled with many of the same traditional constraints as found across the Atlantic. If one examines the writings and speeches of early American leaders or even the major documents of the founding era, a shocking consistency can be noted: virtually nothing new or unique can be found there. For example, Thomas Jefferson borrowed heavily from, among others, John Locke, in penning the Declaration of Independence, and James Madison framed the Constitution with Montesquieu's *Spirit of Laws* as his guide. The United States, however, *was* the first nation founded on basic Enlightenment ideals. Although intellectuals in France, Scotland, and Germany quibbled over the details of theories and philosophic ambiguities, their American counterparts were intent on forming a nation that would place into practice what had been debated over the course of previous centuries.

Fast forward to September 11, 2001, when the United States endured harrowing terrorist attacks on symbols of American economic prosperity and military might that caused many to evaluate the exact nature of American citizenship. As days and months passed after the attack, questions arose, such as: "Why do the terrorists hate us so much?" Such inquiries subsequently led to heated debate about terrorism, the role of the United States in a global community, and, most importantly, the fundamental values of American society. Thus, these books have been compiled with the purpose of identifying the founding principles of the United States and illuminating the evolution of those principles since the American Revolution. The seven principles that are examined in each volume include: equality, virtue, religion, education, republican government, limited government, and economic liberty.

These principles are not intended to be comprehensive but instead focus on the essential components that the editors believe have most profoundly impacted the development of American society.

Acknowledgments

We would like to thank the following reviewers for their valuable input:

Leslie M. Alexander, The Ohio State University

Lesley J. Gordon, University of Akron, Ohio

Murray A. Rubinstein, Baruch College–The City University of New York

Sean Taylor, Minnesota State University, Moorhead

William Benton Whisenhunt, College of Dupage

Introduction to Volume I

From the time of the founding of the United States to the end of Reconstruction, America's founding principles evolved significantly due to a variety of cultural, political, and economic factors. The vast geographic expansion of the United States, the continual friction regarding slavery, and the ultimate outbreak of the Civil War all impacted perceptions about the fundamental direction of America's founding ideals.

Chapter 1: Equality

As defined by the Founding Fathers, equality specifically referred to equality of opportunity, or what Thomas Jefferson termed a "natural aristocracy." Although initially this type of ideal was imperfectly applied exclusively to white men, the first 100 years of America's existence was largely characterized by a gradual journey toward establishing an equitable meritocracy. The readings in this chapter highlight the conflicts and resolutions relating to issues such as eliminating hereditary connections to political power, the elimination of slavery, and the empowerment of women.

Chapter 2: Virtue

The elements of virtue were clearly defined and understood by the Founding Fathers and earlier generations of Americans as relating to temperance, prudence, justice, and fortitude, as well as sacrificing self-interest for the benefit of the multitudes. Although, through the immediate aftermath of the Civil War, most Americans still embraced ideals such as temperance and fortitude, the self-interest component of virtue, as evidenced by the readings in this chapter, became less apparent.

Chapter 3: Religion

Chapter 3 illustrates the religious motives of the first European settlers in America and also the understanding of many of the founders that religion was necessary for the preservation of a free and orderly society. Also represented, however, is the view of some that religion can be a threat to social peace and individual liberty, as well as the early American understanding of the importance of religious liberty. Other selections show the popular understanding of religion's role in a republican government and the belief that America is under God's watchful providence.

Chapter 4: Education

As a founding principle, education was a virtual unanimous point of agreement among those of the founding era and beyond. However, as the readings in this chapter detail, substantial differences were evident in the exact nature of the envisioned educational systems promoted by different individuals. Religion, practicality, and the inclusion of women were all important elements relating to education, as was the increasing democratization of education as the nineteenth century progressed.

Chapter 5: Republican Government

Chapter 5 considers the American commitment to republican government, or government based on the people. The readings trace the founders' initial confidence that republican institutions would protect the rights of all and their subsequent disillusionment and resolution to create constitutional structures that would both embody republicanism and control its worst excesses. Other readings in the chapter illustrate the founders' grappling with the definition of the right to vote, their reasons both for using and later abandoning property qualifications, and Tocqueville's account of the political consequences of universal suffrage. The chapter concludes with a series of readings showing the debate over the attempt to extend the right to vote to the newly freed slaves.

Chapter 6: Limited Government

Several readings in this chapter illustrate the debates over the meaning of, necessity of, and development of constitutional principles intended to contain government power, such as the notion of a federal government of limited powers, the role of the states in our system of Federalism, and the use of a Bill of Rights to protect individual liberties. The chapter concludes with some selections intended to illuminate the difficulties of adhering to limited government during a national crisis like the Civil War.

Chapter 7: Economic Liberty

Arguably the most influential of the founding principles—if not the most inspirational—the right of individuals to acquire and maintain property at a level that would allow for economic independence was an essential component to Revolutionary Era thought. As indicated in the readings in this chapter, from the founding of the United States through the nineteenth century, this quest for economic liberty manifested itself in a variety of ways, including rural development, urban expansion, and the promotion of the market economy.

CHAPTER 1

Equality

1

Acts Passed in the Virginia House of Burgesses Pertaining to Slavery

The Virginia House of Burgesses, founded in 1619, was the first legislative body organized by British Americans in the colonies and was always a tool for the powerful elite of Virginia. By the latter half of the seventeenth century plantation owners' growing dependence on slavery necessitated increasing numbers of laws and regulations by the House of Burgesses addressing slavery and the complexities that arose with the institution. Chattel slavery, as understood by American slaveholders during the eighteenth and nineteenth centuries, had not yet evolved to the point at which distinctions of race and the rights associated with such were clear and immutable. As indicated in the following, Virginians had difficulty reconciling the claim that African Americans could be property in one situation, yet a free citizen with the full spectrum of natural rights in another. Thus, as can be seen in the four readings that follow, the House of Burgesses defines African Americans as maintaining a status somewhere between property and free citizen—a common theme that will emerge later in the chapter as well.

THE STATUS OF CHILDREN
OF MIXED BLOOD (1662)

Whereas some doubts have arisen whether children got by any Englishman upon a negro woman should be slave or free, *Be it therefore enacted and declared by this present grand assembly,* that all children borne in this country shall be held bond or free only according to the condition of the mother, *And* that if any Christian shall commit fornication with a negro man or woman, he or she so offending shall pay double the fines imposed by the former act.

DECLARING BAPTISM DOES NOT GUARANTEE FREEDOM FOR SLAVES (1667)

Whereas some doubts have risen whether children that are slaves by birth, and by the charity and piety of their owners made partakers of the blessed sacrament of baptism, should by virtue of their baptism be made free; *It is enacted and declared by this grand assembly, and the authority thereof,* that the conferring of baptism doth not alter the condition of the person as to his bondage or freedom; that diverse masters, freed from this doubt, may more carefully endeavor the propagation of Christianity by permitting children, though slaves, or those of growth if capable to be admitted to that sacrament.

THE MURDER OF SLAVES (1669)

Whereas the only law in force for the punishment of refractory servants (*a*) resisting their master, mistress or overseer cannot be inflicted upon negroes, nor the obstinacy of many of them by other then violent means suppressed, *Be it enacted and declared by this grand assembly,* if any slave resist his master (or other by his master's order correcting him) and by the extremity of the correction should chance to die, that his death shall not be [a] felony, but the master (or that other person appointed by the master to punish him) be acquit from molestation, since it cannot be presumed that [premeditated] malice (which alone makes murder felony) should induce any man to destroy his own estate.

PROHIBITION AGAINST AFRICAN AMERICANS AND NATIVE AMERICANS FROM PURCHASING CHRISTIAN SLAVES (1670)

Whereas it hath been questioned whither Indians or negroes manumitted, or otherwise free, could be capable of purchasing Christian servants, *It is enacted* that no negro or Indian though baptized and enjoined their own freedom shall be capable of any such purchase of Christians, but yet not debarred from buying any of their own nation.

2

Thomas Jefferson: The Declaration of Independence (1776)

The seminal document of the American Revolution was arguably the clearest and most definitive statement regarding the intellectual direction of the new American nation. The Declaration was meant not only to inform but also to inspire, and although Jefferson was the primary author of the document, he included little original material in it. The famous Virginian instead borrowed heavily from earlier thinkers such as John Locke, who compiled similar ruminations as those found in the first two paragraphs of the Declaration. However, the most notable aspect of the Declaration of Independence was not in its novelty, but in the fact that it was an announcement to the world of the founding of the first nation anywhere in the world based on natural rights and Enlightenment principles.

When in the Course of human events, it becomes necessary for one people to dissolve the political bands which have connected them with another, and to assume among the powers of the earth, the separate and equal station to which the Laws of Nature and of Nature's God entitle them, a decent respect to the opinions of mankind requires that they should declare the causes which impel them to the separation.

We hold these truths to be self-evident, that all men are created equal, that they are endowed by their Creator with certain unalienable Rights, that among these are Life, Liberty and the pursuit of Happiness. —That to secure these rights, Governments are instituted among Men, deriving their just powers from the consent of the governed, —That whenever any Form of Government becomes destructive of these ends, it is the Right of the People to alter or to abolish it, and to institute new Government, laying its foundation on such principles and organizing its powers in such form, as to them shall seem most likely to effect their Safety and Happiness. Prudence, indeed, will dictate that Governments long established should not be changed for light and transient causes; and accordingly all experience hath shewn, that mankind are more disposed to suffer, while evils are sufferable, than to right themselves by abolishing the forms to which they are accustomed. But when a long train of abuses and usurpations, pursuing invariably the same Object evinces a design to reduce them under absolute Despotism, it is their right, it is their duty, to throw off such Government, and to provide new Guards for their future security. —Such has been the patient sufferance of these Colonies; and such is now the necessity which constrains them to alter their former Systems of Government. . . .

3

Thomas Paine: *Common Sense* (1776)

Thomas Paine was one of the most vocal and ardent revolutionaries of his era. He was remarkably progressive and modern in his outlook, even advocating the full equality of women and the elimination of slavery at a time when such positions were not often well received. Paine was also the author of the influential pamphlet Common Sense, *written in an accessible vernacular, which encapsulated American ideological thought at the time of the Revolution and inspired many to oppose British authority in the colonies. In the excerpt that follows, Paine specifically attacks the prevalence of hereditary connections to power that was the foundation of British society.*

. . . Mankind being originally equals in the order of creation, the equality could only be destroyed by some subsequent circumstance; the distinctions of rich, and poor, may in a great measure be accounted for, and that without having recourse to the harsh, ill-sounding names of oppression and avarice. Oppression is often the consequence, but seldom or never the means of riches; and though avarice will preserve a man from being necessitously poor, it generally makes him too timorous to be wealthy.

But there is another and greater distinction for which no truly natural or religious reason can be assigned, and that is, the distinction of men into KINGS and SUBJECTS. Male and female are the distinctions of nature, good and bad the distinctions of heaven; but how a race of men came into the world so exalted above the rest, and distinguished like some new species, is worth enquiring into, and whether they are the means of happiness or of misery to mankind.

To the evil of monarchy we have added that of hereditary succession; and as the first is a degradation and lessening of ourselves, so the second, claimed as a matter of right, is an insult and an imposition on posterity. For all men being originally equals, no one by birth could have a right to set up his own family in perpetual preference to all others for ever, and though himself might deserve some decent degree of honors of his contemporaries, yet his descendants might be far too unworthy to inherit them. One of the strongest natural proofs of the folly of hereditary right in kings, is, that nature disapproves it, otherwise she would not so frequently turn it into ridicule by giving mankind an ass for a lion.

This is supposing the present race of kings in the world to have had an honorable origin; whereas it is more than probable, that could we take off the dark covering of antiquity, and trace them to their first rise, that we should find the first of them nothing better than the principal ruffian of some restless gang, whose savage manners of preeminence in subtlety obtained him the title of chief among plunderers; and who by increasing in power, and extending his depredations, overawed the quiet and defenseless to purchase their safety by frequent contributions. Yet his electors could have no idea of giving hereditary right to his descendants, because such a perpetual exclusion of themselves was incompatible with the free and unrestrained principles they professed to live by. Wherefore, hereditary succession in the early ages of monarchy could not take place as a matter of claim, but as something casual or complemental; but as few or no records were extant in those days, and traditionary history stuffed with fables, it was very easy, after the lapse of a few generations, to trump up some superstitious tale, conveniently timed, Mahomet like, to cram hereditary right down the throats of the vulgar. Perhaps the disorders which threatened, or seemed to threaten on the decease of a leader and the choice of a new one (for elections among ruffians could not be very orderly) induced many at first to favor hereditary pretensions; by which means it happened, as it hath happened since, that what at first was submitted to as a convenience, was afterwards claimed as a right. The nearer any government approaches to a republic the less business there is for a king. . . .

4

Benjamin Franklin: Letter to Sarah Franklin Bache (1784)

Rising from obscurity to one of the most respected men in American history, Benjamin Franklin held strong opinions against hereditary connections to power and authority then prevalent in the Western world. Writing the following letter to his daughter at a time when the permanence of the American nation was tenuous at best, Franklin attacks the Society of Cincinnati—a fraternal organization of Revolutionary War officers formed after the American Revolution that incorporated family ties as a determinant for future membership in the organization.

Your Care in sending me the Newspapers is very agreeable to me. I received by Capt. Barney those relating to the *Cincinnati*. My Opinion of the Institution cannot be of much Importance; I only wonder that, when the united Wisdom of our Nation had, in the Articles of Confederation, manifested their Dislike of establishing Ranks of Nobility, by Authority either of the Congress or of any particular State, a Number of private Persons should think proper to distinguish themselves and their Posterity, from their fellow Citizens, and form an Order of *hereditary Knights,* in direct Opposition to the solemnly declared Sense of their Country! I imagine it must be likewise contrary to the Good Sense of most of those drawn into it by the Persuasion of its Projectors, who have been too much struck with the Ribbands and Crosses they have seen among them hanging to the Buttonholes of Foreign Officers. And I suppose those, who disapprove of it, have not hitherto given it much Opposition, from a Principle somewhat like that of your good Mother, relating to punctilious Persons, who are always exacting little Observances of Respect; that, *"if People can be pleased with small Matters, it is a pity but they should have them."*

... I hope, therefore, that the Order will drop this part of their project, and content themselves, as the Knights of the Garter, Bath, Thistle, St. Louis, and other Orders of Europe do, with a Life Enjoyment of their little Badge and Ribband, and let the Distinction die with those who have merited it. This I imagine will give no offence. For my own part, I shall think it a Convenience, when I go into a Company where there may be Faces unknown to me, if I discover, by this Badge, the Persons who merit some particular Expression of my Respect; and it will save modest Virtue the Trouble of calling for our Regard, by awkward round-about Intimations of having been heretofore employ'd in the Continental Service.

5

Statement by Massachusetts Yeomen Opposing the Constitution (1788)

The framing of the Constitution and the subsequent debates that arose from its structure, wording, and omissions led to a variety of strong arguments both in favor and opposition to the document. At the time, the majority of American leaders did not embrace the concept of democracy, and the Constitution moved the country away from state and local control and more toward centralization. In the following letter, published shortly before the ratification of the Constitution, a number of Massachusetts commoners complain about the potential of elevating the few above the many and offers a warning for those who might want to create an American aristocracy.

... When we see the adherents to this constitution chiefly made up of civil and ecclesiastical gown men, and their dependents, the expedient they have hit upon is not likely to have the intended effect. There are many men destitute of eloquence, yet they can see and hear—They can think and judge, and are therefore not likely to be wheedled out of their senses by the sophistical reasonings of all the advocates for this new constitution in the country combined. We know this is not true; and as we well know the design of such representations, we would have those gentlemen know, that it will not take. They must pull upon some other string, or they must fail. Another thing they tell us, that the constitution must be good, from the characters which composed the Convention that framed it. It is graced with the names of a Washington and a Franklin. Illustrious names, we allow—worthy characters in civil society. Yet we cannot suppose them, to be infallible guides, neither yet that a man must necessarily incur guilt to himself merely by dissenting from them in opinion.

We cannot think the noble general [Washington], has the same ideas with ourselves, with regard to the rules of right and wrong. We cannot think, he acts a very consistent part, or did through the whole of the contest with Great Britain: who, notwithstanding he wielded the sword in defence of American liberty, yet at the same time was, and is to this day, living upon the labours of several hundreds of miserable Africans, as free born as himself; and some of them very likely descended from parents who, in point of property and dignity in their own country, might cope with any man in America. We do not conceive we are to be overborne by the weight of any names, however revered. "ALL MEN ARE BORN FREE AND EQUAL"; if so, every man hath a natural and unalienable right to his own opinion, and, for asserting this right, ought not to be stigmatized with the epithets of tenacious and dogmatical. If we were to pin our faith on any sleeves but our own (without derogating in the least from the merit of any one of the Massachusetts delegates in the federal convention) we should be as likely to pin it on the sleeve of the hon. mr. [Elbridge] Gerry as any one of them. But we mean to see with our own eyes, and thus seeing to act for ourselves. In this view, as a tribute due from us to that hon. gentleman, we must acknowledge his tenderness, his care for the preservation of the liberties of the people, and his desire on all occasions to preserve them from invasion. This hon. gentleman was one who assisted in rearing the pillars of a republican government, he has ever since aided in the support of them, and thus hath acted a much more consistent part than those his brethren, who, after all the expense and fatigue of rearing the building, are now for razing the foundations, destroying instead of repairing the frame, and erecting another, which by no means can answer the good purpose of sheltering the people from storms. But, to lay aside the metaphor—

This gentleman is much more consistent, than those who are for turning our republican government into a hateful aristocracy. And we must think it very dishonourable in the aristocratical party, to treat the worthy gentleman, in the manner they have done in the public papers. We can assure them it has been far from helping their cause. We do not wish to tire the public, but would hint to those gentlemen, who would rob the people of their liberties, that their sophistry is not like to produce the effect. We are willing to have a federal constitution. We are willing another trial should be made; this may be done without derogating from the gentlemen, who composed the late convention. In framing a constitution for this commonwealth, two trials were made before one would stick. We are willing to relinquish so much, as to have a firm, energetic government, and this we are sensible may be done, without becoming slaves, to the capricious fancies of any set of men whatever. It is argued, that there is no danger that the proposed rulers will be disposed to exercise any powers that this constitution puts into their hands, which may enable them to deprive the people of their liberties. But in case, say they, they should make such attempts, the people may, and will rise to arms and prevent it; in answer to which, we have only to say, we have had enough of fighting in the late war, and think it more eligible, to keep our liberties in our own hands, whilst it is in our power thus to do, than to place them in the hands of fallible men, like ourselves, who may if they please, entirely deprive us of them, and so we be at last reduced to the sad alternative of losing them forever, or recovering them back by the point of the sword. The aristocratic party are sensible, that these are the sentiments of the majority of the community, and their conduct plainly evinces the truth of a well known ancient adage—*"Nothing cuts like the truth."*

6

Thomas Jefferson: Letter to John Adams (1813)

In many ways Thomas Jefferson and John Adams were case studies in contrasts. Jefferson was a deistic, slave-owning profligate, whereas Adams was a devoutly Puritan abolitionist who lived relatively modestly. After a long period of animosity between the two that corresponded with the emergence of the Federalist and Democrat-Republican parties, the two great statesmen eventually reconciled and began their relationship anew. The following readings are borrowed from the famous correspondence between Jefferson and Adams on the exact nature of a "natural aristocracy," or equality of opportunity. Jefferson maintains more of an idealized vision of such an arrangement, whereas Adams displays realistic expectations about the practicality of establishing a meritocracy.

. . . For I agree with you that there is a natural aristocracy among men. The grounds of this are virtue and talents. Formerly bodily powers gave place among the aristoi. But since the invention of gunpowder has armed the weak as well as the strong with missile death, bodily strength, like beauty, good humor, politeness and other accomplishments, has become but an auxiliary ground of distinction. There is also an artificial aristocracy founded on wealth and birth, without either virtue or talents; for with these it would belong to the first class. The natural aristocracy I consider as the most precious gift of nature for the instruction, the trusts, and government of society. And indeed it would have been inconsistent in creation to have formed man for the social state, and not to have provided virtue and wisdom enough to manage the concerns of the society. May we not even say that that form of government is the best which provides the most effectually for a pure selection of these natural aristoi into the offices of government? The artificial aristocracy is a mischievous ingredient in government, and provision should be made to prevent its ascendancy. . . .

I think the best remedy is exactly that provided by all our constitutions, to leave to the citizens the free election and separation of the aristoi from the pseudo-aristoi, of the wheat from the chaff. In general they will elect the real good and wise. In some instances, wealth may corrupt, and birth blind them; but not in sufficient degree to endanger the society. . . .

But even in Europe a change has sensibly taken place in the mind of Man. Science had liberated the ideas of those who read and reflect, and the American example had kindled feelings of right in the people. An insurrection has consequently begun, of science, talents and courage against rank and birth, which have fallen into contempt. It has failed in its first effort, because the mobs of the cities, the instrument used for its accomplishment, debased by ignorance, poverty and vice, could not be restrained to rational action. But the world will recover from the panic of this first catastrophe. Science is progressive, and talents and enterprize on the alert. Resort may be had to the people of the country, a more governable power from their principles and subordination; and rank, and birth, and tinsel-aristocracy will finally shrink into insignificance, even there. This however we have no right to meddle with. It suffices for us, if the moral and physical condition of our own citizens qualifies them to select the able and good for the direction of their government, with a recurrence of elections at such short periods as will enable them to displace an unfaithful servant before the mischief he meditates may be irremediable. . . .

7

John Adams to Thomas Jefferson (1813)

We are now explicitly agreed, in one important point, vizt. That "there is a natural Aristocracy among men; the grounds of which are Virtue and Talents. . . ."

But tho' We have agreed in one point, in Words, it is not yet certain that We are perfectly agreed in Sense. Fashion has introduced an indeterminate Use of the Word "Talents." Education, Wealth, Strength, Beauty, Stature, Birth, Marriage, graceful Attitudes and Motions, Gait, Air, Complexion, Physiognomy, are Talents, as well as Genius and Science and learning. Any one of these Talents, that in fact commands or influences true Votes in Society, gives to the Man who possesses it, the Character of an Aristocrat, in my Sense of the Word. . . .

Your distinction between natural and artificial Aristocracy does not appear to me well founded. Birth and Wealth are conferred on some Men, as imperiously by Nature, as Genius, Strength or Beauty. The Heir is honours and Riches, and power has often no more merit in procuring these Advantages, than he has in obtaining an handsome face or an elegant figure. When Aristocracies, are established by human Laws and honour Wealth and Power are made hereditary by municipal Laws and political Institutions, then I acknowledge artificial Aristocracy to commence: but this never commences, till Corruption in Elections becomes dominant and uncontroulable. But this artificial Aristocracy can never last. The everlasting Envys, Jealousies, Rivalries and quarrels among them, their cruel rapacities upon the poor ignorant People their followers, compel these to set up Caesar, a Demagogue to be a Monarch and Master, pour mettre chacun a sa place [to put each one in his place]. Here you have the origin of all artificial Aristocracy, which is the origin of all Monarchy. And both artificial Aristocracy, and Monarchy, and civil, military, political and hierarchical Despotism, have all grown out of the natural Aristocracy of "Virtues and Talents." We, to be sure, are far remote from this. Many hundred years must roll away before We shall be corrupted. Our pure, virtuous, public spirited federative Republick will last for ever, govern the Globe and introduce the perfection of Man, his perfectability being already proved by Price Priestly, Condorcet Rousseau Diderot and Godwin. . . .

Your distinction between the aristoi and pseudo aristoi, will not help the matter. I would trust one as soon as the other with unlimited Power. The Law wisely refuses an Oath as a witness in his own cause to the Saint as well as to the Sinner. . . .

You suppose a difference of Opinion between You and me, on the Subject of Aristocracy. I can find none. I dislike and detest hereditary honours, Offices Emoluments established by Law. So do you. I am for ex[c]luding legal hereditary distinctions from the U.S. as long as possible. So are you. I only say that Mankind have not yet discovered any remedy against irresistable Corruption in Elections to Offices of great Power and Profit, but making them hereditary. . . .

8

James Madison: *Federalist* No. 54 (1788)

Credited as the framer of the Constitution, Madison collaborated primarily with Alexander Hamilton in composing The Federalist Papers, *written at the height of the ratification controversy, to support the ultimate ratification of the Constitution. In the following reading from those papers, Madison seeks to reconcile Northern and Southern interests by arguing on behalf of the "three-fifths" clause in the Constitution, asserting that such an arrangement is a prudent compromise due to the fact that slaves were of "mixed character"—somewhere between strictly property and full citizens.*

. . . Slaves are considered as property, not as persons. They ought therefore to be comprehended in estimates of taxation which are founded on property, and to be excluded from representation which is regulated by a census of persons. This is the objection, as I understand it, stated in its full force. I shall be equally candid in stating the reasoning which may be offered on the opposite side.

"We subscribe to the doctrine," might one of our Southern brethren observe, "that representation relates more immediately to persons, and taxation more immediately to property, and we join in the application of this distinction to the case of our slaves. But we must deny the fact, that slaves are considered merely as property, and in no respect whatever as persons." The true state of the case is, that they partake of both these qualities: being considered by our laws, in some respects, as persons, and in other respects as property. In being compelled to labor, not for himself, but for a master; in being vendible by one master to another master; and in being subject at all times to be restrained in his liberty and chastised in his body, by the capricious will of his owner, the slave may appear to be degraded from the human rank, and classed with those irrational animals which fall under the legal denomination of property. In being protected, on the other hand, in his life and in his limbs, against the violence of all others, even the master of his labor and his liberty; and in being punishable himself for all violence committed against others; the slave is no less evidently regarded by the law as a member of the society, not as a part of the irrational creation; as a moral person, not as a mere article of property. The federal Constitution, therefore, decides with great propriety on the case of our slaves, when it views them in the mixed character of persons and of property. This is in fact their true character. It is the character bestowed on them by the laws under which they live; and it will not be denied, that these are the proper criterion; because it is only under the pretext that the laws have transformed the negroes into subjects of property, that a place is disputed them in the computation of numbers; and it is admitted, that if the laws were to restore the rights which have been taken away, the negroes could no longer be refused an equal share of representation with the other inhabitants. . . .

The qualifications on which the right of suffrage depend are not, perhaps, the same in any two States. In some of the States the difference is very material. In every State, a certain proportion of inhabitants are deprived of this right by the constitution of the State, who will be included in the census by which the federal Constitution apportions the representatives. In this point of view the Southern States might retort the complaint, by insisting that the principle laid down by the convention required that no regard should be had to the policy of particular States towards their own inhabitants; and consequently, that the slaves, as inhabitants, should have been admitted into the census according to their full number, in like manner with other inhabitants, who, by the policy of other States, are not admitted to all the rights of citizens. A rigorous adherence, however, to this principle, is waived by those who would be gainers by it. All that they ask is that equal moderation be shown on the other side. Let the case of the slaves be considered, as it is in truth, a peculiar one. Let the compromising expedient of the Constitution be mutually adopted, which regards them as inhabitants, but as debased by servitude below the equal level of free inhabitants, which regards the SLAVE as divested of two fifths of the MAN.

Such is the reasoning which an advocate for the Southern interests might employ on this subject; and although it may appear to be a little strained in some points, yet, on the whole, I must confess that it fully reconciles me to the scale of representation which the convention have established.

In one respect, the establishment of a common measure for representation and taxation will have a very salutary effect. As the accuracy of the census to be obtained by the Congress will necessarily depend, in a considerable degree on the disposition, if not on the co-operation, of the States, it is of great importance that the States should feel as little bias as possible, to swell or to reduce the amount of their numbers. Were their share of representation alone to be governed by this rule, they would have an interest in exaggerating their inhabitants. Were the rule to decide their share of taxation alone, a contrary temptation would prevail. By extending the rule to both objects, the States will have opposite interests, which will control and balance each other, and produce the requisite impartiality.

9

Judith Sargent Murray:
On the Equality of the Sexes (1790)

Aside from the retention of slavery within the United States, the most glaring inconsistency with American ideals of equality concerned the status of women. Although many, maybe even the majority of women, viewed with pride their position in society as care-takers of the domestic realm, some did express concern about the lack of opportunities accorded to the female sex. Abigail Adams is known for her "remember the ladies" correspondence with her husband, John, but Judith Sargent Murray was arguably the most intelligent voice for women's rights. A publisher and prolific writer, Murray here expounds on the differences and, most importantly, the similarities between the sexes.

Is it upon mature consideration we adopt the idea, that nature is thus partial in her distributions? Is it indeed a fact, that she hath yielded to one half of the human species so unquestionable a mental superiority? I know that to both sexes elevated understandings, and the reverse, are common. But suffer me to ask, in what the minds of females are so notoriously deficient, or unequal. May not the intellectual powers be ranged under their four heads—imagination, reason, memory and judgment? The province of imagination has long since been surrendered up to us, and we have been crowned undoubted sovereigns of the regions of fancy. . . .

Are we deficient in reason? We can only reason from what we know, and if opportunity of acquiring knowledge hath been denied us, the inferiority of our sex cannot fairly be deduced from thence. Memory, I believe, will be allowed us in common, since everyone's experience must testify, that a loquacious old woman is as frequently met with, as a communicative old man; their subjects are alike drawn from the fund of other times, and the transactions of their youth, or of maturer life, entertain, or perhaps fatigue you, in the evening of their lives. "But our judgment is not so strong—we do not distinguish so well." Yet it may be questioned, from what doth this superiority, in this discriminating faculty of the soul, proceed? May we not trace its source in the difference of education, and continued advantages? Will it be said that the judgment of a male of two years old, is more sage than that of a female's of the same age? I believe the reverse is generally observed to be true. But from that period what partiality! How is the one exalted and the other depressed, by the contrary modes of education which are adopted! The one is taught to aspire, and the other is early confined and limited. As their years increase, the sister must be wholly domesticated, while the brother is led by the hand through all the flowery paths of science. Grant that their minds are by nature equal, yet who shall wonder at the apparent superiority, if indeed custom becomes second nature; nay if it taketh place of nature, and that it doth, the experience of each day will evince. At length arrived at womanhood, the uncultivated fair one feels a void, which the employments allotted her are by no means capable of filling. What can she do? To books, she may not apply; or if she doth, to those only of the novel kind, lest she merit the appellation of a learned lady; and what ideas have been affixed to this term, the observation of many can testify. Fashion, scandal, and sometimes what is still more reprehensible, are then called in to her relief; and who can say what lengths the liberties she takes may proceed. Meantime she herself is most unhappy; she feels the want of a cultivated mind. Is she single, she in vain seeks to fill up time from sexual employments or amusements. Is she united to a person whose soul nature made equal to her own, education hath set him so far above her, that in those entertainments which are productive of such rational felicity, she is not qualified to accompany him. She experiences a mortifying consciousness of inferiority, which embitters every enjoyment. . . .

[W]hile we are pursuing the needle, or the superintendency of the family, I repeat, that our minds are at full liberty for reflection; that imagination may exert itself in full vigor; and that if a just foundation early laid, our ideas will then be worthy of rational beings. If we were industrious we might easily find time to arrange them upon paper, or should avocations press too hard for such an indulgence, the hours allotted for conversation would at least become more refined and rational. Should it still be vociferated, "Your domestic employments are sufficient"—I would calmly ask, is it reasonable, that a candidate for immortality, for the joys of heaven, an intelligent being, who is to spend an eternity in contemplating the works of the Deity, should at present be so degraded, as to be allowed no other ideas, than those which are suggested by the mechanism of a pudding, or the sewing the seams of a garment? Pity that all such censurers of female improvement do not go one step further, and deny their future existence; to be consistent they surely ought.

Yes, ye lordly, ye haughty sex, our souls are by nature equal to yours; the same breath of God animates, enlivens, and invigorates us; and that we are not fallen lower than yourselves, let those witness who have greatly towered above the various discouragements by which they have been so heavily oppressed; and though I am unacquainted with the list of celebrated characters on wither side, yet from the observations I have made in the contracted circle in which I have moved, I dare confidently believe, that form the commencement of time to the present day, there hath been as many females, as males, who, by the mere force of natural powers, have merited the crown of applause; who thus unassisted, have seized the wreath of fame.

I know there are those who assert, that as the animal powers of the one sex are superior, of course their mental faculties must also be stronger; thus attributing strength of mind to the transient organization of this earth born tenement. But if this reasoning is just, man must be content to yield the palm to many of the brute creation, since by not a few of his brethren of the field, he is far surpassed in bodily strength. Moreover, was this argument admitted, it would prove too much, for ocular demonstration evinceth, that there are many robust masculine ladies, and effeminate gentlemen. . . . Besides, were we to grant that animal strength proved anything, taking into consideration the accustomed impartiality of nature, we should be induced to imagine, that she had invested the female mind with superiour strength as an equivalent for the bodily powers of man. But waiving this however palpable advantage, for equality only, we wish to contend. . . .

10

John C. Calhoun: Speech in the Senate on the Oregon Bill (1848)

In 1848, Congress witnessed a series of heated debates regarding the admission of the territory of Oregon as a state. The most contentious portions of the debates centered on the antislavery provision present in the bill elevating Oregon to statehood. Senator John C. Calhoun of South Carolina was one of the most eloquent and passionate advocates for states' rights and, by association, the preservation of slavery in the United States. In the following reading, Calhoun attacks the notion of equality as a founding principle, making reference to the inconsistencies of the America's fascination with the subject.

If he should possess a philosophical turn of mind, and be disposed to look to more remote and recondite causes, he will trace it to a proposition which originated in a hypothetical truism, but which, as now expressed and now understood, is the most false and dangerous of all political errors. The proposition to which I allude, has become an axiom in the minds of a vast majority on both sides of the Atlantic, and is repeated daily from tongue to tongue, as an established and incontrovertible truth; it is that "all men are born free and equal." I am not afraid to attack error, however deeply it may be entrenched, or however widely extended, whenever it becomes my duty to do so, as I believe it to be on this subject and occasion.

Taking the proposition literally (it is in that sense it is understood), there is not a word of truth in it. It begins with "all men are born," which is utterly untrue. Men are not born. Infants are born. They grow to be men. And concludes with asserting that they are born "free and equal," which is not less false. They are not born free. While infants they are incapable of freedom, being destitute alike of the capacity of thinking and acting, without which there can be no freedom. Besides, they are necessarily born subject to their parents and remain so among all people, savage and civilized until the development of their intellect and physical capacity enables them to take care of themselves. They grow to all the freedom of which the condition in which they were born permits, by growing to be men. Nor is it less false that they are born "equal." They are not so in any sense in which it can be regarded; and thus, as I have asserted, there is not a word of truth in the whole proposition, as expressed and generally understood. If we trace it back, we shall find the proposition (that "all men are born free and equal") differently expressed in the Declaration of

Independence. That asserts that "all men are created equal." The form of expression, though less dangerous, is not less erroneous. All men are not created. According to the Bible, only two, a man and a woman, ever were, and of these one was pronounced subordinate to the other. All others have come into the world by being born, and in no sense, as I have shown, either free or equal. But this form of expression being less striking and popular has given way to the present, and under the authority of a document put forth on so great an occasion, and leading to such important consequences, has spread far and wide, and fixed itself deeply in the public mind. It was inserted in our Declaration of Independence without any necessity. It made no necessary part of our justification in separating from the parent country, and declaring ourselves independent. Breach of our chartered privileges, and lawless encroachment on our acknowledged and well-established rights by the parent country, were the real causes, and of themselves sufficient, without resorting to any other, to justify the step. Nor had it any weight in constructing the governments which were substituted in the place of the colonial. They were formed of the old materials and on practical and well-established principles, borrowed for the most part from our own experience and that of the country from which we sprang.

. . . of all men having the same right to liberty and equality, as is claimed by those who hold that they are all born free and equal, liberty is the noble and highest reward bestowed on mental and moral development, combined with favorable circumstances. Instead, then, of liberty and equality being born with man; instead of all men and all classes and descriptions being equally entitled to them, they are prizes to be won, and are in their most perfect state, not only the highest reward that can be bestowed on our race, but the most difficult to be won—and when won, the most difficult to be preserved.

11

Daniel Webster: Speech to the United States Senate on Slavery (1850)

By 1850 the United States was very much a divided nation, primarily because of the issue of slavery. The annexation of new states due to population expansion and dispersion caused conflicts between pro- and antislavery factions, culminating in the violence surrounding the Kansas-Nebraska Act and, ultimately, the Civil War. Daniel Webster was a fiery senator from Massachusetts and a devoted abolitionist who spoke loudly and often on the evils of slavery throughout his stellar career. In the following reading, Webster specifically outlines his desire to see slavery extinguished in the United States to preserve the liberty promised by American government and principles.

. . . It is not to be denied that we live in the midst of strong agitations, and are surrounded by very considerable dangers to our institutions and government.

The imprisoned winds are let loose. The East, the North, and the stormy South combine to throw the whole sea into commotion, to toss its billows to the skies, and disclose its profoundest depths. . . .

We all know, Sir, that slavery has existed in the world from time immemorial. There was slavery, in the earliest periods of history, among the Oriental nations. There was slavery among the Jews; the theocratic government of that people issued no injunction against it. There was slavery among the Greeks; and the ingenious philosophy of the Greeks found, or sought to find, a justification for it exactly upon the grounds which have been assumed for such a justification in this country; that is, a natural and original difference among the races of mankind, and the inferiority of the black or colored race to the white. The Greeks justified their system of slavery upon that idea, precisely. They held the African and some of the Asiatic tribes to be inferior to the white race; but they did not show, I think, by any close process of logic, that, if this were true, the more intelligent and the stronger had therefore a right to subjugate the weaker.

Now, Sir, upon the general nature and influence of slavery there exists a wide difference of opinion between the northern portion of this country and the southern. It is said on the one side, that, although not the subject of any injunction or direct prohibition in the New Testament, slavery is a wrong; that it is founded merely in the right of the strongest; and that it is an oppression, like unjust wars, like all those conflicts by which a powerful nation subjects a weaker to its will; and that, in its nature, whatever may be said of it in the modifications which have taken place, it is not according to the meek spirit of the Gospel. It is not "kindly affection"; it does not "seek another's, and not its own"; it does not "let the oppressed go free." These are sentiments that are cherished, and of late with greatly augmented force, among the people of the Northern States. They have taken hold of the religious sentiment of that part of the country, as they have, more or less, taken hold of the religious feelings of a considerable portion of mankind. The South, upon the other side, having been accustomed to this relation between the two races all their lives, from their birth, having been taught, in general, to treat the subjects of this bondage with care and kindness, and I believe, in general, feeling great kindness for them, have not taken the view of the subject which I have mentioned. There are thousands of religious men, with consciences as tender as any of their brethren at the North, who do not see the unlawfulness of slavery; and there are more thousands, perhaps, that, whatsoever they may think of it in its origin, and as a matter depending upon natural right, yet take things as they are, and finding slavery to be an established relation of the society in which they live, can see no way in which, let their opinions on the abstract question be what they may, it is in the power of the present generation to relieve themselves from this relation. And candor obliges me to say, that I believe they are just as conscientious, many of them, and the religious people, all of them, as they are at the North who hold different opinions. . . .

But we must view things as they are. Slavery does exist in the United States. It did exist in the States before the adoption of this Constitution, and at that time. Let us, therefore, consider for a moment what was the state of sentiment, North and South, in regard to slavery, at the time this Constitution was adopted. A remarkable change has taken place since; but what did the wise and great men of all parts of the country think of slavery then? In what estimation did they hold it at the time when this Constitution was adopted? It will be found, Sir, if we will carry ourselves by historical research back to that day, and ascertain men's opinions by authentic records still existing among us, that there was then no diversity of opinion between the North and South upon the subject of slavery. It will be found that both parts of the country held it equally an evil, a moral and political evil. It will not be found that, either at the North or at the South, there was much, though there was some, invective against slavery as inhuman and cruel. The great ground of objection to it was political; that it weakened the social fabric; that, taking the place of free labor, society became less strong and labor less productive; and therefore we find from all the eminent men of the time the clearest expression of their opinion that slavery is an evil. They ascribed its existence here, not without truth, and not without some acerbity of temper and force of language, to the injurious policy of the mother country, who, to favor the navigator, had entailed these evils upon the Colonies. I need hardly refer, Sir, particularly to the publications of the day. They are matters of history on the record. The eminent men, the most eminent men, and nearly all the conspicuous politicians of the South, held the same sentiments; that slavery was an evil, a blight, a scourge, and a curse. There are no terms of reprobation of slavery so vehement in the North at that day as in the South. The North was not so much excited against it as the South; and the reason is, I suppose, that there was much less of it at the North, and the people did not see, or think they saw, the evils so prominently as they were seen, or thought to be seen, at the South.

Then, Sir, when this Constitution was framed, this was the light in which the Federal Convention viewed it. That body reflected the judgment and sentiments of the great men of the South. A member of the other house, whom I have not the honor to know, has, in a recent speech, collected extracts from these public documents. They prove the truth of what I am saying, and the question then was, how to deal with it, and how to deal with it as an evil. They came to this general result. They thought that slavery could not be continued in the country if the importation of slaves were made to cease, and therefore they provided that, after a certain period, the importation might be prevented by the act of the new government. The period of twenty years was proposed by some gentleman from the North, I think, and many members of the Convention from the South opposed it as being too long. Mr. Madison especially was somewhat warm against it. He said it would bring too much of this mischief into the country to allow the importation of slaves for such a period. Because we must take along with us, in the whole of this discussion, when we are considering the sentiments and opinions in which the constitutional provision originated, that the conviction of all men was, that, if the importation of slaves ceased, the white race would multiply faster than the black race, and that slavery would therefore gradually wear out and expire. It may not be improper here to allude to that, I had almost said, celebrated opinion of Mr. Madison. You observe, Sir, that the term slave, or slavery, is not used in the Constitution. The Constitution does not require that "fugitive slaves" shall be delivered up. It requires that persons held to service in one State, and escaping into another, shall be delivered up. Mr. Madison opposed the introduction of the term slave, or slavery, into the Constitution; for he said that he did not wish to see it recognized by the Constitution of the United States of America that there could be property in men. . . .

I have one other remark to make. In my observations upon slavery as it has existed in this country, and as it now exists, I have expressed no opinion of the mode of its extinguishment or melioration. I will say, however, though I have nothing to propose, because I do not deem myself so competent as other gentlemen to take the lead on this subject, that if any gentleman from the South shall propose a scheme, to be carried on by this government upon a large scale, for the transportation of free colored people to any colony or any place in the world, I should be quite disposed to incur almost any degree of expense to accomplish that object. Nay, Sir, following an example set more than twenty years ago by a great man, then a Senator from New York, I would return to Virginia, and through her to the whole South, the money received from the lands and territories ceded by her to this government, for any such purpose as to remove, in whole or in part, or in any way to diminish or deal beneficially with, the free colored population of the Southern States. I have said that I honor Virginia for her cession of this territory. There have been received into the treasury of the United States eighty millions of dollars, the proceeds of the sales of the public lands ceded by her. If the residue should be sold at the same rate, the whole aggregate will exceed two hundred millions of dollars. If Virginia and the South see fit to adopt any proposition to relieve themselves from the free people of color among them, or such as may be made free, they have my full consent that the government shall pay them any sum of money out of the proceeds of that cession which may be adequate to the purpose. . . .

We have a great, popular, constitutional government guarded by law and by judicature, and defended by the affections of the whole people. No monarchical throne presses these States together, no iron chain of military power encircles them; they live and stand under a government popular in its form, representative in its character, founded upon principles of equality, and so constructed, we hope, as to last for ever. In all its history it has been beneficent; it has trodden down no man's liberty; it has crushed no State. Its daily respiration is liberty and patriotism; its yet youthful veins are full of enterprise, courage, and honorable love of glory and renown. . . .

12

Stephen Douglas: Speech on Slavery and the Founding (1858)

In a hotly contested race for a Senate seat in Illinois in 1858, Stephen Douglas and Abraham Lincoln engaged in a series of debates that transcended state politics. The debates thrust Lincoln onto a national stage and allowed for his ascension to the presidency two years later. Of the many topics addressed during the debates, the topic of slavery was one that illustrated the stark differences between the candidates. In the two speeches that follow, Douglas proclaims that the Founding Fathers did not intend to grant African Americans equality, whereas Lincoln illustrates that such an assertion is illogical and inconsistent with America's founding principles.

. . . I tell you that this Chicago doctrine of Lincoln's—declaring that the negro and the white man are made equal by the Declaration of Independence and by Divine Providence—is a monstrous heresy. The signers of the Declaration of Independence never dreamed of the negro when they were writing that document. They referred to white men, to men of European birth and European descent, when they declared the equality of all men. I see a gentleman there in the crowd shaking his head. Let me remind him that when Thomas Jefferson wrote that document he was the owner, and so continued until his death, of a large number of slaves. Did he intend to say in that Declaration that his negro slaves, which he held and treated as property, were created his equals by divine law, and that he was violating the law of God every day of his life by holding them as slaves? It must be borne in mind that when that Declaration was put forth, every one of the thirteen colonies were slaveholding colonies, and every man who signed that instrument represented a slaveholding constituency. Recollect, also, that no one of them emancipated his slaves, much less put them on an equality with himself, after he signed the Declaration. On the contrary, they all continued to hold their negroes as slaves during the Revolutionary War. Now, do you believe—are you willing to have it said—that every man who signed the Declaration of Independence declared the negro his equal, and then was hypocrite enough to hold him as a slave, in violation of what he believed to be the divine law? And yet when you say that the Declaration of Independence includes the negro, you charge the signers of it with hypocrisy.

I say to you frankly, that in my opinion this government was made by our fathers on the white basis. It was made by white men for the benefit of white men and their posterity forever, and was intended to be administered by white men in all time to come. But while I hold that under our Constitution and political system the negro is not a citizen, cannot be a citizen, and ought not to be a citizen, it does not follow by any means that he should be a slave. On the contrary, it does follow that the negro as an inferior race ought to possess every right, every privilege, every immunity which he can safely exercise consistent with the safety of the society in which he lives. Humanity requires, and Christianity commands, that you shall extend to every inferior being, and every dependent being, all the privileges, immunities, and advantages which can be granted to them consistent with the safety of society. If you ask me the nature and extent of these privileges, I answer that that is a question which the people of each State must decide for themselves. . . .

13

Abraham Lincoln: Speech on Slavery and the Founding (1858)

. . . [Stephen Douglas] has alluded to the Declaration of Independence, and insisted that negroes are not included in that Declaration; and that it is, a slander upon the framers of that instrument to suppose that negroes were meant therein; and he asks you: Is it possible to believe that Mr. Jefferson, who penned the immortal paper, could have supposed himself applying the language of that instrument to the negro race, and yet held a portion of that race in slavery? Would he not at once have freed them? I only have to remark upon this part of the Judge's speech (and that, too, very briefly, for I shall not detain myself, or you, upon that point for any great length of time), that I believe the entire records of the world, from the date of the Declaration of Independence up to within three years ago, may be searched in vain for one single affirmation, from one single man, that the negro was not included in the Declaration of Independence; I think I may defy Judge Douglas to show that he ever said so, that Washington ever said so, that any president ever said so, that any member of Congress ever said so, or that any living man upon the whole earth ever said so, until the necessities of the present policy of the Democratic party, in regard to slavery, had to invent that affirmation. And I will remind Judge Douglas and this audience that while Mr. Jefferson was the owner of slaves, as undoubtedly he was, in speaking upon this very subject, he used the strong language that "he trembled for his country when he remembered that God was just"; and I will offer the highest premium in my power to Judge Douglas if he will show that he, in all his life, ever uttered a sentiment at all akin to that of Jefferson.

14

Abraham Lincoln: Speech on the Kansas-Nebraska Act (1854)

During the spring of 1854 Congress passed the highly controversial Kansas-Nebraska Act, which invalidated the Missouri Compromise and allowed for the possibility of slavery spreading into the territories of Kansas and Nebraska. The act was crafted and supported by Abraham Lincoln's political nemesis, Stephen Douglas, and Abraham Lincoln became an outspoken opponent of the act and its incompatibility with the concept of free government. Following, Lincoln expounds on his distaste of slavery and especially the expansion of the institution into formerly free territories.

. . . The doctrine of self-government is right,—absolutely and eternally right,—but it has no just application as here attempted. Or perhaps I should rather say that whether it has such application depends upon whether a negro is not or is a man. If he is not a man, in that case he who is a man may as a matter of self-government do just what he pleases with him. But if the negro is a man, is it not to that extent a total destruction of self-government to say that he too shall not govern himself. When the white man governs himself, that is self-government; but when he governs himself and also governs another man, that is more than self-government—that is despotism. If the negro is a man, why then my ancient faith teaches me that "all men are created equal," and that there can be no moral right in connection with one man's making a slave of another.

Judge Douglas frequently, with bitter irony and sarcasm, paraphrases our argument by saying: "The white people of Nebraska are good enough to govern themselves, but they are not good enough to govern a few miserable negroes!"

Well! I doubt not that the people of Nebraska are and will continue to be as good as the average of people elsewhere. I do not say the contrary. What I do say is that no man is good enough to govern another man without that other's consent. I say this is the leading principle, the sheet-anchor of American republicanism. Our Declaration of Independence says:

We hold these truths to be self-evident: That all men are created equal; that they are endowed by their Creator with certain inalienable rights; that among these are life, liberty and the pursuit of happiness. That to secure these rights, governments are instituted among men, DERIVING THEIR JUST POWERS FROM THE CONSENT OF THE GOVERNED.

I have quoted so much at this time merely to show that, according to our ancient faith, the just powers of governments are derived from the consent of the governed. Now the relation of master and slave is *pro tanto* a total violation of this principle. The master not only governs the slave without his consent, but he governs him by a set of rules altogether different from those which he prescribes for himself. Allow all the governed an equal voice in the government, and that, and that only, is self-government.

Let it not be said I am contending for the establishment of political and social equality between the whites and blacks. I have already said the contrary. I am not combating the argument of necessity, arising from the fact that the blacks are already among us; but I am combating what is set up as moral argument for allowing them to be taken where they have never yet been—arguing against the extension of a bad thing, which, where it already exists, we must of necessity manage as we best can.

In support of his application of the doctrine of self-government, Senator Douglas has sought to bring to his aid the opinions and examples of our Revolutionary fathers. I am glad he has done this. I love the sentiments of those old-time men, and shall be most happy to abide by their opinions. He shows us that when it was in contemplation for the colonies to break off from Great Britain, and set up a new government for themselves, several of the States instructed their delegates to go for the measure, provided each State should be allowed to regulate its domestic concerns in its own way. I do not quote; but this is substance. This was right; I see nothing objectionable in it. I also think it probable that it had some reference to the existence of slavery among them. I will not deny that it had. But had it any reference to the carrying of slavery into new countries? That is the question, and we will let the fathers themselves answer it.

This same generation of men, and mostly the same individuals of the generation who declared this principle, who declared independence, who fought the war of the Revolution through, who afterward made the Constitution under which we still live—these same men passed the ordinance of '87, declaring that slavery should never go to the Northwest Territory. I have no doubt Judge Douglas thinks they were very inconsistent in this. It is a question of discrimination between them and him. But there is not an inch of ground left for his claiming that their opinions, their example, their authority, are on his side in the controversy. . . .

I particularly object to the new position which the avowed principle of this Nebraska law gives to slavery in the body politic. I object to it because it assumes that there can be moral right in the enslaving of one man by another. I object to it as a dangerous dalliance for a free people—a sad evidence that, feeling prosperity, we forget right; that liberty, as a principle, we have ceased to revere. I object to it because the fathers of the republic eschewed and rejected it. The argument of "necessity" was the only argument they ever admitted in favor of slavery; and so far, and so far only, as it carried them did they ever go. They found the institution existing among us, which they could not help, and they cast blame upon the British king for having permitted its introduction. Before the Constitution they prohibited its introduction into the Northwestern Territory, the only country we owned then free from it. At the framing and adoption of the Constitution, they forbore to so much as mention the word "slave" or "slavery" in the whole instrument. In the provision for the recovery of fugitives, the slave is spoken of as a "person held to service or labor." In that prohibiting the abolition of the African slave-trade for twenty years, that trade is spoken of as "the migration or importation of such persons as any of the States now existing shall think proper to admit," etc. These are the only provisions alluding to slavery. Thus the thing is hid away in the Constitution, just as an afflicted man hides away a wen or cancer which he dares not cut out at once, lest he bleed to death,—with the promise, nevertheless, that the cutting may begin at a certain time. Less than this our fathers could not do, and more they would not do. Necessity drove them so far, and further they would not go. But this is not all. The earliest Congress under the Constitution took the same view of slavery. They hedged and hemmed it in to the narrowest limits of necessity. . . .

15

Alexis de Tocqueville: *Democracy in America* (1840)

After visiting the United States in 1831 to study the American penal system, Alexis de Tocqueville penned his famous Democracy in America, which highlighted various aspects of American culture. While visiting the United States, he was at various times fascinated, appalled, and surprised by what he witnessed. Although critical of many aspects of American culture, in the following reading Tocqueville conveys a positive image of the role of women in the United States and the unique station they enjoyed in America compared to their European counterparts.

There are people in Europe who, confounding together the different characteristics of the sexes, would make man and woman into beings not only equal but alike. They would give to both the same functions, impose on both the same duties, and grant to both the same rights; they would mix them in all things—their occupations, their pleasures, their business. It may readily be conceived that by thus attempting to make one sex equal to the other, both are degraded, and from so preposterous a medley of the works of nature nothing could ever result but weak men and disorderly women.

It is not thus that the Americans understand that species of democratic equality which may be established between the sexes. They admit that as nature has appointed such wide differences between the physical and moral constitution of man and woman, her manifest design was to give a distinct employment to their various faculties; and they hold that improvement does not consist in making beings so dissimilar do pretty nearly the same things, but in causing each of them to fulfill their respective tasks in the best possible manner. The Americans have applied to the sexes the great principle of political economy which governs the manufacturers of our age, by carefully dividing the duties of man from those of woman in order that the great work of society may be the better carried on. In no country has such constant care been taken as in America to trace two clearly distinct lines of action for the two sexes and to make them keep pace one with the other, but in two pathways that are always different. American women never manage the outward concerns of the family or conduct a business or take a part in political life; nor are they, on the other hand, ever compelled to perform the rough labor of the fields or to make any of those laborious efforts which demand the exertion of physical strength. No families are so poor as to form an exception to this rule. If, on the one hand, an American woman cannot escape from the quiet circle of domestic employments, she is never forced, on the other, to go beyond it. Hence it is that the women of America, who often exhibit a masculine strength of understanding and a manly energy, generally preserve great delicacy of personal appearance and always retain the manners of women although they sometimes show that they have the hearts and minds of men.

Nor have the Americans ever supposed that one consequence of democratic principles is the subversion of marital power or the confusion of the natural authorities in families. They hold that every association must have a head in order to accomplish its object, and that the natural head of the conjugal association is man. They do not therefore deny him the right of directing his partner, and they maintain that in the smaller association of husband and wife as well as in the great social community the object of democracy is to regulate and legalize the powers that are necessary, and not to subvert all power.

This opinion is not peculiar to one sex and contested by the other; I never observed that the women of America consider conjugal authority as a fortunate usurpation of their rights, or that they thought themselves degraded by submitting to it. It appeared to me, on the contrary, that they attach a sort of pride to the voluntary surrender of their own will and make it their boast to bend themselves to the yoke, not to shake it off. Such, at least, is the feeling expressed by the most virtuous of their sex; the others are silent; and in the United States it is not the practice for a guilty wife to clamor for the rights of women while she is trampling on her own holiest duties. It has often been remarked that in Europe a certain degree of contempt lurks even in the flattery which men lavish upon women; although a European frequently affects to be the slave of woman, it may be seen that he never sincerely thinks her his equal. In the United States men seldom compliment women, but they daily show how much they esteem them. They constantly display an entire confidence in the understanding of a wife and a profound respect for her freedom; they have decided that her mind is just as fitted as that of a man to discover the plain truth, and her heart as firm to embrace it; and they have never sought to place her virtue, any more than his, under the shelter of prejudice, ignorance, and fear.

It would seem in Europe, where man so easily submits to the despotic sway of women, that they are nevertheless deprived of some of the greatest attributes of the human species and considered as seductive but imperfect beings; and (what may well provoke astonishment) women ultimately look upon themselves in the same light and almost consider it as a privilege that they are entitled to show themselves futile, feeble, and timid. The women of America claim no such privileges.

Again, it may be said that in our morals we have reserved strange immunities to man, so that there is, as it were, one virtue for his use and another for the guidance of his partner, and that, according to the opinion of the public, the very same act may be punished alternately as a crime or only as a fault. The Americans do not know this iniquitous division of duties and rights; among them the seducer is as much dishonored as his victim. It is true that the Americans rarely lavish upon women those eager attentions which are commonly paid them in Europe, but their conduct to women always implies that they suppose them to be virtuous and refined; and such is the respect entertained for the moral freedom of the sex that in the presence of a woman the most guarded language is used lest her ear should be offended by an expression. In America a young unmarried woman may alone and without fear undertake a long journey.

The legislators of the United States, who have mitigated almost all the penalties of criminal law, still make rape a capital offense, and no crime is visited with more inexorable severity by public opinion. This may be accounted for; as the Americans can conceive nothing more precious than a woman's honor and nothing which ought so much to be respected as her independence, they hold that no punishment is too severe for the man who deprives her of them against her will. In France, where the same offense is visited with far milder penalties, it is frequently difficult to get a verdict from a jury against the prisoner. Is this a consequence of contempt of decency or contempt of women? I cannot but believe that it is a contempt of both.

Thus the Americans do not think that man and woman have either the duty or the right to perform the same offices, but they show an equal regard for both their respective parts; and though their lot is different, they consider both of them as beings of equal value. They do not give to the courage of woman the same form or the same direction as to that of man, but they never doubt her courage; and if they hold that man and his partner ought not always to exercise their intellect and understanding in the same manner, they at least believe the understanding of the one to be as sound as that of the other, and her intellect to be as clear. Thus, then, while they have allowed the social inferiority of woman to continue, they have done all they could to raise her morally and intellectually to the level of man; and in this respect they appear to me to have excellently understood the true principle of democratic improvement.

As for myself, I do not hesitate to avow that although the women of the United States are confined within the narrow circle of domestic life, and their situation is in some respects one of extreme dependence, I have nowhere seen woman occupying a loftier position; and if I were asked, now that I am drawing to the close of this work, in which I have spoken of so many important things done by the Americans, to what the singular prosperity and growing strength of that people ought mainly to be attributed, I should reply: To the superiority of their women.

16

Elizabeth Cady Stanton: The Seneca Falls Declaration (1848)

By the middle of the nineteenth century many women in the United States had begun to mobilize to obtain basic citizenship rights such as the right to vote and to pursue gainful employment outside of the home. Although often overshadowed by abolitionist crusades in the years leading up to the Civil War, feminist leaders such as Elizabeth Cady Stanton were extremely active in promoting equality for women. Issued during the Seneca Falls Convention in New York, the declaration that follows borrows heavily from the Declaration of Independence in demanding a higher level of respect for women's rights.

1. DECLARATION OF SENTIMENTS

When, in the course of human events, it becomes necessary for one portion of the family of man to assume among the people of the earth a position different from that which they have hitherto occupied, but one to which the laws of nature and of nature's God entitle them, a decent respect to the opinions of mankind requires that they should declare the causes that impel them to such a course.

We hold these truths to be self-evident: that all men and women are created equal; that they are endowed by their Creator with certain inalienable rights; that among these are life, liberty, and the pursuit of happiness; that to secure these rights governments are instituted, deriving their just powers from the consent of the governed. Whenever any form of government becomes destructive of these ends, it is the right of those who suffer from it to refuse allegiance to it, and to insist upon the institution of a new government, laying its foundation on such principles, and organizing its powers in such form, as to them shall seem most likely to effect their safety and happiness. Prudence, indeed, will dictate that governments long established should not be changed for light and transient causes; and accordingly all experience hath shown that mankind are more disposed to suffer while evils are sufferable, than to right themselves by abolishing the forms to which they are accustomed. But when a long train of abuses and usurpations, pursuing invariably the same object, evinces a design to reduce them under absolute despotism, it is their duty to throw off such government, and to provide new guards for their future security. Such has been the patient sufferance of the women under this government, and such is now the necessity which constrains them to demand the equal station to which they are entitled. The history of mankind is a history of repeated injuries and usurpations on the part of man toward woman, having in direct object the establishment of an absolute tyranny over her. To prove this, let facts be submitted to a candid world.

- He has never permitted her to exercise her inalienable right to the elective franchise.
- He has compelled her to submit to laws, in the formation of which she had no voice.
- He has withheld from her rights which are given to the most ignorant and degraded men both natives and foreigners.
- Having deprived her of this first right of a citizen, the elective franchise, thereby leaving her without representation in the halls of legislation, he has oppressed her on all sides.
- He has made her, if married, in the eye of the law, civilly dead. He has taken from her all right in property, even to the wages she earns.
- He has made her, morally, an irresponsible being. as she can commit many crimes with impunity, provided they be done in the presence of her husband.
- In the covenant of marriage, she is compelled to promise obedience to her husband, he becoming, to all intents and purposes, her master, the law giving him power to deprive her of her liberty. and to administer chastisement.
- He has so framed the laws of divorce, as to what shall be the proper causes, and in case of separation, to whom the guardianship of the children shall be given, as to be wholly regardless of the happiness of women, the law, in all cases, going upon a false supposition of the supremacy of man, and giving all power into his hands.
- After depriving her of all rights as a married woman, if single, and the owner of property, he has taxed her to support a government which recognizes her only when her property can be made profitable to it.
- He has monopolized nearly all the profitable employments, and from those she is permitted to follow, she receives but a scanty remuneration. He closes against her all the avenues to wealth and distinction which he considers most honorable to himself. As a teacher of theology, medicine, or law, she is not known.
- He has denied her the facilities for obtaining a thorough education, all colleges being closed against her.
- He allows her in Church, as well as State, but a subordinate position, claiming Apostolic authority for her exclusion from the ministry, and, with some exceptions, from any public participation in the affairs of the Church.
- He has created a false public sentiment by giving to the world a different code of morals for men and women, by which moral delinquencies which exclude women from society, are not only tolerated, but deemed of little account in man.

- He has usurped the prerogative of Jehovah himself, claiming it as his right to assign for her a sphere of action, when that belongs to her conscience and to her God.

- He has endeavored, in every way that he could, to destroy her confidence in her own powers, to lessen her self-respect and to make her willing to lead a dependent and abject life.

Now, in view of this entire disfranchisement of one-half the people of this country, their social and religious degradation, in view of the unjust laws above mentioned, and because women do feel themselves aggrieved, oppressed, and fraudulently deprived of their most sacred rights, we insist that they have immediate admission to all the rights and privileges which belong to them as citizens of the United States.

In entering upon the great work before us, we anticipate no small amount of misconception, misrepresentation, and ridicule; but we shall use every instrumentality within our power to effect our object. We shall employ agents, circulate tracts, petition the State and National legislatures, and endeavor to enlist the pulpit and the press in our behalf. We hope this Convention will be followed by a series of Conventions embracing every part of the country.

17

Statement to the People of the State of South Carolina by the Colored State Convention (1865)

The conclusion of the Civil War resulted in the immediate emancipation of millions of African Americans and the beginning of assimilation for many freedmen. With over half of its population composed of African Americans, the state of South Carolina was in a unique and potentially dangerous position of having to incorporate massive changes in its social structure in a short period of time. In the aftermath of the war, a group of African American religious leaders issued a statement to the people of South Carolina stating their disappointment with the emergence of the "black codes," but the group also outlined their goals, expectations, and optimistic vision for the future.

Fellow Citizens:—We have assembled as delegates representing the colored people of the State of South Carolina, in the capacity of State Convention, to confer together and to deliberate upon our intellectual, moral, industrial, civil, and political condition as affected by the great changes which have taken place in this State and throughout this whole country, and to devise ways and means which may, through the blessing of God, tend to our improvement, elevation, and progress; fully believing that our cause is one which commends itself to all good men throughout the civilized world; that it is the sacred cause of truth and righteousness; that it particularly appeals to those professing to be governed by that religion which teaches to "do unto all men as you would have them do unto you."

These principles we conceive to embody the great duty of man to his fellow man; and, *as men,* we ask only to be included in a practical application of this principle.

We feel that the *justness* of our cause is sufficient apology for our course at this time. Heretofore we have had no avenues opened to us or our children— we have had no firesides that we could call our own; none of those incentives to work for the development of our minds and the aggrandizement of our race in common with other people. The measures which have been adopted for the development of white men's children have been denied to us and ours. The laws which have made white men great, have degraded us, because we were colored, and because we were reduced to chattel slavery. But now that we are freemen, now that we have been lifted up by the providence of God to manhood, we have resolved to come forward, and, like MEN, speak and act for ourselves. We fully recognize the truth of the maxim that "God helps those who help themselves." In making this appeal to you, we adopt the language of the immortal Declaration of Independence, "that all men are created equal," and that "life, liberty, and the pursuit of happiness" are the right of all; that taxation and representation should go together; that governments are to protect, not to destroy the rights of mankind; that the Constitution of the United States was formed to establish justice, to promote the general welfare, and secure the blessings of liberty to all the people of this country; that resistance to tyrants is obedience to God are American principles and maxims; and together they form the constructive elements of the American Government.

We think we fully comprehend and duly appreciate the principles and measures which compose this platform; and all that we desire or ask for is to be placed in a position that we could conscientiously and legitimately defend, with you, those principles against the surges of despotism to the last drop of our blood. We have not come together in battle array to assume a boastful attitude and to talk loudly of high-sounding principles or unmeaning platforms, nor do we pretend to any great boldness; for we know your wealth and greatness, and our poverty and weakness; and although we feel keenly our wrongs, still we come together, we trust, in a spirit of meekness and of patriotic good-will to all the people of the State. But yet it is some consolation to know (and it inspires us with hope when we reflect) that our cause is not alone the cause of five millions of colored men in this country, but we are intensely alive to the fact that it is also the cause of millions of oppressed men in other "parts of God's beautiful earth," who are now struggling to be free in the fullest sense of that word; and God and nature are pledged in its triumph. We are Americans by birth, and we assure you that we are Americans in feeling. . . .

Thus we would address you, not as enemies, but as friends and fellow-countrymen, who desire to dwell among you in peace, and whose destinies are interwoven, and linked with those of the American people, and hence must be fulfilled in this country. As descendants of a race feeble and long oppressed, we might with propriety appeal to a great and magnanimous people like

Americans, for special favors and encouragement, on the principle that the strong should aid the weak, the learned should teach the unlearned.

But it is for no such purposes that we raise our voices to the people of South Carolina on this occasion. We ask for no special privileges or peculiar favors. We ask only for *even-handed Justice*, or for the removal of such positive obstructions and disabilities as past, and the recent Legislators have seen fit to throw in our way, and heap upon us. Without any rational cause or provocation on our part, of which we are conscious, as a people, we, by the action of your Convention and Legislature, have been virtually, and with few exceptions excluded from, first, the rights of citizenship, which you cheerfully accord to strangers, but deny to us who have been born and reared in your midst, who were faithful while your greatest trials were upon you, and have done nothing since to merit your disapprobation.

We are denied the right of giving our testimony in like manner with that of our white fellow-citizens, in the courts of the State, by which our persons and property are subject to every species of violence, insult and fraud without redress.

We are also by the present laws, not only denied the right of citizenship, the inestimable right of voting for those who rule over us in the land of our birth, but by the so-called Black Code we are deprived the rights of the meanest profligate in the country—the right to engage in any legitimate business free from any restraints, save those which govern all other citizens of this State.

You have by your Legislative actions placed barriers in the way of our educational and mechanical improvement; you have given us little or no encouragement to pursue agricultural pursuits, by refusing to sell to us lands, but organize societies to bring foreigners to your country, and thrust us out or reduce us to a serfdom, intolerable to men born amid the progress of American genius and national development.

Your public journals charge the freedmen with destroying the products of the country since they have been made free, when they know that the destruction of the products was brought about by the ravages of war of four years duration. How unjust, then, to charge upon the innocent and helpless, evils in which they had no hand, and which may be traced to where it properly belongs.

We simply desire that we shall be recognized as men; that we have no obstructions placed in our way; that the same laws which govern white men shall direct colored men; that we have the right of trial by a jury of our peers, that schools be opened or established for our children; that we be permitted to acquire homesteads for ourselves and children; that we be dealt with as others, in equity and justice.

We claim the confidence and good-will of all classes of men; we ask that the same chances be extended to us that freemen should demand at the hands of their fellow-citizens. We desire the prosperity and growth of this State and the well-being of all men, and shall be found ever struggling to elevate ourselves and add to the national character; and we trust the day will not be distant when you will acknowledge that by our rapid progress in moral, social, religious and intellectual development that you will cheerfully accord to us the high commendation that we are worthy, with you, to enjoy all political emoluments—when we shall realize the truth that "all men are endowed by their Creator with inalienable rights," and that on the American continent this is the right of all, whether he come from east, west, north or south; and, although complexions may differ, "a mans a man for a that."

DISCUSSION QUESTIONS FOR CHAPTER 1

1. How do you think Jefferson reconciled the state of enslaved African Americans with the principle "All men are created equal" that was embedded in the Declaration of Independence? What components of slavery would enable an otherwise just individual to rationalize the oppression of another human being? How does Madison define the nature of African American slaves in the United States?

2. Why were most early Americans so intent on eliminating hereditary connections to political power? Is it unexpected that the American elite as well as commoners would advocate protecting against a hereditary aristocracy? How do the opinions of Jefferson and Adams differ on the subject of a "natural aristocracy"?

3. How does the status of women in the early national period relate to the founding principle of equality? How do the opinions of Judith Sargent Murray, Tocqueville, and the components of the Seneca Falls Declaration differ in their perspectives on women's rights?

4. How did the debate on the existence of slavery evolve during the nineteenth century? What events were occurring domestically and even internationally that brought slavery to the forefront of American consciousness? Who constructs a stronger argument on the connection between slavery and the Founding Fathers—Douglas or Lincoln?

5. In the final reading, what seems to be the main objective of the petitioners? Why do you think they maintained such a measured tone in their demands?

CHAPTER 2

Virtue

1

William Penn: Letter to His Children (1682)

A vigilant Quaker as well as the founder of the colony of Pennsylvania, William Penn was one of the most influential Americans of the colonial period. Because of his religious background and the emphasis Quakerism placed on simplicity and modesty, Penn was wary of the luxury and decadence that tended to affect wealthy and powerful individuals. In the following letter, Penn exhorts his children to avoid situations or individuals that betray characteristics of modesty, obedience, and temperance.

. . . And now, my dear children that are the gifts and mercies of the God of your tender father, hear my counsel and lay it up in your hearts. Love it more than treasure and follow it, and you shall be blessed here and happy hereafter. . . .

. . . [B]e obedient to your dear mother, a woman whose virtue and good name is an honor to you; for she has been exceeded by none in her time for her plainness, integrity, industry, humanity, virtue, and good understanding, qualities not usual among women of her worldly condition and quality. Therefore, honor and obey her, my dear children, as your mother, and your father's love and delight; nay, love her too, for she loved your father with a deep and upright love, choosing him before all her many suitors. And though she be of a delicate constitution and noble spirit, yet she descended to the utmost tenderness and care for you, performing in painfulness acts of service to you in your infancy, as a mother and a nurse too. I charge you before the Lord, honor and obey, love and cherish, your dear mother.

Next betake yourselves to some honest, industrious course of life; and that not of sordid covetousness, but for example and to avoid idleness. And if you change your condition and marry, choose with the knowledge and consent of your mother, if living, guardians, or those that have the charge of you. Mind neither beauty nor riches, but the fear of the Lord and a sweet and amiable disposition, such as you can love above all this world and that may make your habitations pleasant and desirable to you. And being married, be tender, affectionate, and patient, and meek. Live in the fear of the Lord, and

He will bless you and your offspring. Be sure to live within compass; borrow not, neither be beholden to any. Ruin not yourselves by kindness to others, for that exceeds the due bounds of friendship; neither will a true friend expect it. Small matters I heed not.

Let your industry and parsimony go no farther than for a sufficiency for life, and to make a provision for your children (and that in moderation, if the Lord gives you any). I charge you to help the poor and needy. Let the Lord have a voluntary share of your income, for the good of the poor, both in our Society and others; for we are all His creatures, remembering that he that gives to the poor, lends to the Lord. Know well your incomings, and your outgoings may be the better regulated. Love not money, nor the world. Use them only and they will serve you; but if you love them, you serve them, which will debase your spirits as well as offend the Lord. Pity the distressed, and hold out a hand of help to them; it may be your case, and as you mete to others, God will mete to you again. Be humble and gentle in your conversation; of few words, I charge you; but always pertinent when you speak, hearing out before you attempt to answer, and then speaking as if you would persuade, not impose. Affront none, neither revenge the affronts that are done to you; but forgive, and you shall be forgiven of your Heavenly Father.

In making friends, consider well, first; and when you are fixed, be true, not wavering by reports nor deserting in affliction, for that becomes not the good and virtuous.

Watch against anger; neither speak nor act in it, for like drunkenness, it makes a man a beast and throws people into desperate inconveniences.

Avoid flatterers; for they are thieves in disguise. Their praise is costly, designing to get by those they bespeak. They are the worst of creatures; they lie to flatter and flatter to cheat, and, which is worse, if you believe them, you cheat yourselves most dangerously. But the virtuous—though poor—love, cherish, and prefer. . . .Next, my children, be temperate in all things: in your diet, for that is physic by prevention; it keeps, nay, it makes people healthy and their generation sound. This is exclusive of the spiritual advantage it brings. Be also plain in your apparel; keep out that lust which reigns too much over some. Let your virtues be your ornaments; remembering, life is more than food, and the body than raiment. Let your furniture be simple and cheap. Avoid pride, avarice, and luxury. Read my *No Cross, No Crown;* there is instruction. Make your conversation with the most eminent for wisdom and piety; and shun all wicked men, as you hope for the blessing of God, and the comfort of your father's living and dying prayers. Be sure you speak no evil of any; no, not of the meanest, much less of your superiors, as magistrates, guardians, tutors, teachers, and elders in Christ.

Be no busybodies; meddle not with other folks' matters but when in conscience and duly pressed, for it procures trouble, and is ill-mannered, and very unseemly to wise men.

In your families, remember Abraham, Moses, and Joshua, their integrity to the Lord; and do as [if] you have them for your examples. Let the fear and service of the living God be encouraged in your houses, and that plainness, sobriety, and moderation in all things, as becomes God's chosen people. And, as I advise you, my beloved children, do you counsel yours, if God should give you any. Yea, I counsel and command them, as my posterity, that they love and serve the Lord God with an upright heart, that He may bless you and yours, from generation to generation.

And as for you who are likely to be concerned in the government of Pennsylvania and my parts of East Jersey, especially the first, I do charge you before the Lord God and his only angels that you be lowly, diligent, and tender; fearing God, loving the people, and hating covetousness. Let justice have its impartial course, and the law free passage. Though to your loss, protect no man against it, for you are not above the law, but the law above you. Live therefore the lives yourselves you would have the people live; and then you have right and boldness to punish the transgressor. Keep upon the square, for God sees you; therefore do your duty; and be sure you see with your own eyes, and hear with your own ears. Entertain no lurchers; cherish no informers for gain or revenge; use no tricks, fly to no devices to support or cover injustice, but let your hearts be upright before the Lord, trusting in Him above the contrivances of men, and none shall be able to hurt or supplant. . . .

If you thus behave yourselves, and so become a terror to evildoers and a praise to them that do well, God, my God, will be with you, in wisdom and a sound mind, and make you blessed instruments in His hand for the settlement of some of those desolate parts of the world—which my soul desires above all worldly honors and riches, both for you that go and you that stay, you that govern and you that are governed—that in the end you may be gathered with me to the rest of God.

Finally, my children, love one another with a true and endeared love, and your dear relations on both sides; and take care to preserve tender affection in your children to each other, often marrying within themselves, so [long] as it be without the bounds forbidden in God's law. That so they may not, like the forgetting and unnatural world, grow out of kindred and as cold as strangers; but, as becomes a truly natural and Christian stock, you and yours after you may live in the pure and fervent love of God toward one another, as becomes brethren in the spiritual and natural relation. . . .

2

Benjamin Franklin: *Autobiography* (1771)

Benjamin Franklin was arguably the most logical and pragmatic of the Founding Fathers, renowned for his intellect and his tendency to scientifically examine various aspects of human behavior. Throughout his career as a printer and public servant, Franklin continually promoted, though did not always practice, principles of republican virtue. In this excerpt from his Autobiography, *which was not published until years after his death, Franklin lists the virtues that he felt were most important in molding the character of productive citizens.*

. . . I included under thirteen names of virtues all that at that time occurr'd to me as necessary or desirable, and annexed to each a short precept, which fully express'd the extent I gave to its meaning. These names of virtues, with their precepts, were:

1. **Temperance**. Eat not to dullness; drink not to elevation.
2. **Silence**. Speak not but what may benefit others or yourself; avoid trifling conversation.
3. **Order**. Let all your things have their places; let each part of your business have its time.
4. **Resolution**. Resolve to perform what you ought; perform without fail what you resolve.
5. **Frugality**. Make no expense but to do good to others or yourself; i.e., waste nothing.
6. **Industry**. Lose no time; be always employ'd in something useful; cut off all unnecessary actions.
7. **Sincerity**. Use no hurtful deceit; think innocently and justly, and, if you speak, speak accordingly.
8. **Justice**. Wrong none by doing injuries, or omitting the benefits that are your duty.
9. **Moderation**. Avoid extreams; forbear resenting injuries so much as you think they deserve.
10. **Cleanliness**. Tolerate no uncleanliness in body, cloaths, or habitation.
11. **Tranquillity**. Be not disturbed at trifles, or at accidents common or unavoidable.
12. **Chastity**. Rarely use venery but for health or offspring, never to dullness, weakness, or the injury of your own or another's peace or reputation.
13. **Humility**. Imitate Jesus and Socrates. . . .

3

Samuel Adams: Letter in the *Boston Gazette* (1772)

A true revolutionary and strident republican, Samuel Adams, often allying with his cousin and future president John Adams, wielded an inordinate amount of influence in the colonies in the years leading up to and during the Revolution. Although Adams's reluctance to support a united alliance of states following the Revolution caused him to quickly lose his status as a national spokesman, he nevertheless was an eloquent and tireless advocate for republican virtue until his death in 1803. In the following reading,

Adams stresses the need for the promotion of morality among American citizens. Note especially his poem at the conclusion of his declaration.

... Is it not High Time for the People of this Country explicitly to declare, whether they will be Freemen or Slaves? It is an important Question, which ought to be decided. It concerns us more than any Thing in this Life. The Salvation of our Souls is interested in the Event: For wherever Tyranny is establish'd, Immorality of every Kind comes in like a Torrent. It is in the Interest of Tyrants to reduce the People to Ignorance and Vice. For they cannot live in any Country where Virtue and Knowledge prevail. The Religion and public Liberty of a People are intimately connected; their Interests are interwoven, they cannot subsist separately; and therefore they rise and fall together. For this Reason, it is always observable, that those who are combin'd to destroy the People's Liberties, practice every Art to poison their Morals. How greatly then does it concern us, at all Events, to put a Stop to the Progress of Tyranny. It is advanced already by far too many Strides. We are at this moment upon a precipice. The next step may be fatal to us. Let us then act like wise Men; calmly took around us and consider what is best to be done. Let us converse together upon this most interesting Subject and open our minds freely to each other. Let it be the topic of conversation in every social Club. Let every Town assemble. Let Associations & Combinations be everywhere set up to consult and recover our just Rights.

> The Country claims our active Aid.
> That let us roam; & where we find a Spark
> Of public Virtue, blow it into Flame.

4

Samuel Langdon: A Government Corrupted by Vice and Recovered by Righteousness (1775)

Samuel Langdon was a respected Congregational minister from Massachusetts and an ardent supporter of America's right to declare independence during the Revolutionary War. Langdon also later partook in many of the debates regarding the Constitution before its adoption and was especially concerned about the moral direction of the American people. Issued at a time when he was the president of Harvard College (later Harvard University), the following speech was given shortly after the first shots of the Revolutionary War were fired. As evidenced by his constant religious references, Langdon married religion and public virtue and was deeply concerned that the continuation of a relationship with Great Britain would prove detrimental to the morality of Americans.

... When a government is in its prime, the public good engages the attention of the whole; the strictest regard is paid to the qualifications of those who hold the offices of the state; virtue prevails; everything is managed with justice, prudence, and frugality; the laws are founded on principles of equity rather than mere policy, and all the people are happy. But vice will increase with the riches and glory of an empire; and this gradually tends to corrupt the constitution, and in time bring on its dissolution. This may be considered not only as the natural effect of vice, but a righteous judgment of Heaven, especially upon a nation which has been favored with the blessings of religion and liberty, and is guilty of undervaluing them, and eagerly going into the gratification of every lust. . . .

We have rebelled against God. We have lost the true spirit of Christianity, though we retain the outward profession and form of it. We have neglected and set light by the glorious gospel of our Lord Jesus Christ, and his holy commands and institutions. The worship of many is but mere compliment to the Deity, while their hearts are far from him. By many the gospel is corrupted into a superficial system of moral philosophy, little better than ancient Platonism; and, after all the pretended refinements of moderns in the theory of Christianity, very little of the pure practice of it is to be found among those who once stood foremost in the profession of the gospel. In a general view of the present moral state of Great Britain it may be said, "There is no truth, nor mercy, nor knowledge of God in the land. By swearing, and lying, and killing, and stealing, and committing adultery," their wickedness breaks out, and one murder after another is committed, under the connivance and encouragement even of that authority by which such crimes ought to be punished, that the purposes of oppression and despotism may be answered. As they have increased, so have they sinned; therefore God is changing their glory into shame. The general prevalence of vice has changed the whole face of things in the British government.

The excellency of the constitution has been the boast of Great Britain and the envy of neighboring nations. In former times the great departments of the state, and the various places of trust and authority, were filled with men of wisdom, honesty, and religion, who employed all their powers, and were ready to risk their fortunes and their lives, for the public good. They were faithful counselors to kings; directed their authority and majesty to the happiness of the nation, and opposed every step by which despotism endeavored to advance. They were fathers of the people, and sought the welfare and prosperity of the whole body. They did not exhaust the national wealth by luxury and bribery, or convert it to their own private benefit or the maintenance of idle, useless officers and dependents, but improved it faithfully for the proper purposes—for the necessary support of government and defense of the kingdom. Their laws were dictated by wisdom and equality, and justice was administered with impartiality. Religion discovered its general influence among all ranks, and kept out great corruptions from places of power.

But in what does the British nation now glory?—In a mere shadow if its ancient political system—in titles of dignity without virtue—in vast public treasures continually lavished in corruption till every fund is exhausted, notwithstanding the mighty streams perpetually flowing in—in the many artifices to stretch the prerogatives of the crown beyond all constitutional bounds, and make the king an absolute monarch, while the people are deluded with a mere phantom of liberty....

Would not a reverend regard to the authority of divine revelation, a hearty belief of the gospel of the grace of God, and a general reformation of all those vices which bring misery and ruin upon individuals, families, and kingdoms, and which have provoked Heaven to bring the nation into such perplexed and dangerous circumstances, be the surest way to recover the sinking state, and make it again rich and flourishing? ...

But, alas! have not the sins of America, and of New England in particular, had a hand in bringing down upon us the righteous judgments of Heaven? Wherefore is all this evil come upon us? Is it not because we have forsaken the Lord? Can we say we are innocent of crimes against God? No, surely. It becomes us to humble ourselves under his mighty hand, that he may exalt us in due time. However unjustly and cruelly we have been treated by man, we certainly deserve, at the hand of God, all the calamities in which we are now involved. Have we not lost much of that spirit of genuine Christianity which so remarkably appeared in our ancestors, for which God distinguished them with the signal favors of providence when they fled from tyranny and persecution into this western desert? Have we not departed from their virtues? Though I hope and am confident that as much true religion, agreeable to the purity and simplicity of the gospel, remains among us among any people in the world, yet, in the midst of the present great apostasy of the nations professing Christianity, have not we likewise been guilty of departing from the living God? Have we not made light of the gospel of salvation, and too much affected the cold, formal, fashionable religion of countries grown old in vice, and overspread with infidelity? Do not our follies and iniquities testify against us? Have we not, especially in our seaports, gone much too far into the pride and luxuries of life? Is it not a fact, open to common observation, that profaneness, intemperance, unchastity, the love of pleasure, fraud, avarice, and other vices, are increasing among us from year to year? And have not even these young governments been in some measure infected with the corruptions of European courts? Has there been no flattery, no bribery, no artifices practiced, to get into places of honor and profit, or carry a vote to serve a particular interest, without regard to right or wrong? Have our statesmen always acted with integrity, and every judge with impartiality, in the fear of God? In short, have all ranks of men showed regard to the divine commands, and joined to promote the Redeemer's kingdom and the public welfare? I wish we could more fully justify ourselves in all these respects. If such sins have not been so notorious among us as in older countries, we must nevertheless remember that the sins of a people who have been remarkable for the profession of godliness, are more aggravated by all the advantages and favors they have enjoyed, and will receive more speedy and signal punishment; as God says of Israel: "You only have I known of all the families of the earth, therefore will I punish you for all your iniquities."

5

Thomas Paine: *The American Crisis* (1780)

As seen in Chapter 1 in the selection from Common Sense, *Thomas Paine clearly saw great potential in the envisioned United States and its attempt to establish a new nation based on Enlightenment principles. By 1780, however, the Revolutionary War was not proceeding exceptionally well for the American forces, and some wondered whether the colonists would soon be crushed by superior British military might. As with his pamphlet* Common Sense *several years earlier, Paine attempted to rally Americans around the cause of independence with his piece* The American Crisis. *The selection that follows highlights the desperate situation of the war, yet implores Americans to embrace the virtues of "perseverance and fortitude" that Paine claims to have witnessed among the rebel forces.*

. . . I turn with the warm ardor of a friend to those who have nobly stood, and are yet determined to stand the matter out: I call not upon a few, but upon all: not on this state or that state, but on every state: up and help us; lay your shoulders to the wheel; better have too much force than too little, when so great an object is at stake. Let it be told to the future world, that in the depth of winter, when nothing but hope and virtue could survive, that the city and the country, alarmed at one common danger, came forth to meet and to repulse it. Say not that thousands are gone, turn out your tens of thousands; throw not the burden of the day upon Providence, but "show your faith by your works," that God may bless you. It matters not where you live, or what rank of life you hold, the evil or the blessing will reach you all. The far and the near, the home counties and the back, the rich and the poor, will suffer or rejoice alike. The heart that feels not now is dead; the blood of his children will curse his cowardice, who shrinks back at a time when a little might have saved the whole, and made them happy. I love the man that can smile in trouble, that can gather strength from distress, and grow brave by reflection. 'Tis the business of little minds to shrink; but he whose heart is firm, and whose conscience approves his conduct, will pursue his principles unto death. My own line of reasoning is to myself as straight and clear as a ray of light. Not all the treasures of the world, so far as I believe, could have induced me to support an offensive war, for I think it murder; but if a thief breaks into my house, burns and destroys my property, and kills or threatens to kill me, or those that are in it, and to "bind me in all cases whatsoever" to his absolute will, am I to suffer it? What signifies it to me, whether he who does it is a king or a common man; my countryman or not my countryman; whether it be done by an individual villain, or an army of them? If we reason to the root of things we shall find no difference; neither can any just cause be assigned why we should punish in the one case and pardon in the other. Let them call me rebel and welcome, I feel no concern from it; but I should suffer the misery of devils, were I to make a whore of my soul by swearing allegiance to one whose character is that of a sottish, stupid, stubborn, worthless, brutish man. I conceive likewise a horrid idea in receiving mercy from a being, who at the last day shall be shrieking to the rocks and mountains to cover him, and fleeing with terror from the orphan, the widow, and the slain of America. . . .

I thank God, that I fear not. I see no real cause for fear. I know our situation well, and can see the way out of it. While our army was collected, Howe dared not risk a battle; and it is no credit to him that he decamped from the White Plains, and waited a mean opportunity to ravage the defenceless Jerseys; but it is great credit to us, that, with a handful of men, we sustained an orderly retreat for near an hundred miles, brought off our ammunition, all our field pieces, the greatest part of our stores, and had four rivers to pass. None can say that our retreat was precipitate, for we were near three weeks in performing it, that the country might have time to come in. Twice we marched back to meet the enemy, and remained out till dark. The sign of fear was not seen in our camp, and had not some of the cowardly and disaffected inhabitants spread false alarms through the country, the Jerseys had never been ravaged. Once more we are again collected and collecting; our new army at both ends of the continent is recruiting fast, and we shall be able to open the next campaign with sixty thousand men, well armed and clothed. This is our situation, and who will may know it. By perseverance and fortitude we have the prospect of a glorious issue; by cowardice and submission, the sad choice of a variety of evils-a ravaged country—a depopulated city—habitations without safety, and slavery without hope-our homes turned into barracks and bawdy-houses for Hessians, and a future race to provide for, whose fathers we shall doubt of. Look on this picture and weep over it! and if there yet remains one thoughtless wretch who believes it not, let him suffer it unlamented.

6

Benjamin Franklin:
Dangers of a Salaried Bureaucracy (1787)

As mentioned previously, Benjamin Franklin was one of the most outspoken proponents of his era on behalf of republican principles, one of which included the practice of virtuous and wise individuals serving the public with no pecuniary rewards. Republican theorists such as Franklin and Thomas Jefferson foresaw a nation with an elite class of "guardians" who would, by their talents and virtues, rise to a status in society in which financial matters were no longer of concern and, thus, they could then involve themselves impartially in public affairs. Franklin, in fact, followed this aspect of republican thought and did not fully become a public servant until he was financially comfortable and could retire from his occupation as a printer. In the following speech given at the Constitutional Convention, the famous Pennsylvanian exhorts his colleagues to embrace restrictions on the payment of public servants—a plea that eventually was ignored.

It is with reluctance that I rise to express a disapprobation of any one article of the plan for which we are so much obliged to the honorable gentlemen who laid it before us. From its first reading I have borne a good will to it, and, in general, wished it success. In this particular of salaries to the executive branch, I happen to differ; and, as my opinion may appear new and chimerical, it is only from a persuasion that it is right, and from a sense of duty, that I hazard it. The committee will judge of my reasons when they have heard them, and their judgment may possibly change mine. I think I see inconveniences in the appointment of salaries; I see none in refusing them, but, on the contrary, great advantages.

Sir, there are two passions which have a powerful influence in the affairs of men. These are ambition and avarice—the love of power and the love of money. Separately, each of these has great force in prompting men to action; but, when united in view of the same object, they have, in many minds, the most violent effects. Place before the eyes of such men a post of honor, that shall, at the same time, be a place of profit, and they will move heaven and earth to obtain it. . . .

And of what kind are the men that will strive for this profitable preeminence, through all the bustle of cabal, the heat of contention, the infinite mutual abuse of parties, tearing to pieces the best of characters? It will not be the wise and moderate, the lovers of peace and good order, the men fittest for the trust. It will be the bold and the violent, the men of strong passions and indefatigable activity in their selfish pursuits. These will thrust themselves into your government and be your rulers. And these, too, will be mistaken in the expected happiness of their situation, for their vanquished competitors, of the same spirit, and from the same motives, will perpetually be endeavoring to distress their administration, thwart their measures, and render them odious to the people. . . .

To bring the matter nearer home, have we not seen the greatest and most important of our offices, that of general of our armies, executed for eight years together, without the smallest salary, by a patriot whom I will not now offend by any other praise; and this, through fatigues and distresses, in common with the other brave men, his military friends and companions, and the constant anxieties peculiar to his station? And shall we doubt finding three or four men in all the United States with public spirit enough to bear sitting in peaceful council, for, perhaps, an equal term, merely to preside over our civil concerns, and see that our laws are duly executed?

Sir, I have a better opinion of our country. I think we shall never be without a sufficient number of wise and good men to undertake and execute well and faithfully the office in question.

Sir, the saving of the salaries, that may at first be proposed, is not an object with me. The subsequent mischiefs of proposing them are what I apprehend. And, therefore, it is that I move the amendment. If it be not seconded or accepted, I must be contented with the satisfaction of having delivered my opinion frankly and done my duty.

7

George Washington: Inaugural Address (1789)

Never considered as intellectually sophisticated as some of the other American leaders of his era, including Benjamin Franklin, James Madison, Thomas Jefferson, and John Adams, George Washington was, nonetheless, an individual who inspired Americans and was able to crystallize the complexities of republican thought. One of the facets of Washington's character that was so appealing to the masses was that he was an essentialist. He believed in "immutable principles" that governed the universe and this, to many, simplified the multidimensional nature of political and social movements then influencing American society at the time of the founding. In the readings that follow, excerpted from both his inaugural and farewell addresses, Washington emphasizes what he felt was one of the most important essentials to establishing a progressive and enduring nation—a virtuous citizenry.

. . . In these honorable qualifications, I behold the surest pledges, that as on one side, no local prejudices, or attachments; no separate views, nor party animosities, will misdirect the comprehensive and equal eye which ought to watch over this great Assemblage of communities and interests: so, on another, that the foundations of our national policy, will be laid in the pure and immutable principles of private morality; and the pre-eminence of free Government, be exemplified by all the attributes which can win the affections of its Citizens, and command the respect of the world. I dwell on this prospect with every satisfaction which an ardent love for my Country can inspire: since there is no truth more thoroughly established, than that there exists in the economy and course of nature, an indissoluble union between virtue and happiness, between duty and advantage, between the genuine maxims of an honest and magnanimous policy, and the solid rewards of public prosperity and felicity: Since we ought to be no less persuaded that the propitious smiles of Heaven, can never be expected on a nation that disregards the eternal rules of order and right, which Heaven itself has ordained: And since the preservation of the sacred fire of liberty, and the destiny of the Republican model of Government, are justly considered as deeply, perhaps as finally staked, on the experiment entrusted to the hands of the American people.

8

George Washington: Farewell Address (1796)

. . . It is substantially true, that virtue or morality is a necessary spring of popular government. The rule indeed extends with more or less force to every species of Free Government. Who that is a sincere friend to it, can look with indifference upon attempts to shake the foundation of the fabric.

Promote then as an object of primary importance, Institutions for the general diffusion of knowledge. In proportion as the structure of a government gives force to public opinion, it is essential that public opinion should be enlightened. . . .

Observe good faith & justice towards all Nations. Cultivate peace & harmony with all—Religion & morality enjoin this conduct; and can it be that good policy does not equally enjoin it? It will be worthy of a free, enlightened, and, at no distant period, a great Nation, to give to mankind the magnanimous and too novel example of a People always guided by an exalted justice & benevolence. Who can doubt that in the course of time and things the fruits of such a plan would richly repay any temporary advantages which might be lost by a steady adherence to it? Can it be, that Providence has not connected the permanent felicity of a Nation with its virtue? The experiment, at least, is recommended by every sentiment which ennobles human Nature. Alas! is it rendered impossible by its vices?. . .

9

Thomas Jefferson: Letter to His Grandson, Thomas Jefferson Randolph (1808)

Arguably the Founding Father most influenced by Classical thought, Jefferson drew inspiration from the great Greek and Roman thinkers from antiquity, such as Cicero, who was famous for, among other things, identifying the main precepts of republican virtue: prudence, temperance, justice, and fortitude. In the following letter to his grandson, Jefferson reflects on all of these components of virtue to varying degrees.

. . . I have mentioned good humor as one of the preservatives of our peace and tranquillity. It is among the most effectual, and its effect is so well imitated and aided artificially by politeness, that this also becomes an acquisition of first rate value. In truth, politeness is artificial good humor, it covers the natural want of it, and ends by rendering habitual a substitute nearly equivalent to the real virtue. It is the practice of sacrificing to those whom we meet in society all the little conveniences and preferences which will gratify them, and deprive us of nothing worth a moment's consideration; it is the giving a pleasing and flattering turn to our expressions which will conciliate others, and make them pleased with us as well as themselves. How cheap a price for the good will of another! When this is in return for a rude thing said by another, it brings him to his senses, it mortifies and corrects him in the most salutary way, and places him at the feet of your good nature in the eyes of the company. But in stating prudential rules for our government in society I must not omit the important one of never entering into dispute or argument with another. I never yet saw an instance of one of two disputants convincing the other by argument. I have seen many on their getting warm, becoming rude, and shooting one another. Conviction is the effect of our own dispassionate reasoning, either in solitude, or weighing within ourselves dispassionately what we hear from others standing uncommitted in argument ourselves. It was one of the rules which above all others made Doctr. Franklin the most amiable of men in society, 'never to contradict any body.' If he was urged to announce an opinion, he did it rather by asking questions, as if for information, or by suggesting doubts. When I hear another express an opinion, which is not mine, I say to myself, He has a right to his opinion, as to mine; why should I question it. His error does me no injury, and shall I become a Don Quixote to bring all men by force of argument, to one opinion? If a fact be misstated, it is probable he is gratified by a belief of it, and I have no right to deprive him of the gratification. If he wants information he will ask it, and then I will give it in measured terms; but if he still believes his own story, and shows a desire to dispute the fact with me, I hear him and say nothing. It is his affair, not mine, if he prefers error. There are two classes of disputants most frequently to be met with among us. The first is of young students just entered the threshold of science, with a first view of its outlines, not yet filled up with the details and modifications which a further progress would bring to their knowledge. The other consists of the ill-tempered and rude men in society who have taken up a passion for politics. (Good humor and politeness never introduce into mixed society a question on which they foresee there will be a difference of opinion.) From both of these classes of disputants, my dear Jefferson, keep aloof, as you would from the infected subjects of yellow fever or pestilence. Consider yourself, when with them, as among the patients of Bedlam needing medical more than moral counsel. Be a listener only, keep within yourself, and endeavor to establish with yourself the habit of silence, especially in politics. In the fevered state of our country, no good can ever result from any attempt to set one of these fiery zealots to rights either in fact or principle. They are determined as to the facts they will believe, and the opinions on which they will act. Get by them, therefore as you would by an angry bull: it is not for a man of sense to dispute the road with such an animal. You will be more exposed than others to have these animals shaking their horns at you, because of the relation in which you stand with me and to hate me as a chief in the antagonist party your presence will be to them what the vomit-grass is to the sick dog a nostrum for producing an ejaculation. Look upon them exactly with that eye, and pity them as objects to whom you can administer only occasional ease. My character is not within their power. It is in the hands of my fellow citizens at large, and will be consigned to honor or infamy by the verdict of the republican mass of our country, according to what themselves will have seen, not what their enemies and mine shall have said. Never therefore consider these puppies in politics as requiring any notice from you, and always shew that you are not afraid to leave my character to the umpirage of public opinion. Look steadily to the pursuits which have carried you to Philadelphia, be very select in the society you attach yourself to; avoid taverns, drinkers, smokers, and idlers and dissipated persons generally; for it is with such that broils and contentions arise, and you will find your path more easy and tranquil. The limits of my paper warn me that it is time for me to close with my affectionate Adieux. . . .

10

Lyman Beecher: *Six Sermons on Intemperance* (1828)

A controversial clergyman who often fell into disfavor with conservative religious bodies in New England, Lyman Beecher was concerned about what he saw as the moral decline of society. Issues such as alcoholism and prostitution had long been targets for attack, though new social ills such as urban poverty and wealthy extravagance were beginning to afflict certain areas of the United States. In one of his famous diatribes, excerpts of which follow, Beecher outlines the evils of alcohol abuse and connects such behavior to the erosion of virtue and republican values.

But of all the ways to hell, which the feet of deluded mortals tread, that of the intemperate is the most dreary and terrific. The demand for artificial stimulus to supply the deficiencies of healthful aliment, is like the rage of thirst, and the ravenous demand of famine. It is famine: for the artificial excitement has become as essential now to strength and cheerfulness, as simple nutrition once was. But nature, taught by habit to require what once she did not need, demands gratification now with a decision inexorable as death, and to most men as irresistible. The denial is a living death. The stomach, the head, the heart, and arteries, and veins, and every muscle, and every nerve, feel the exhaustion, and the restless, unutterable wretchedness which puts out the light of life, and curtains the heavens, and carpets the earth with sackcloth. All these varieties of sinking nature, call upon the wretched man with trumpet tongue, to dispel this darkness, and raise the ebbing tide of life, by the application of the cause which produced these woes, and after a momentary alleviation will produce them again with deeper terrors, and more urgent importunity; for the repetition, at each time renders the darkness deeper, and the torments of self-denial more irresistible and intolerable. . . .

These sufferings, however, of animal nature, are not to be compared with the moral agonies which convulse the soul. It is an immortal being who sins, and suffers; and as his earthly house dissolves, he is approaching the judgment seat, in anticipation of a miserable eternity. He feels his captivity, and in anguish of spirit clanks his chains and cries for help. Conscience thunders, remorse goads, and as the gulf opens before him, he recoils, and trembles, and weeps, and prays, and resolves, and promises, and reforms, and "seeks it yet again,"— again resolves, and weeps, and prays, and "seeks it yet again!" Wretched man, he has placed himself in the hands of a giant, who never pities, and never relaxes his iron gripe. He may struggle, but he is in chains. He may cry for release, but it comes not; and lost! lost! may be inscribed upon the door posts of his dwelling. . . .

Upon national industry the effects of intemperance are manifest and mischievous. The results of national industry depend on the amount of well-directed intellectual and physical power. But intemperance paralyses and prevents both these springs of human action.

In the inventory of national loss by intemperance, may be set down—the labor prevented by indolence, by debility, by sickness, by quarrels and litigation, by gambling and idleness, by mistakes and misdirected effort, by improvidence and wastefulness, and by the shortened date of human life and activity. Little wastes in great establishments constantly occurring may defeat the energies of a mighty capital. But where the intellectual and muscular energies are raised to the working point daily by ardent spirits, until the agriculture, and commerce, and arts of a nation move on by the power of artificial stimulus, that moral power cannot be maintained, which will guaranty fidelity, and that physical power cannot be preserved and well directed, which will ensure national prosperity. The nation whose immense enterprise is thrust forward by the stimulus of ardent spirits, cannot ultimately escape debility and bankruptcy. . . .

The prospect of a destitute old age, or of a suffering family, no longer troubles the vicious portion of our community. They drink up their daily earnings, and bless God for the poor-house, and begin to look upon it as, of right, the drunkard's home, and contrive to arrive thither as early as idleness and excess will give them a passport to this sinecure of vice. Thus is the insatiable destroyer of industry marching through the land, rearing poor-houses, and augmenting taxation: night and day, with sleepless activity, squandering property, cutting the sinews of industry, undermining vigor, engendering disease, paralysing intellect, impairing moral principle, cutting short the date of life, and rolling up a national debt, invisible, but real and terrific as the debt of England: continually transferring larger and larger bodies of men, from the class of contributors to the national income, to the class of worthless consumers. . . .

It is admitted that intelligence and virtue are the pillars of republican institutions, and that the illumination of schools, and the moral power of religious institutions, are indispensable to produce this intelligence and virtue. But who are found so uniformly in the ranks of irreligion as the intemperate? Who like these violate the Sabbath, and set their mouth against the heavens—neglecting the education of their families—and corrupting their morals? Almost the entire amount of national ignorance and crime is the offspring of intemperance. Throughout the land, the intemperate are hewing down the pillars, and undermining the foundations of our national edifice. Legions have besieged it, and upon every gate the battle-axe rings; and still the sentinels sleep.

Should the evil advance as it has done, the day is not far distant when the great body of the laboring classes of the community, the bones and sinews of the nation, will be contaminated; and when this is accomplished, the right of suffrage becomes the engine of self-destruction. For the laboring classes constitute an immense majority, and when these are perverted by intemperance, ambition needs no better implements with which to dig the grave of our liberties, and entomb our glory.

Such is the influence of interest, ambition, fear, and indolence, that one violent partisan, with a handful of disciplined troops, may overrule the influence of five hundred temperate men, who act without concert. Already is the disposition to temporize, to tolerate, and even to court the intemperate, too apparent, on account of the apprehended retribution of their perverted suffrage. The whole power of law, through the nation, sleeps in the statute book, and until public sentiment is roused and concentrated, it may be doubted whether its execution is possible. Where is the city, town, or village, in which the laws are not openly violated, and where is the magistracy that dares to carry into effect the laws against the vending or drinking of ardent spirits? Here then an aristocracy of bad influence has already risen up, which bids defiance to law, and threatens the extirpation of civil liberty. As intemperance increases, the power of taxation will come more and more into the hands of men of intemperate habits and desperate fortunes; of course the laws gradually will become subservient to the debtor, and less efficacious in protecting the rights of property. This will be a vital stab to liberty—to the security of which property is indispensable. For money is the sinew of war—and when those who hold the property of a nation cannot be protected in their rights, they will change the form of government, peaceably if they may, by violence if they must.

11

Abraham Lincoln: Address to the Washington Temperance Society in Springfield, Illinois (1842)

Two decades before his ascension to the White House, Abraham Lincoln had already exhibited a remarkable ability to endear himself to people of various backgrounds and political persuasions. By the 1840s, the temperance movement had gained momentum, spawning hundreds of local organizations around the country. In the following reading, Lincoln warmly addresses the Washington Temperance Society, which was composed of reformed alcoholics seeking to combat alcohol abuse.

Although the Temperance cause has been in progress for near twenty years, it is apparent to all, that it is, just now, being crowned with a degree of success, hitherto unparalleled. . . .

On this point, [you] greatly excel the temperance advocates of former times. Those whom [you] desire to convince and persuade, are [your] old friends and companions. [You] know they are not demons, nor even the worst of men. [You] know that generally, they are kind, generous and charitable, even beyond the example of their more staid and sober neighbors. They are practical philanthropists; and they glow with a generous and brotherly zeal, that mere theorizers are incapable of feeling. Benevolence and charity possess their hearts entirely; and out of the abundance of their hearts, their tongues give utterance. "Love through all their actions runs, and all their words are mild." In this spirit they speak and act, and in the same, they are heard and regarded. And when such is the temper of the advocate, and such of the audience, no good cause can be unsuccessful. . . .

[One] error, as it seems to me, into which the old reformers fell, was, the position that all habitual drunkards were utterly incorrigible, and therefore, must be turned adrift, and damned without remedy, in order that the grace of temperance might abound to the temperate then, and to all mankind some hundred years thereafter. There is in this something so repugnant to humanity, so uncharitable, so cold-blooded and feelingless, that it never did, nor ever can enlist the enthusiasm of a popular cause. We could not love the man who taught it—we could not hear him with patience. The heart could not throw open its portals to it. The generous man could not adopt it. It could not mix with his blood. It looked so fiendishly selfish, so like throwing fathers and brothers overboard, to lighten the boat for our security—that the noble minded shrank from the manifest meanness of the thing. . . .

By the Washingtonians, this system of consigning the habitual drunkard to hopeless ruin, is repudiated. They adopt a more enlarged philanthropy. They go for present as well as future good. They labor for all now living, as well as all hereafter to live. They teach hope to all—despair to none. As applying to their cause, they deny the doctrine of unpardonable sin. As in Christianity it is taught, so in this they teach, that

> While the lamp holds out to burn,
> The vilest sinner may return.

To these new champions, and this new system of tactics, our late success is mainly owing; and to them we must chiefly look for the final consummation. The ball is now rolling gloriously on, and none are so able as they to increase its speed, and its bulk—to add to its momentum, and its magnitude. Even though unlearned in letters, for this task, none others are so well educated. To fit them for this work, they have been taught in the true school. They have been in that gulf, from which they would teach others the means of escape. They have passed that prison wall, which others have long declared impassable; and who that has not, shall dare to weigh opinions with them, as to the mode of passing. . . .

But it is said by some, that men will think and act for themselves; that none will disuse spirits or any thing else, merely because his neighbors do; and that moral influence is not that powerful engine contended for. Let us examine this. Let me ask the man who would maintain this position most stiffly, what compensation he will accept to go to church some Sunday and sit during the sermon with his wife's bonnet upon his head? Not a trifle, I'll venture. And why not? There would be nothing irreligious in it: nothing immoral, nothing uncomfortable. Then why not? Is it not because there would be something egregiously unfashionable in it? Then it is the influence of fashion; and what is the influence of fashion, but the influence that other people's actions have [on our own?] actions, the strong inclination each of us feels to do as we see all our neighbors do? Nor is the influence of fashion confined to any particular thing or class of things. It is just as strong on one subject as another. Let us make it as unfashionable to withhold our names from the temperance pledge as for husbands to wear their wives bonnets to church, and instances will be just as rare in the one case as the other. . . .

Indeed, I believe, if we take habitual drunkards as a class, their heads and their hearts will bear an advantageous comparison with those of any other class. There seems ever to have been a proneness in the brilliant, and the warm-blooded, to fall into this vice. The demon of intemperance ever seems to have delighted in sucking the blood of genius and of generosity. What one of us but can call to mind some dear relative, more promising in youth than all his fellows, who has fallen a sacrifice to his rapacity? He ever seems to have gone forth, like the Egyptian angel of death, commissioned to slay if not the first, the fairest born of every family. Shall he now be arrested in his desolating career? In that arrest, all can give aid that will; and who shall be excused that can, and will not? Far around as human breath has ever blown, he keeps our fathers, our brothers, our sons, and our friends, prostrate in the chains of moral death. To all the living every where, we cry, "come sound the moral resurrection trump, that these may rise and stand up, an exceeding great army"— "Come from the four winds, O breath! and breathe upon these slain, that they may live."

If the relative grandeur of revolutions shall be estimated by the great amount of human misery they alleviate, and the small amount they inflict, then, indeed, will this be the grandest the world shall ever have seen. Of our political revolution of '76, we all are justly proud. It has given us a degree of political freedom, far exceeding that of any other of the nations of the earth. In it the world has found a solution of that long mooted problem, as to the capability of man to govern himself. In it was the germ which has vegetated, and still is to grow and expand into the universal liberty of mankind.

But with all these glorious results, past, present, and to come, it had its evils too. It breathed forth famine, swam in blood and rode on fire; and long, long after, the orphan's cry, and the widow's wail, continued to break the sad silence that ensued. These were the price, the inevitable price, paid for the blessings it bought.

Turn now, to the temperance revolution. In it, we shall find a stronger bondage broken; a viler slavery, manumitted; a greater tyrant deposed. In it, more of want supplied, more disease healed, more sorrow assuaged. By it no orphans starving, no widows weeping. By it, none wounded in feeling, none injured in interest. Even the dram-maker, and dram seller, will have glided into other occupations so gradually, as never to have felt the shock of change; and will stand ready to join all others in the universal song of gladness. . . .

12

William A. Alcott: *The Young Wife* (1838)

By the middle of the nineteenth century, Victorian culture, which stressed the need for women to actively promote and cultivate virtue within their families, had begun to significantly impact American society. Like other Victorians, William Alcott believed that the role of women in society should be to promote a civilizing influence, and he published widely on that topic. In the following reading, Alcott describes what, in his opinion, are the proper qualities of a virtuous woman— supportive, patient, and passive, yet assertive and diligent in promoting moral improvement.

. . . Every wife has it in her power to make her husband either better or worse. This result is accomplished, not merely by giving advice, nor by advice and instruction alone. Both these have their influence; and as means of improvement, should not be neglected. But it is by the general tone and spirit of her conversation, as manifesting the temper and disposition of the heart, that she makes the most abiding impressions. These are modifying his character daily and hourly; sometimes even when absent. The thought of what a wife wishes or expects, especially when a letter or paper is occasionally received from her or from some member of the family, is silently and perhaps unconsciously changing a husband's character. . . .

It is by no means denied that the influence, in the matrimonial state, is reciprocal. No doubt it is. But I am not writing now for husbands, directly. Besides, however great may be the changes wrought in the wife by the husband, those which are wrought in the latter by the wife are frequently more surprising as well as more permanent.

But if it be true that woman is thus silently changing the current of man's affections, and the tenor of his thoughts and habits, how important that she should be well taught! How worthy of consideration the claims which have been urged in the preceding pages, and the motives which I have endeavored to present for her improvement! And how important—nay, how just—in this point of view, was the remark of Mr. Flint, in one of the numbers of the Western Review—"If this world," said he, "is ever to become a better and a happier world, woman, properly educated and truly wise enough to exert it aright, must be the original mover in the great work. . . ."

It has been said of the wife of Jonathan Edwards, that by enabling him to put forth his powers unembarrassed, she conferred a greater benefit upon mankind, than all the female public characters that ever lived or ever will live. A similar remark might be applied to the mother of almost every great and good man. Woman's true greatness consists, so it seems to me, in rendering others useful, rather than in being directly useful herself. Or, in other words, it is less her office to be seen and known in society, than to make others seen and known, and their influence felt. . . .

[N]o one is more forward than myself in opposing the idea of merging her own individuality in that of her husband. I insist on her forming for herself a character quite independent of his and a perfect one, too. In becoming a wife, I say again, no individual is to dispossess herself of any trait of character which was hers before. She is still an independent woman, notwithstanding: just as I am none the less an independent man, by becoming a member of some association. My new character and the new duties are superinduced—added to the duties which existed before. In the same way we lose nothing—dispossess ourselves of nothing—when we form new relations. No person is the less a brother, a sister, a child, a neighbor, or a citizen, because he or she has entered into the bonds of matrimony. New duties are indeed added, and new obligations imposed; but the old ones remain. We have, in effect, so many different characters to sustain; and marriage only adds one—though a very important one—to the number already existing. The wife, in becoming one with her husband, and forming, in one point of view, a new and more perfect character, loses nothing, of necessity, of her individuality; nor does her husband. Nay, more—much more than all this—the latter is, or at least ought to become so much the more perfect by it. . . .

Hence the spirit of speculation, which everywhere prevails, and which has even seized on hearts of many who profess to be governed better motives. I fear there are some professing christians who do not hesitate to enter into any of speculation which the public sentiment does not denounce, provided they have a strong hope of filling their pockets by it. . . .

Is it asked how this concerns the young wife? Surely such a question is not necessary. Has she no influence in continuing this lamentable state of things? On the contrary, is it not in her power to extend and promote, or to limit and even to suppress it, at her option? Has God given her the power to mould the character of her husband almost as she will, and has she no sort of control over his love for making money?

That it may require a great deal of time to turn the current of thought in a worldly young man—such as most young men are supposed to be, at marriage, and give it a more rational direction, is most true; but that it cannot be done at all, no one will pretend who has the least knowledge of human nature as it is, or of the motives which govern human action. And when I see a man go on from the day of his marriage to the end of life, in one continued series of effort to lay up property, as the principal object worth possessing, and when, above all, I see aged men, like aged trees, I cannot forbear to conclude that no effort has been made, worth the name, to prevent such a state of things, and to fear that the mania has possessed not only the husband, but also the wife.

The last suggestion—suspicion rather—may be revolting to some minds. Female avarice is, I confess, particularly shocking. But such a thing there is, shocking as it may be. There are females, there are wives even, to be found, not a whit less avaricious than their husbands. For the honor of human nature, however, we may hope their number is not large. . . .

In short, unless you love your husband as you ought, and have caught the spirit of improvement, you will never succeed in finding anything worthy the name of happiness below the sun. But with this love and this spirit, and a good fund of plain common sense, you will not, you cannot fail to be happy. With this, all external circumstances will be pleasant—at least comparatively so. Life will be such as will be likely to secure life's great end; and death will be but the door to a better and more enduring state of happiness. . . .

13

"Friend of Virtue": "The Just Treatment of Licentious Men. Addressed to Christian Mothers, Wives, Sisters, and Daughters" (1838)

As indicated previously, by the middle part of the nineteenth century, many Americans were concerned that the United States was becoming a haven for decadence and moral degradation. With the increasing numbers of impoverished, urban dwelling women, by the 1830s many cities became centers of prostitution. In the following reading, a "Friend of Virtue" implores women to remain valiant in their attempts to avoid licentious men and to work together to strengthen the moral foundations of women everywhere.

Dear sisters:

As members with us of the body of the Lord Jesus Christ, we take the liberty of addressing you on a subject near our hearts, and of the deepest interest to our sex. We ask your serious attention, while we press upon your consciences the inquiry, "Is it right to admit to the society of virtuous females, those unprincipled and licentious men, whose conduct is fraught with so much evil to those who stand in the relation to us of sisters?" True, God designed that man should be our protector, the guardian of our peace, our happiness, and our honor; but how often has he proved himself a traitor to his trust, and the worst enemy of our sex? The deepest degradation to which many of our sex have been reduced, the deepest injuries they have suffered, have been in consequence of his perfidy. He has betrayed, and robbed, and forsaken his victim, and left her to endure alone the untold horrors of a life embittered by self-reproach, conscious ignomiminy, and exclusion from every virtuous circle. Is there a woman among us, whose heart has not been pained at the fall and fate of some one sister of her sex? Do you say the guilty deserve to suffer and must expect it? Granted. But why not let a part of this suffering fall on the destroyer? Why is he caressed and shielded from scorn by the countenance of the virtuous, and encouraged to commit other acts of perfidy and sin, while his victim, for one offence, is trampled upon, despised and banished from all virtuous society; The victim thus crushed, yields herself to despair, and becomes a practical illustration of the proverb that, "A bad woman is the worst of all God's creatures." Surely, if she is worse, after her fall, than man equally fallen, is there not reason to infer that in her nature there is something more chaste, more pure and refined, and exalted than in his? Is it then not worth while to do something to prevent her from becoming a prey to the perfidy and baseness of unprincipled man, and a disgrace to her sex? Do you ask, what can woman do, and reply as have some others, "We must leave this work for the men?" Can we expect the wolf, ravenous for his prey, to throw up a barrier to protect the defenceless sheep? As well might we expect this, as to expect that men as a body will take measures to redress the wrongs of woman.

Dear sisters, women have commenced this work, and women must see it carried through. Commenced by women? No it was commenced by one who is now, we trust, a sainted spirit in heaven, and who sacrificed his life in the cause. Yes, he fell a martyr in the conflict, but not till he had effectually roused the women of the nation to enlist in the cause he had commenced. Moral Reform is the first of causes to our sex. It involves principles, which if faithfully and perseveringly applied, will preserve the rights and elevate the standing of our sex in society. As times have been, the libertine has found as ready a passport to the society of the virtuous, as any one, and he has as easily obtained a good wife, as the more virtuous man. But a new era has commenced. Woman has erected a standard, and laid down the principle, that man shall not trample her rights, and on the honor of her sex with impunity. She has undertaken to banish licentious men from all virtuous society. And mothers, wives, sisters, and daughters will you lend your influence to this cause? Prompt action in the form of association will accomplish this work. Females in this manner must combine their strength and exert their influence. Will you not join one of these bands of the pious? The cause has need of your interest, your prayers, and your funds. Come then to our help, and let us pray and labor together.

14

Susan B. Anthony: Speech on Social Purity (1875)

The late eighteenth century was the apex of Victorian culture in America, characterized, most notably, by concern over improving the collective morality of society. The period was also significant for the tremendous upsurge in women's rights movements, which often contradicted goals of traditional Victorians, who believed that women should remain in the domestic realm. Nevertheless, the following reading by suffragette stalwart Susan B. Anthony finds some common ground on issues of drunkenness and prostitution. Note, however, Anthony's solution to the problem—the education and independence of women—which most Victorians found unpalatable.

Though women, as a class, are much less addicted to drunkenness and licentiousness than men, it is universally conceded that they are by far the greater sufferers from these evils. Compelled by their position in society to depend on men for subsistence, for food, clothes, shelter, for every chance even to earn a dollar, they have no way of escape from the besotted victims of appetite and passion with whom their lot is cast. They must endure, if not endorse, these twin vices, embodied, as they so often are, in the person of father, brother, husband, son, employer. No one can doubt that the sufferings of the sober, virtuous woman, in legal subjection to the mastership of a drunken, immoral husband and father over herself and children, not only from physical abuse, but from spiritual shame and humiliation, must be such as the man himself can not possibly comprehend. . . .

The prosecutions on our courts for breach of promise, divorce, adultery, bigamy, seduction, rape; the newspaper reports every day of every year of scandals and outrages, of wife murders and paramour shooting, of abortions and infanticides, are perpetual reminders of men's incapacity to cope successfully with this monster evil of society. The statistics of New York show the murder of professional prostitutes in that city to be over twenty thousand. Add to these the thousands and tens of thousands of Boston, Philadelphia, Washington, New Orleans, St. Louis, Chicago, San Francisco, and all our cities, great and small, from ocean to ocean, and what a holocaust of the womanhood of this nation is sacrificed to the insatiate Moloch of lust. And yet more: those myriads of wretched women, publicly known as prostitutes, constitute but a small portion of the numbers who actually tread the paths of vice and crime. For, as the oft-broken ranks of the vast army of common drunkards are steadily filled by the boasted moderate drinkers, so are the ranks of professional prostitution continually replenished by discouraged, seduced deserted unfortunates, who can no longer hide the terrible secret of their lives. . . .

To license certain persons to keep brothels and saloons is but to throw around them and their traffic the shield of law, and thereby to blunt the edge of all moral and social efforts against them. Nevertheless, in every large city, brothels are virtually licensed. When "Maggie Smith" is made to appear before the police court at the close of each quarter, to pay her fine of $10, $25 or $100, as an inmate or a keeper of a brothel, and allowed to continue her vocation, so long as she pays her fine, that is license. When a grand jury fails to find cause for indictment against a well-known keeper of a house of ill-fame, that too, is permission for her and all her class to follow their trade, against the statue laws of the State, and with impunity.

The work of woman is not to lessen the severity or the certainty of the penalty for the violation of the moral law, but to prevent this violation by the removal of the causes, which lead to it. These causes are said to be wholly different with the sexes. The acknowledged incentive to this vice on the part of man is his own abnormal passion; while on the part of woman, in the great majority of causes, it is conceded to be destitution—absolute want of the necessaries of life. Lecky, the famous historian of European morals, says: "The statistics of prostitution show that a great proportion of those women who have fallen into it have been impelled by the most extreme poverty, in many instances verging on starvation." All other conscientious students of this terrible problem, on both continents, agree with Mr. Lecky. Hence, there is no escape from the conclusion that, while woman's want of bread induces her to purpose this vice, man's love of the vice itself leads him into it and holds him there. While statistics show no lessening of the passional demand on the part of man, they reveal a most frightful increase of the temptations, the necessities, on the part of woman.

In the olden times, when the daughters of the family, as well as the wife, were occupied with useful and profitable work in the household, getting the meals and washing the dishes three times in every day of every year, doing the baking, the brewing, the washing and the ironing, the whitewashing, the butter and cheese and soap making, the mending and the making of clothes for the entire family, the carding, spinning and weaving of the cloth—when everything to eat, to drink and to wear was manufactured in the home, almost no young women "went out to work." But now, when nearly all these handicrafts are turned over to men and to machinery, tens of thousands, nay, millions, of the women of both hemispheres are thrust into the world's outer market of work to earn their own subsistence. Society, ever slow to change its conditions, presents to these millions but few and meager chances. Only the barest necessaries, and oftentimes not even those, can be purchased with the proceeds of the most excessive and exhausting labor.

Hence, the reward of virtue for the homeless, friendless, penniless woman is ever a scanty larder, a pinched, patched, faded wardrobe, a dank basement or rickety garret, with the colder, shabbier scorn and neglect of the more fortunate of her sex. Nightly, as weary and worn from her day's toil she wends her way through the dark alleys toward her still darker abode, where only cold and hunger await her, she sees on ever side and at ever turn the gilded hand of vice and crime outstretched, beckoning her to food and clothed and shelter; hears the whisper in softest accents, "Come with me and I will give you all comforts, pleasures and luxuries that love and wealth can bestow." Since the vast multitudes of human being, women like men, are not born to the courage or conscience of the martyr, can we wonder that so many poor girls fall, that so many accept material ease and comfort at the expense of spiritual purity and peace? Should we not wonder, rather, that so many escape the sad fate?

Clearly, then, the first step forward solving this problem is to this vast army of poverty-stricken women who now crowd our cities, above the temptation, the necessity, to sell themselves, in marriage or out, for bread and shelter. To do that, girls, like boys, must be educated to some lucrative employment; women, like men, must have equal chances to earn a living. If the plea that poverty is the cause of woman's prostitution be not true, perfect equality of chances to earn honest bread will demonstrate the falsehood by removing that pretext and placing her on the same plane with man. Then, if she is found in the ranks of vice and crime, she will be there for the same reason that man is and, from an object of pity, she, like him, will become a fit subject of contempt. From being the party sinned against, she will become an equal sinner, if not the greater of the two. Women, like men, must not only have "fair play" in the world of work and self-support, but, like men, must be eligible to all the honors and emoluments of society and government. Marriage, to women as to men, must be a luxury, not a necessity; an incident of life, not all of it. And the only possible way to accomplish this great change is to accord to women equal power in the making, shaping and controlling of the circumstances of life.

That equality of rights and privileges is vested in the ballot, the symbol of power in a republic. Hence, our first and most urgent demand—that women shall be protected in the exercise of their inherent, personal, citizen's right to a voice in the government, municipal, state, national. . . .

Whoever controls work and wages, controls morals. Therefore, we must have women employers, superintendents, legislators; wherever girls go to seek the means of subsistence, there must be some woman. Nay, more; we must have women preachers, lawyers, doctors—that wherever women go to seek counsel—spiritual, legal, physical—there, too, they will be sure to find the best and noblest of their own sex to minister to them. . . .

As the fountain can rise no higher than the spring that feeds it, so a legislative body will enact or enforce no law above the average sentiment of the people who created it. Any and every reform work is sure to lead women to the ballot-box. It is idle for them to hope to battle successfully against the monster evils of society until they shall be armed with weapons equal to those of the enemy—votes and money. Archimedes said, "Give to me a fulcrum on which to plant my lever, and I will move the world." And I say, give to woman the ballot, the political fulcrum, on which to plant her moral lever, and she will lift the world into a nobler purer atmosphere. . . .

15

Alexis de Tocqueville: *Democracy in America* (1840)

By the time of Tocqueville's visit to the United States in the 1830s, many Americans were concerned that the United States had become a free-for-all with everyone seeking to further their own interests at the expense of others. Those of the founding generation who lived to witness the rapid expansion of the United States during the first few decades of the nineteenth century lamented the abandonment of strict republican virtue as a collective ideal, which stressed the need for citizens to consider the impact of their actions on society as a whole. Tocqueville, however, notes below in his famous work Democracy in America *that self-interest, when properly practiced, is an admirable virtue in and of itself.*

. . . In the United States hardly anybody talks of the beauty of virtue, but they maintain that virtue is useful and prove it every day. The American moralists do not profess that men ought to sacrifice themselves for their fellow creatures because it is noble to make such sacrifices, but they boldly aver that such sacrifices are as necessary to him who imposes them upon himself as to him for whose sake they are made.

They have found out that, in their country and their age, man is brought home to himself by an irresistible force; and, losing all hope of stopping that force, they turn all their thoughts to the direction of it. They therefore do not deny that every man may follow his own interest, but they endeavor to prove that it is the interest of every man to be virtuous. I shall not here enter into the reasons they allege, which would divert me from my subject; suffice it to say that they have convinced their fellow countrymen.

Montaigne said long ago: "Were I not to follow the straight road for its straightness, I should follow it for having found by experience that in the end it is commonly the happiest and most useful track." The doctrine of interest rightly understood is not then new, but among the Americans of our time it finds universal acceptance; it has become popular there; you may trace it at the bottom of all their actions, you will remark it in all they say. It is as often asserted by the poor man as by the rich. In Europe the principle of interest is much grosser than it is in America, but it is also less common and especially it is less avowed; among us, men still constantly feign great abnegation which they no longer feel.

The Americans, on the other hand, are fond of explaining almost all the actions of their lives by the principle of self-interest rightly understood; they show with complacency how an enlightened regard for themselves constantly prompts them to assist one another and inclines them willingly to sacrifice a portion of their time and property to the welfare of the state. In this respect I think they frequently fail to do themselves justice, for in the United States as well as elsewhere people are sometimes seen to give way to those disinterested and spontaneous impulses that are natural to man; but the Americans seldom admit that they yield to emotions of this kind; they are more anxious to do honor to their philosophy than to themselves. . . .

The principle of self-interest rightly understood produces no great acts of self-sacrifice, but it suggests daily small acts of self-denial. By itself it cannot suffice to make a man virtuous; but it disciplines a number of persons in habits of regularity, temperance, moderation, foresight, self-command; and if it does not lead men straight to virtue by the will, it gradually draws them in that direction by their habits. If the principle of interest rightly understood were to sway the whole moral world, extraordinary virtues would doubtless be more rare; but I think that gross depravity would then also be less common. The principle of interest rightly understood perhaps prevents men from rising far above the level of mankind, but a great number of other men, who were falling far below it, are caught and restrained by it. Observe some few individuals, they are lowered by it; survey mankind, they are raised.

I am not afraid to say that the principle of self-interest rightly understood appears to me the best suited of all philosophical theories to the wants of the men of our time, and that I regard it as their chief remaining security against themselves. Towards it, therefore, the minds of the moralists of our age should turn; even should they judge it to be incomplete, it must nevertheless be adopted as necessary.

I do not think, on the whole, that there is more selfishness among us than in America; the only difference is that there it is enlightened, here it is not. Each American knows when to sacrifice some of his private interests to save the rest; we want to save everything, and often we lose it all. Everybody I see about me seems bent on teaching his contemporaries, by precept and example, that what is useful is never wrong. Will nobody undertake to make them understand how what is right may be useful?

No power on earth can prevent the increasing equality of conditions from inclining the human mind to seek out what is useful or from leading every member of the community to be wrapped up in himself. It must therefore be expected that personal interest will become more than ever the principal if not the sole spring of men's actions; but it remains to be seen how each man will understand his personal interest. If the members of a community, as they become more equal, become more ignorant and coarse, it is difficult to foresee to what pitch of stupid excesses their selfishness may lead them; and no one can foretell into what disgrace and wretchedness they would plunge themselves lest they should have to sacrifice something of their own well-being to the prosperity of their fellow creatures.

I do not think that the system of self-interest as it is professed in America is in all its parts self-evident, but it contains a great number of truths so evident that men, if they are only educated, cannot fail to see them. Educate, then, at any rate, for the age of implicit self-sacrifice and instinctive virtues is already flitting far away from us, and the time is fast approaching when freedom, public peace, and social order itself will not be able to exist without education.

16

William Ellery Channing: On the Elevation of the Laboring Classes (1840)

By the 1840s, the concept of republican simplicity as an essential American virtue had not completely disappeared. A devoutly religious Unitarian, William Ellery Channing believed in the genuine goodness of human nature and in activist attempts to alleviate suffering. Addressed to apprentices and manual laborers, the following reading reveals Channing's disillusionment with free market capitalism and his opinions on the need for working-class families to make sound moral and financial decisions.

. . . I am naturally, almost necessarily, led to address you on a topic which must insure the attention of such an audience: namely, the elevation of that portion of the community who subsist by the labor of the hands. This work, I have said, is going on. I may add, that it is advancing nowhere so rapidly as in this city. I do not believe that, on the face of the earth, the spirit of improvement has anywhere seized so strongly on those who live by the sweat of the brow as among ourselves. . . .

[L]abor in due proportion is an important part of our present lot. It is the condition of all outward comforts and improvements, whilst, at the same time, it conspires with higher means and influences in ministering to the vigor and growth of the soul. Let us not fight against it. We need this admonition, because the present moment there is a general disposition to shun labor; and this ought to be regarded as a bad sign of our times. The city is thronged with adventurers from the country, and the liberal professions are overstocked, in the hope of escaping the primeval sentence of living by the sweat of the brow; and to this crowding of men into trade we owe not only the neglect of agriculture, but, what is far worse, the demoralization of the community. It generates excessive competition, which of necessity generates fraud. Trade is turned to gambling; and a spirit of mad speculation exposes public and private interests to a disastrous instability. . . . Let us learn to regard manual toil as the true discipline of a man. Not a few of the wisest, grandest spirits have toiled at the work-bench and the plough. . . .

I now proceed to my main subject. I have said that the elevation of a man is to be sought, or rather consists, first, in force of thought exerted for the acquisition of truth; and to this I ask your serious attention. Thought, thought, is the fundamental distinction of mind, and the great work of life. All that a man does outwardly is but the expression and completion of his inward thought. To work effectually, he must think clearly. To act nobly, he must think nobly. Intellectual force is a principal element of the soul's life, and should be proposed by every man as a principal end of his being. It is common to distinguish between the intellect and the conscience, between the power of thought and virtue, and to say that virtuous action is worth more than strong thinking. But we mutilate our nature by thus drawing lines between actions or energies of the soul, which are intimately, indissolubly bound together. The head and the heart are not more vitally connected than thought and virtue. Does not conscience include, as a part of itself, the noblest action of the intellect or reason? Do we not degrade it by making it a mere feeling? Is it not something more? Is it not a wise discernment of the right, the holy, the good? Take away thought from virtue, and what remains worthy of a man? Is not high virtue more than blind instinct? Is it not founded on, and does it not include clear, bright perceptions of what is lovely and grand in character and action? Without power of thought, what we call conscientiousness, or a desire to do right, shoots out into illusion, exaggeration, pernicious excess. The most cruel deeds on earth have been perpetrated in the name of conscience. Men have hated and murdered one another from a sense of duty. The worst frauds have taken the name of pious. Thought, intelligence, is the dignity of a man, and no man is rising but in proportion as he is learning to think clearly and forcibly, or directing the energy of his mind to the acquisition of truth. Every man, in whatsoever condition, is to be a student. No matter what other vocation he may have, his chief vocation is to Think. . . .

That some should be richer than others is natural and is necessary, and could only be prevented by gross violations of right. Leave men to the free use of their powers, and some will accumulate more than their neighbors. But to be prosperous is not to be superior; and should form no barrier between men. Wealth ought not to secure to the prosperous the slightest consideration. The only distinctions which should be recognized are those of the soul, of strong principle, of incorruptible integrity, of usefulness, of cultivated intellect, of fidelity in seeking for truth. A man in proportion as he has these claims, should be honored and welcomed everywhere. I see not why such a man, however coarsely if neatly dressed, should not be a respected guest in the most splendid mansions, and at the most brilliant meetings. A man is worth infinitely more than the saloons, and the costumes, and the show of the universe. He was made to tread all these beneath his feet. What an insult to humanity is the present deference to dress and upholstery, as if silk-worms, and looms, and scissors, and needles could produce something nobler than a man! Every good man should protest against a caste founded on outward prosperity, because it exalts the outward above the inward, the material above the spiritual; because it springs from and cherishes a contemptible pride in superficial and transitory distinctions; because it alienates man from his brother, breaks the tie of common humanity, and breeds jealousy, scorn, and mutual ill-will. Can this be needed to social order? . . .

Another consideration, in reply to the objection, is, that as yet no community has seriously set itself to the work of improving all its members, so that what is possible remains to be ascertained. No experiment has been made to determine how far liberal provision can be made at once for the body and mind of the laborer. The highest social art is yet in its infancy. Great minds have nowhere solemnly, earnestly undertaken to resolve the problem, how the multitude of men may be elevated. The trial is to come. Still more, the multitude have nowhere comprehended distinctly the true idea of progress, and resolved deliberately and solemnly to reduce it to reality. This great thought, however, is gradually opening on them, and it is destined to work wonders. From themselves their salvation must chiefly come. Little can be done for them by others, till a spring is touched in their own breasts; and this being done, they cannot fail. The people, as history shows us, can accomplish miracles under the power of a great idea. How much have they often done and suffered in critical moments for country, for religion! The great idea of their own elevation is only beginning to unfold itself within them, and its energy is not to be foretold. A lofty conception of this kind, were it once distinctly seized, would be a new life breathed into them. Under this impulse they would create time and strength for their high calling, and would not only regenerate themselves, but the community. . . .

I will mention one more cause of the depressed condition of many laborers, and that is, sloth, "the sin which doth most easily beset us." How many are there who, working languidly and reluctantly, bring little to pass, spread the work of one hour over many, shrink from difficulties which ought to excite them, keep themselves poor, and thus doom their families to ignorance as well as to want!

In these remarks I have endeavored to show that the great obstacles to the improvement of the laboring classes are in themselves, and many therefore be overcome. They want nothing but the will. Outward difficulty will shrink and vanish before them, just as far as they are bent on progress, just as far as the great idea of their own elevation shall take possession of their minds. I know that many will smile at the suggestion, that the laborer may be brought to practise thrift and self-denial, for the purpose of becoming a nobler being. But such sceptics, having never experienced the power of a grand thought or generous purpose, are no judges of others. They may be assured, however, that enthusiasm is not wholly a dream, and that it is not wholly unnatural for individuals or bodies to get the idea of something higher and more inspiring than their past attainments. . . .

DISCUSSION QUESTIONS FOR CHAPTER 2

1. What was the motivation for so many early American leaders to promote the classical virtues of prudence, temperance, justice, and fortitude? How do you reconcile the fact that many of the most outspoken proponents of such behavior—Benjamin Franklin, for example—did not always follow their own advice?

2. In Thomas Paine's reading, which virtue is he extolling? Why did he feel that this characteristic was so vital to the survival of the United States?

3. Do you notice any similarities and/or differences in George Washington's inaugural and farewell addresses? What does he argue is a necessity for a government to properly meet the needs of the populace? How does Franklin's warning against paying public officials reconcile with Washington's opinions on government?

4. Why do you think that the nineteenth century witnessed such a strong temperance movement? How did this correspond with an increasing concern over sexual mores? Why did the burden of organizing and mobilizing many of the groups that promoted social purity and temperance fall mainly on women? How did Susan B. Anthony's views differ from the other readings' relating to the role of women in improving the moral fiber of society?

5. How did Tocqueville equate "self-interest" with commonly held perceptions of virtue? What virtues does Channing promote, and how do these virtues correspond with Tocqueville's comments?

CHAPTER 3

Religion

1

John Winthrop: Excerpt from "A Model of Christian Charity" (1630)

John Winthrop was the first governor of the colony of Massachusetts. His "Model of Christian Charity," a sermon written at sea during the trip from England, illustrates the great importance of religion to the original European settlers of North America, many of whom took religion, or the worship of God, as the primary purpose of the political communities they set out to establish.

Herein are four things to be propounded; first the persons, secondly the work, thirdly the end, fourthly the means. 1. For the persons. We are a company professing ourselves fellow members of Christ, in which respect only though we were absent from each other many miles, and had our employments as far distant, yet we ought to account ourselves knit together by this bond of love, and, live in the exercise of it, if we would have comfort of our being in Christ. . . . Secondly for the work we have in hand. It is by a mutual consent, through a special overvaluing providence and a more than an ordinary approbation of the Churches of Christ, to seek out a place of cohabitation and Consortship under a due form of Government both civil and ecclesiastical. In such cases as this, the care of the public must oversway all private respects, by which, not only conscience, but mere civil policy, doth bind us. For it is a true rule that particular estates cannot subsist in the ruin of the public. Thirdly. The end is to improve our lives to do more service to the Lord; the comfort and increase of the body of Christ, whereof we are members; that ourselves and posterity may be the better preserved from the common corruptions of this evil world, to serve the Lord and work out our Salvation under the power and purity of his holy ordinances. Fourthly for the means whereby this must be effected. They are twofold, a conformity with the work and end we aim at. These we see are extraordinary, therefore we must not content ourselves with usual ordinary means. Whatsoever we did, or ought to have, done, when we lived in England, the same must we do, and more also, where we go. That which the most in their churches maintain as truth in profession only, we must bring into familiar and constant practice; as in this duty of love, we must love brotherly without dissimulation, we must love one another with a pure heart fervently. We must bear one another's burdens. We must not look only on our own things, but also on the things of our brethren. Neither must we think that the Lord will bear with such failings at our hands as he doth from those among whom we have lived; and that for these three reasons; 1. In regard of the more near bond of marriage between him and us, wherein he hath taken us to be his, after a most strict and peculiar manner, which will make them the more jealous of our love and obedience. So he tells the people of Israel, "you only have I known of all the families of the Earth, therefore will I punish you for your transgressions." Secondly, because the Lord will be sanctified in them that come near him. We know that there were many that corrupted the service of the Lord; some setting up altars before his own; others offering both strange fire and strange sacrifices also; yet there came no fire from heaven, or other sudden judgment upon them, as did upon Nadab and Abihu, who yet we may think did not sin presumptuously. Thirdly. When God gives a special commission he looks to have it strictly observed in every article; When he gave Saul a commission to destroy Amaleck, He indented with him upon certain articles, and because he failed in one of the least, and that upon a fair pretence, it lost him the kingdom, which should have been his reward, if he had observed his commission. Thus stands the cause between God and us. We are entered into Covenant with Him for this work. We have taken out a commission. The Lord hath given us leave to draw our own articles. We have professed to enterprise these and those accounts, upon these and those ends. We have hereupon besought Him of favor and blessing. Now if the Lord shall please to hear us, and bring us in peace to the place we desire, then hath he ratified this covenant and sealed our Commission, and will expect a strict performance of the articles contained in it; but if we shall neglect the observation of these articles which are the ends we have propounded, and, dissembling with our God, shall fall to embrace this present world and prosecute our carnal intentions, seeking great things for ourselves and our posterity, the Lord will surely break out in wrath against us; be revenged of such a people and make us know the price of the breach of such a covenant.

Now the only way to avoid this shipwreck, and to provide for our posterity, is to follow the counsel of Micah, to do justly, to love mercy, to walk humbly with our God. For this end, we must be knit together, in this work, as one man. We must entertain each other in brotherly affection. We must be willing to abridge ourselves of our superfluities, for the supply of others' necessities. We must uphold a familiar commerce together in all meekness, gentleness, patience and liberality. We must delight in each other; make others' conditions our own; rejoice together, mourn together, labor and suffer together, always having before our eyes our commission and community in the work, as members of the same body. So shall we keep the unity of the spirit in the bond of peace. The Lord will be our God, and delight to dwell among us, as His own people, and will command a blessing upon us in all our ways, so that we shall see much more of His wisdom, power, goodness and truth, than formerly we have been acquainted with. We shall find that the God of Israel is among us, when ten of us shall be able to resist a thousand of our enemies; when He shall make us a praise and glory that men shall say of succeeding plantations, "may the Lord make it like that of New England." For we must consider that we shall be as a city upon a hill. The eyes of all people are upon us. So that if we shall deal falsely with our God in this work we have undertaken, and so cause Him to withdraw His present help from us, we shall be made a story and a by-word through the world. We shall open the mouths of enemies to speak evil of the ways of God, and all professors for God's sake. We shall shame the faces of many of God's worthy servants, and cause their prayers to be turned into curses upon us till we be consumed out of the good land whither we are going.

And to shut this discourse with that exhortation of Moses, that faithful servant of the Lord, in his last farewell to Israel, Deut. 30. "Beloved, there is now set before us life and death, good and evil," in that we are commanded this day to love the Lord our God, and to love one another, to walk in his ways and to keep his Commandments and his ordinance and his laws, and the articles of our Covenant with Him, that we may live and be multiplied, and that the Lord our God may bless us in the land whither we go to possess it. But if our hearts shall turn away, so that we will not obey, but shall be seduced, and worship other Gods, our pleasure and profits, and serve them; it is propounded unto us this day, we shall surely perish out of the good land whither we pass over this vast sea to possess it. Therefore let us choose life, that we and our seed may live, by obeying His voice and cleaving to Him, for He is our life and our prosperity.

2

John Adams: An Excerpt from His Diary (1756)

Between the time of the initial colonization and the later emergence of the founding generation, some Americans came to a somewhat different understanding of religion. On this view, religion is less as an end in itself than a means to other ends. The purpose of the political community is not the worship and service of God but the maintenance of a peaceful and prosperous society. Although noticeably more worldly in its aims, this position nevertheless continues to emphasize the political importance of religion as a necessary support for the morality that makes for a decent and orderly society. This understanding of the political role of religion is illustrated in the following passage from the diary of John Adams, one of the key leaders of the American Revolution and later the third president of the United States.

Suppose a nation in some distant region should take the Bible for their only law book, and every member should regulate his conduct by the precepts there exhibited! Every member would be obliged, in conscience, to temperance and frugality and industry; to justice and kindness and charity towards his fellow men; and to piety, love and reverence towards Almighty God. In this commonwealth, no man would impair his health by gluttony, drunkenness, or lust; no man would sacrifice his most precious time to cards or any other trifling and mean amusement; no man would steal, or lie, or in any way defraud his neighbor, but would live in peace and good will with all men; no man would blaspheme his Maker or profane his worship; but a rational and manly, a sincere and unaffected piety and devotion would reign in all hearts. What a Utopia; what a Paradise would this region be.

3

Benjamin Franklin: Reasons Against Satirizing Religion (1757)

Sharing Adams's concern with the moral and political usefulness of religion, Benjamin Franklin, another important figure in the Revolutionary War and later in the Constitutional Convention, here rebukes a fellow citizen for advancing an argument that would tend to undermine religious belief. Franklin thus suggests that it is the part of a good citizen to respect religion, at least in public, even if he or she does not believe in it.

I have read your manuscript with some attention. By the argument it contains against a particular Providence, though you allow a general Providence, you strike at the foundations of all religion. For, without the belief of a Providence that takes cognizance of, guards, and guides, and may favor particular persons, there is no motive to worship a Deity, to fear his displeasure, or to pray for his protection. I will not enter into any discussion of your principles, though you seem to desire it. At present I shall only give you my opinion that, though your reasons are subtle, and may prevail with some readers, you will not succeed so as to change the general sentiments of mankind on that subject, and the consequence of printing this piece will be, a great deal of odium drawn upon yourself, mischief to you, and no benefit to others. He that spits against the wind spits in his own face.

But were you to succeed, do you imagine any good would be done by it? You yourself may find it easy to live a virtuous life, without the assistance afforded by religion; you having a clear perception of the advantage of virtue, and the disadvantages of vice, and possessing a strength of resolution sufficient to enable you to resist common temptations. But think how great a portion of mankind consists of weak and ignorant men and women, and of inexperienced, inconsiderate youth of both sexes, who have need of the motives of religion to restrain them from vice, to support their virtue, and retain them in the practice of it till it becomes habitual, which is the great point for its security. And perhaps you are indebted to her originally, that is to your religious education, for the habits of virtue upon which you now justly value yourself. You might easily display your excellent talents of reasoning upon a less hazardous subject, and thereby obtain a rank with our most distinguished authors. For among us it is not necessary, as among the Hottentots, that a youth, to be raised into the company of men, should prove his manhood by beating his mother.

I would advise you, therefore, not to attempt unchaining the tiger, but to burn this piece before it is seen by any other person, whereby you will save yourself a great deal of mortification by the enemies it may raise against you, and perhaps a great deal of regret and repentance. If men are so wicked *with religion*, what would they be *if without it?*

4

Benjamin Franklin: An Excerpt from His *Autobiography* (1771)

In the following passage, Franklin, by his emphasis on morality and his indifference to purely theological doctrines, further clarifies his primarily political understanding of religion.

I had been religiously educated as a Presbyterian; and though some of the dogmas of that persuasion, such as the eternal decrees of God, election, reprobation, etc., appeared to me unintelligible, others doubtful, and I early absented myself from the public assemblies of the sect, Sunday being my studying day, I never was without some religious principles. I never doubted, for instance, the existence of the Deity; that he made the world, and governed it by his Providence; that the most acceptable service of God was the doing good to man; that our souls are immortal; and that all crime will be punished, and virtue rewarded, either here or hereafter. These I esteemed the essentials of every religion; and, being to be found in all the religions we had in our country, I respected them all, though with different degrees of respect, as I found them more or less mixed with other articles, which, without any tendency to inspire, promote, or confirm morality, served principally to divide us, and make us unfriendly to one another. This respect to all, with an opinion that the worst had some good effects, induced me to avoid all discourse that might tend to lessen the good opinion another might have of his own religion; and as our province increased in people, and new places of worship were continually wanted, and generally erected by voluntary contributions, my mite for such purpose, whatever might be the sect, was never refused.

Though I seldom attended any public worship, I had still an opinion of its propriety, and of its utility when rightly conducted, and I regularly paid my annual subscription for the support of the only Presbyterian minister or meeting we had in Philadelphia. He used to visit me sometimes as a friend, and admonish me to attend his administrations, and I was now and then prevailed on to do so, once for five Sundays successively. Had he been in my opinion a good preacher, perhaps I might have continued, notwithstanding the occasion I had for the Sunday's leisure in my course of study; but his discourses were chiefly either polemic arguments, or explications of the peculiar doctrines of our sect, and were all to me very dry, uninteresting, and unedifying, since not a single moral principle was inculcated or enforced, their aim seeming to be rather to make us Presbyterians than good citizens.

5

James Madison: Letter to Thomas Jefferson (1787)

Although Madison played an important part in the Constitutional Convention, Jefferson was in France as America's Ambassador. Madison wrote his friend to report on the work of the Convention, here explaining why it sought to use self-interest to moderate tyrannical majorities. As this passage indicates, some members of the founding generation were less than impressed with religion's ability to foster morality and in fact tended to view religion more as a political problem than a public benefit.

Religion. The inefficacy of this restraint on individuals is well known. The conduct of every popular Assembly, acting on oath, the strongest of religious ties, shows that individuals join without remorse in acts against which their consciences would revolt, if proposed to them separately in their closets. When indeed Religion is kindled into enthusiasm, its force like that of other passions is increased by the sympathy of a multitude. But enthusiasm is only a temporary state of Religion, and whilst it lasts will hardly be seen with pleasure at the helm. Even in its coolest state, it has been much oftener a motive to oppression than a restraint from it.

6

James Madison: Excerpts from the Memorial and Remonstrance (1785)

Madison sought to mitigate religion's potential political divisiveness by confining it as much as possible to the private sphere. In the following work, he contends that government promotion of religion is a violation of the natural rights of individuals as well as a threat to public peace. Notice, however, that he also shows a concern for the well-being of religion itself, arguing that it is harmed more than helped by state support.

To the Honorable General Assembly of the Commonwealth of Virginia:

We the subscribers, citizens of the said Commonwealth, having taken into serious consideration, a Bill printed by order of the last Session of General Assembly, entitled "A Bill establishing a provision for Teachers of the Christian Religion," and conceiving that the same if finally armed with the sanctions of a law, will be a dangerous abuse of power, are bound as faithful members of a free State to remonstrate against it, and to declare the reasons by which we are determined. We remonstrate against the said Bill,

1. Because we hold it for a fundamental and undeniable truth, "that religion or the duty which we owe to our Creator and the manner of discharging it, can be directed only by reason and conviction, not by force or violence." The Religion then of every man must be left to the conviction and conscience of every man; and it is the right of every man to exercise it as these may dictate. This right is in its nature an unalienable right. It is unalienable, because the opinions of men, depending only on the evidence contemplated by their own minds cannot follow the dictates of other men: It is unalienable also, because what is here a right towards men, is a duty towards the Creator. It is the duty of every man to render to the Creator such homage and such only as he believes to be acceptable to him. This duty is precedent, both in order of time and in degree of obligation, to the claims of Civil Society. Before any man can be considered as a member of Civil Society, he must be considered as a subject of the Governor of the Universe: And if a member of Civil Society, do it with a saving of his allegiance to the Universal Sovereign. We maintain therefore that in matters of Religion, no man's right is abridged by the institution of Civil Society and that Religion is wholly exempt from its cognizance. True it is, that no other rule exists, by which any question which may divide a Society, can be ultimately determined, but the will of the majority; but it is also true that the majority may trespass on the rights of the minority.

2. Because Religion be exempt from the authority of the Society at large, still less can it be subject to that of the Legislative Body. The latter are but the creatures and vicegerents of the former. . . .

3. Because it is proper to take alarm at the first experiment on our liberties. . . . Who does not see that the same authority which can establish Christianity, in exclusion of all other Religions, may establish with the same ease any particular sect of Christians, in exclusion of all other Sects? that the same authority which can force a citizen to contribute three pence only of his property for the support of any one establishment, may force him to conform to any other establishment in all cases whatsoever?

4. Because the Bill violates the equality which ought to be the basis of every law, and which is more indispensable, in proportion as the validity or expediency of any law is more liable to be impeached. If "all men are by nature equally free and independent," all men are to be considered as entering into Society on equal conditions; as relinquishing no more, and therefore retaining no less, one than another, of their natural rights. Above all are they to be considered as retaining an "equal title to the free exercise of Religion according to the dictates of Conscience." Whilst we assert for ourselves a freedom to embrace, to profess and to observe the Religion which we believe to be of divine origin, we cannot deny an equal freedom to those whose minds have not yet yielded to the evidence which has convinced us. If this freedom be abused, it is an offence against God, not against man: To God, therefore, not to man, must an account of it be rendered. . . .

5. Because the Bill implies either that the Civil Magistrate is a competent Judge of Religious Truth; or that he may employ Religion as an engine of Civil policy. The first is an arrogant pretension falsified by the contradictory opinions of Rulers in all ages, and throughout the world: the second an unhallowed perversion of the means of salvation.

6. Because the establishment proposed by the Bill is not requisite for the support of the Christian Religion. To say that it is, is a contradiction to the Christian Religion itself, for every page of it disavows a dependence on the powers of this world: it is a contradiction to fact; for it is known that this Religion both existed and flourished, not only without the support of human laws, but in spite of every opposition from them, and not only during the period of miraculous aid, but long after it had been left to its own evidence and the ordinary care of Providence. . . . It is moreover to weaken in those who profess this Religion a pious confidence in its innate excellence and the patronage of its Author; and to foster in those who still reject it, a suspicion that its friends are too conscious of its fallacies to trust it to its own merits.

7. Because experience witnesseth that ecclesiastical establishments, instead of maintaining the purity and efficacy of Religion, have had a contrary operation. During almost fifteen centuries has the legal establishment of Christianity been on trial. What have been its fruits? More or less in all places, pride and indolence in the Clergy, ignorance and servility in the laity, in both, superstition, bigotry and persecution. . . .

8. Because the establishment in question is not necessary for the support of Civil Government. If it be urged as necessary for the support of Civil Government only as it is a means of supporting Religion, and it be not necessary for the latter purpose, it cannot be necessary for the former. If Religion be not within the cognizance of Civil Government how can its legal establishment be necessary to Civil Government? . . . A just Government instituted to secure & perpetuate it needs them not. Such a Government will be best supported by protecting every Citizen in the enjoyment of his Religion with the same equal hand which protects his person and his property; by neither invading the equal rights of any Sect, nor suffering any Sect to invade those of another. . . .

11. Because it will destroy that moderation and harmony which the forbearance of our laws to intermeddle with Religion has produced among its several sects. Torrents of blood have been split in the old world, by vain attempts of the secular arm, to extinguish Religious discord, by proscribing all difference in Religious opinion. Time has at length revealed the true remedy. Every relaxation of narrow and rigorous policy, wherever it has been tried, has been found to assuage the disease. The American Theatre has exhibited proofs that equal and complete liberty, if it does not wholly eradicate it, sufficiently destroys its malignant influence on the health and prosperity of the State. If with the salutary effects of this system under our own eyes, we begin to contract the bounds of Religious freedom, we know no name that will too severely reproach our folly. At least let warning be taken at the first fruits of the threatened innovation. The very appearance of the Bill has transformed

"that Christian forbearance, love and charity," which of late mutually prevailed, into animosities and jealousies, which may not soon be appeased. What mischiefs may not be dreaded, should this enemy to the public quiet be armed with the force of a law?

12. Because the policy of the Bill is adverse to the diffusion of the light of Christianity. The first wish of those who enjoy this precious gift ought to be that it may be imparted to the whole race of mankind. Compare the number of those who have as yet received it with the number still remaining under the dominion of false Religions; and how small is the former! Does the policy of the Bill tend to lessen the disproportion? No; it at once discourages those who are strangers to the light of revelation from coming into the Region of it; and countenances by example the nations who continue in darkness, in shutting out those who might convey it to them. Instead of Leveling as far as possible, every obstacle to the victorious progress of Truth, the Bill with an ignoble and unchristian timidity would circumscribe it with a wall of defense against the encroachments of error.

7

A Bill for Establishing Religious Freedom (1786)

Something like Madison's understanding of the proper posture of government toward religion became law in Virginia with the passage of the Bill for Establishing Religious Freedom. Thomas Jefferson was the bill's principal author, and to the end of his life he considered it one of his greatest accomplishments. The bill enjoys an enduring significance in American politics because it, along with Madison's Memorial and Remonstrance, has been taken by the modern Supreme Court as a key to the proper interpretation of the First Amendment's religion clauses.

SECTION I

Well aware that the opinions and belief of men depend not on their own will, but follow involuntarily the evidence proposed to their minds; that Almighty God hath created the mind free, and manifested his supreme will that free it shall remain by making it altogether insusceptible of restraint; that all attempts to influence it by temporal punishments, or burdens, or by civil incapacitations, tend only to beget habits of hypocrisy and meanness, and are a departure from the plan of the holy author of our religion, who being lord both of body and mind, yet chose not to propagate it by coercions on either, as was in his Almighty power to do, but to extend it by its influence on reason alone; that the impious presumption of legislators and rulers, civil as well as ecclesiastical, who, being themselves but fallible and uninspired men, have assumed dominion over the faith of others, setting up their own opinions and modes of thinking as the only true and infallible, and as such endeavoring to impose them on others, hath established and maintained false religions over the greatest part of the world and through all time: That to compel a man to furnish contributions of money for the propagation of opinions which he disbelieves and abhors, is sinful and tyrannical; that even the forcing him to support this or that teacher of his own religious persuasion, is depriving him of the comfortable liberty of giving his contributions to the particular pastor whose morals he would make his pattern, and whose powers he feels most persuasive to righteousness; and is withdrawing from the ministry those temporary rewards, which proceeding from an approbation of their personal conduct, are an additional incitement to earnest and unremitting labors for the instruction of mankind; that our civil rights have no dependence on our religious opinions, any more than our opinions in physics or geometry; that therefore the proscribing any citizen as unworthy the public confidence by laying upon him an incapacity of being called to offices of trust and emolument, unless he profess or renounce this or that religious opinion, is depriving him injuriously of those privileges and advantages to which, in common with his fellow citizens, he has a natural right; that it tends also to corrupt the principles of that very religion it is meant to encourage, by bribing, with a monopoly of worldly honors and emoluments, those who will externally profess and conform to it; that though indeed these are criminal who do not withstand such temptation, yet neither are those innocent who lay the bait in their way; that the opinions of men are not the object of civil government, nor under its jurisdiction; that to suffer the civil magistrate to intrude his powers into the field of opinion and to restrain the profession or propagation of principles on supposition of their ill tendency is a dangerous fallacy, which at once destroys all religious liberty, because he being of course judge of that tendency will make his opinions the rule of judgment, and approve or condemn the sentiments of others only as they shall square with or differ from his own; that it is time enough for the rightful purposes of civil government for its officers to interfere when principles break out into overt acts against peace and good order; and finally, that truth is great and will prevail if left to herself; that she is the proper and sufficient antagonist to error, and has nothing to fear from the conflict unless by human interposition disarmed of her natural weapons, free argument and debate; errors ceasing to be dangerous when it is permitted freely to contradict them.

SECTION II

We the General Assembly of Virginia do enact that no man shall be compelled to frequent or support any religious worship, place, or ministry whatsoever, nor shall be enforced, restrained, molested, or burdened in his body or goods, nor shall otherwise suffer, on account of his religious opinions or belief; but that all men shall be free to profess, and by argument to maintain, their opinions in matters of religion, and that the same shall in no wise diminish, enlarge, or affect their civil rights.

SECTION III

And though we well know that this Assembly, elected by the people for the ordinary purposes of legislation only, have no power to restrain the acts of succeeding Assemblies, constituted with powers equal to our own, and that therefore to declare this act irrevocable would be of no effect in law; yet we are free to declare, and do declare, that the rights hereby asserted are of the natural rights of mankind, and that if any act shall be hereafter passed to repeal the present or to narrow its operation, such act will be an infringement of natural right.

8

George Washington: Thanksgiving Proclamation (1789)

The First Amendment to the Constitution provides that Congress shall make no law respecting an establishment of religion, nor prohibiting the free exercise thereof. Although the Amendment clearly intends to limit the federal government's involvement with religion, many of the founding generation understood it as nevertheless permitting some government support for religious belief. As this official pronouncement indicates, the first president saw no Constitutional bar to his use of the office to encourage religious exercises. Similar proclamations were issued by subsequent presidents, including Adams and Madison.

Whereas it is the duty of all Nations to acknowledge the providence of Almighty God, to obey his will, to be grateful for his benefits, and humbly to implore his protection and favor—and whereas both Houses of Congress have by their joint Committee requested me to recommend to the People of the United States a day of public thanksgiving and prayer to be observed by acknowledging with grateful hearts the many signal favors of Almighty God especially by affording them an opportunity peaceably to establish a form of government for their safety and happiness.

Now therefore I do recommend and assign Thursday the 26th day of November next to be devoted by the People of these States to the service of that great and glorious Being, who is the beneficent Author of all the good that was, that is, or that will be—That we may then all unite in rendering unto him our sincere and humble thanks—for his kind care and protection of the

People of this Country previous to their becoming a Nation—for the signal and manifold mercies, and the favorable interpositions of his Providence which we experienced in the course and conclusion of the late war—for the great degree of tranquility, union, and plenty, which we have since enjoyed—for the peaceable and rational manner, in which we have been enabled to establish constitutions of government for our safety and happiness, and particularly the national One now lately instituted—for the civil and religious liberty with which we are blessed; and the means we have of acquiring and diffusing useful knowledge; and in general for all the great and various favors which he hath been pleased to confer upon us.

And also that we may then unite in most humbly offering our prayers and supplications to the great Lord and Ruler of Nations and beseech him to pardon our national and other transgressions—to enable us all, whether in public or private stations, to perform our several and relative duties properly and punctually—to render our national government a blessing to all the people, by constantly being a Government of wise, just, and constitutional laws, discreetly and faithfully executed and obeyed—to protect and guide all Sovereigns and Nations (especially such as have shown kindness unto us) and to bless them with good government, peace, and concord—To promote the knowledge and practice of true religion and virtue, and the increase of science among them and us—and generally to grant unto all Mankind such a degree of temporal prosperity as he alone knows to be best.

9

George Washington: An Excerpt from the Farewell Address (1796)

Washington's desire to encourage religious belief was no doubt informed by his agreement with Adams and Franklin that religion supports the morality necessary to a healthy society. In his Farewell Address, published near the end of his second and final term as president, Washington contends that a religiously supported morality is especially necessary to a popular and free government.

Of all the dispositions and habits which lead to political prosperity, religion and morality are indispensable supports. In vain would that man claim the tribute of patriotism, who should labor to subvert these great pillars of human happiness, these firmest props of the duties of men and citizens. The mere politician, equally with the pious man, ought to respect and to cherish them. A volume could not trace all their connections with private and public felicity. Let it simply be asked: Where is the security for property, for reputation, for life, if the sense of religious obligation desert the oaths which are the instruments of investigation in courts of justice? And let us with caution indulge the supposition that morality can be maintained without religion. Whatever may be conceded to the influence of refined education on minds of peculiar structure, reason and experience both forbid us to expect that national morality can prevail in exclusion of religious principle.

It is substantially true that virtue or morality is a necessary spring of popular government. The rule, indeed, extends with more or less force to every species of free government. Who that is a sincere friend to it can look with indifference upon attempts to shake the foundation of the fabric?

10

George Washington: Letter to Hebrew Congregation at Newport (1790)

Respect for religious liberty was important not only to Madison and Jefferson, but also to those among the founders who viewed religion as publicly beneficial and who therefore approved of some government support for it. Here Washington praises America precisely because its institutions recognize the rights of those who do not share the majority's religious beliefs.

The citizens of the United States of America have a right to applaud themselves for having given to mankind examples of an enlarged and liberal policy—a policy worthy of imitation. All possess alike liberty of conscience and immunities of citizenship.

It is now no more that toleration is spoken of as if it were the indulgence of one class of people that another enjoyed the exercise of their inherent natural rights, for, happily, the Government of the United States, which gives to bigotry no sanction, to persecution no assistance, requires only that they who live under its protection should demean themselves as good citizens in giving it on all occasions their effectual support.

It would be inconsistent with the frankness of my character not to avow that I am pleased with your favorable opinion of my administration and fervent wishes for my felicity.

May the children of the stock of Abraham who dwell in this land continue to merit and enjoy the good will of the other inhabitants—while every one shall sit in safety under his own vine and fig tree and there shall be none to make him afraid.

May the father of all mercies scatter light, and not darkness, upon our paths, and make us all in our several vocations useful here, and in His own due time and way everlastingly happy.

11

Thomas Jefferson: Letter to the Danbury Baptist Association (1802)

The founders do not appear to have been in complete agreement on the meaning of the First Amendment's religion clauses. Although Washington thought it permitted some government support for religion, Jefferson thought it created a "wall of separation between Church and State," a formulation adopted by the modern Supreme Court in its interpretation of the First Amendment.

Believing with you that religion is a matter which lies solely between Man and his God, that he owes account to none other for his faith or his worship, that the legitimate powers of government reach actions only, and not opinions, I contemplate with sovereign reverence that act of the whole American people which declared that their legislature should "make no law respecting an establishment of religion, or prohibiting the free exercise thereof," thus building a wall of separation between Church and State. Adhering to this expression of the supreme will of the nation in behalf of the rights of conscience, I shall see with sincere satisfaction the progress of those sentiments which tend to restore to man all his natural rights, convinced he has no natural right in opposition to his social duties.

I reciprocate your kind prayers for the protection and blessing of the common father and creator of man, and tender you for yourselves and your religious association, assurances of my high respect and esteem.

12

Thomas Jefferson: Letter to Rev. Samuel Miller (1808)

In keeping with his view of the religion clauses, Jefferson declined, as president, to issue a Thanksgiving Proclamation. In the following letter he explains his reasons, which are based not only on the First Amendment, but also on the Tenth Amendment and Jefferson's understanding of the limits of the national government's powers within the Constitution's scheme of Federalism.

I consider the government of the U.S. as interdicted by the Constitution from intermeddling with religious institutions, their doctrines, discipline, or exercises. This results not only from the provision that no law shall be made respecting the establishment, or free exercise, of religion, but from that also which reserves to the states the powers not delegated to the U.S. Certainly no power to prescribe any religious exercise, or to assume authority in religious discipline, has been delegated to the general government. It must then rest with the states, as far as it can be in any human authority. But it is only proposed that I should *recommend*, not prescribe a day of fasting and prayer. That is, that I should *indirectly* assume to the U.S. an authority over religious exercises which the Constitution has directly precluded them from. It must be meant too that this recommendation is to carry some authority, and to be sanctioned by some penalty on those who disregard it; not indeed of fine and imprisonment, but of some degree of proscription perhaps in public opinion. And does the change in the nature of the penalty make the recommendation the less a law of conduct for those to whom it is directed? I do not believe it is for the interest of religion to invite the civil magistrate to direct its exercises, its discipline, or its doctrines; nor of the religious societies that the general government should be invested with the power of effecting any uniformity of time or matter among them. Fasting and prayer are religious exercises. The enjoining them an act of discipline. Every religious society has a right to determine for itself the times for these exercises, and the objects proper for them, according to their own particular tenets; and this right can never be safer than in their own hands, where the constitution has deposited it.

I am aware that the practice of my predecessors may be quoted. But I have ever believed that the example of state executives led to the assumption of that authority by the general government, without due examination, which would have discovered that what might be a right in a state government, was a violation of that right when assumed by another. Be this as it may, every one must act according to the dictates of his own reason, and mine tells me that civil powers alone have been given to the President of the U.S. and no authority to direct the religious exercises of his constituents.

13

Mercy Otis Warren: An Excerpt from *History of the Rise, Progress, and Termination of the American Revolution* (1805)

A prolific writer, Mercy Otis Warren was probably the most prominent woman's voice during the founding generation. She was a member of a family of activist Patriots (or revolutionaries) in Massachusetts during the American War of Independence. During the debate over the merits of the proposed new Constitution, she aligned herself with the Anti-Federalist opponents of ratification. In the following passages, taken from her three-volume history of the American Revolution, she contends that republican freedom is not the cause of disdain for religion and suggests that religion is necessary for the preservation of republican freedom.

In the outset of the American Revolution, the arm of foreign power was opposed by a people uncontaminated by foreign luxury, the intricacies of foreign politics, or the theological jargon of metaphysical skeptics of foreign extract. Philosophy then conveyed honorable ideas of science, of religion, and morals: the character is since degraded by the unprincipled sarcasms of men of letters, who assume the dignity of philosophic thought. Instead of unfolding the sources of knowledge, and inculcating truth, they often confound without convincing, and by their sophistical reasonings leave the superficial reader, their newly initiated disciple, on the comfortless shores of annihilation.

These observations are not confined to any particular nation or character; the historians of Britain and the philosophers and poets of France, Germany, and England are perhaps equally culpable; and it is to be regretted that America has not preserved a national character of her own, free from any symptoms of pernicious deviation from the purest principles on morals, religion, and civil liberty. She has been conducted through a revolution that will be ever memorable, both for its origin, its success, and the new prospects it has opened both at home and abroad. The consequences of this revolution have not been confined to one quarter of the globe, but the dissemination of more liberal principles in government, and more honorable opinions of the rights of man, and the melioration of his condition have been spread over a considerable part of the world.

But men, prone to abuse the best advantages, lent by the beneficent hand of Providence, sometimes sport them away, or confound causes with effects, which lead to the most erroneous conclusions. Thus it has been the recent fashion of courtiers, and of a great part of the clergy, under monarchic governments, to impute the demoralization and skepticism that prevails to the spirit of free inquiry, as it regards the rights of civil society. This fashion has been adopted by all anti-republicans in America; but it may be asked whether the declamation and clamor against the dissemination of republican opinions on civil government, as originating the prevalence of atheistic folly, is founded on the basis of truth.

Examine the history of the ancient republics of Greece and the splendid commonwealth of Rome; was not the strictest regard paid to the worship of their gods and a sacred observance of their religious rites enjoined, until the Grecian republics were overthrown by ambitious individuals? It was then that skeptical disputes more generally employed the philosophers; in consequence of which, the rulers and the people sunk into an indifference to all religion. The rich city of Athens particularly, was early corrupted by the influx of wealth, the influence of aristocratic nobles, and the annihilation of every principle connected with religion.

Survey the Roman commonwealth before its decline, when it was most worthy of the imitation of republicans. Was not a general regard paid to the worship of their deities among this celebrated people, and a superstitious attention observed relative to omens, prodigies, and judgments, as denounced and executed by their gods, until republicanism was extinguished, the commonwealth subverted, and the scepter of a single sovereign was stretched over that vast empire? It was then that Caligula set up his horse to be worshipped, as a burlesque on religion, and the sycophants of the court encouraged every caprice of their emperor. The people did not become so universally corrupt as to throw off all regard for religion, and all homage to the deities of their ancestors, until the libidinous conduct of their august sovereigns and the nobles of the court set the example.

Nor do we read in more sacred history, through all the story of the Israelites, that the fool ever said in his heart that there is no God, until under the dominion of kings.

It may be observed in the character of more modern republics that religion has been the grand palladium of their institutions. Through all the free states of Italy, democracy and religion have been considered in union; some of them have indeed been darkened by superstition and bigotry, yet not equally hoodwinked under republican governments, as are the neighboring kingdoms of Spain and Portugal, subjected to monarchic despotism. . . .

It is neither a preference to republican systems, nor an attachment to monarchic or aristocratic forms of government, that disseminates the wild opinions of infidelity. It is the licentious manners of courts of every description, the unbridled luxury of wealth, and the worst passions of men let loose on the multitude by the example of their superiors. Bent on gratification, at the expense of every moral tie, they have broken down the barriers of religions, and the spirit of infidelity is nourished at the fount; thence the poisonous streams run through every grade that constitutes the mass of nations.

It may be further observed that there is a variety of additional causes which have led to a disposition among some part of mankind to reject the obligations of religion and even to deny their God. This propensity in some may easily be elucidated without casting any part of the odium on the spirit of free inquiry relative to civil and political liberty, which had been widely disseminated and had produced two such remarkable revolutions as those of America and France. It may be imputed to the love of novelty, the pride of opinion, and an extravagant propensity to speculate and theorize on subjects beyond the comprehension of mortals, united with a desire of being released from the restraints on their appetites and passions: restraints dictated both by reason and revelation, and which, under the influence of sober reflection, forbid the indulgence of all gratifications that are injurious to man. Further elucidations, or more abstruse causes, which contribute to lead the vain inquirer, who steps over the line prescribed by the Author of nature, to deviations from, and forgetfulness of its Creator, and to involve him a labyrinth of darkness, from which his weak reasonings can never disentangle him, may be left to those who delight in metaphysical disquisitions.

The world might reasonably have expected, from the circumstances connected with the first settlement of the American colonies, which was in consequence of their attachment to the religion of their fathers, united with a spirit of independence relative to civil government, that there would have been no observable dereliction of those honorable principles for many ages to come. From the sobriety of their manners, their simple habits, their attention to the education and moral conduct of their children, they had the highest reason to hope that it might have been long, very long, before the faith of their religion was shaken, or their principles corrupted either by the manners, opinions, or habits of foreigners, bred in the courts of despotism or the schools of licentiousness.

This hope shall not yet be relinquished. There has indeed been some relaxation of manners, and the appearance of a change in public opinion not contemplated when revolutionary scenes first shook the western world. But it must be acknowledged that the religious and moral character of Americans yet stands on a higher grade of excellence and purity than that of most other nations. It has been observed [by Montesquieu] that "a violation of manners has destroyed more states than the infraction of laws." It is necessary for every *American* with becoming energy to endeavor to stop the dissemination of principles evidently destructive of the cause for which they have bled. It must be the combined virtue of the rulers and of the people to do this, and to rescue and save their civil and religious rights from the out-stretched arm of tyranny, which may appear under any mode or form of government.

Let not the frivolity of the domestic taste of the children of Columbia, nor the examples of strangers of high or low degree, that may intermix among them, or the imposing attitude of distant nations, or the machinations of the bloody tyrants of Europe, who have united themselves and to the utmost are exerting their strength to extirpate the very name of *republicanism*, rob them of their character, their morals, their religion, or their liberty.

14

Justice Joseph Story: An Excerpt from the *Commentaries on the Constitution of the United States* (1833)

Story was an influential member of the Supreme Court in its early period and also the author of a highly regarded set of commentaries on the meaning of the Constitution. In the following section on the First Amendment, Story lays out what he takes to be the founding generation's consensus of understanding of the religion clauses.

§ 1865.   How far any government has a right to interfere in matters touching religion, has been a subject much discussed by writers upon public and political law. The right and the duty of the interference of government, in matters of religion, have been maintained by many distinguished authors, as well those, who were the warmest advocates of free government, as those, who were attached to governments of a more arbitrary character. Indeed, the right of a society or government to interfere in matters of religion will hardly be contested by any persons, who believe that piety, religion, and morality are intimately connected with the well being of the state, and indispensable to the administration of civil justice. The promulgation of the great doctrines of religion, the being, and attributes, and providence of one Almighty God; the responsibility to him for all our actions, founded upon moral freedom and accountability; a future state of rewards and punishments; the cultivation of all the personal, social, and benevolent virtues—these never can be a matter of indifference in any well ordered community. It is, indeed, difficult to conceive, how any civilized society can well exist without them. And at all events, it is impossible for those, who believe in the truth of Christianity, as a divine revelation, to doubt, that it is the especial duty of government to foster, and encourage it among all the citizens and subjects. This is a point wholly distinct from that of the right of private judgment in matters of religion, and of the freedom of public worship according to the dictates of one's conscience.

§ **1866.**   The real difficulty lies in ascertaining the limits, to which government may rightfully go in fostering and encouraging religion. Three cases may easily be supposed. One, where a government affords aid to a particular religion, leaving all persons free to adopt any other; another, where it creates an ecclesiastical establishment for the propagation of the doctrines of a particular sect of that religion, leaving a like freedom to all others; and a third, where it creates such an establishment, and excludes all persons, not belonging to it, either wholly, or in part, from any participation in the public honors, trusts, emoluments, privileges, and immunities of the state. For instance, a government may simply declare, that the Christian religion shall be the religion of the state, and shall be aided, and encouraged in all the varieties of sects belonging to it; or it may declare, that the Catholic or Protestant religion shall be the religion of the state, leaving every man to the free enjoyment of his own religious opinions; or it may establish the doctrines of a particular sect, as of Episcopalians, as the religion of the state, with a like freedom; or it may establish the doctrines of a particular sect, as exclusively the religion of the state, tolerating others to a limited extent, or excluding all, not belonging to it, from all public honors, trusts, emoluments, privileges, and immunities. . . .

§ **1868.**   Probably at the time of the adoption of the constitution, and of the amendment to it, now under consideration, the general, if not the universal, sentiment in America was, that Christianity ought to receive encouragement from the state, so far as was not incompatible with the private rights of conscience, and the freedom of religious worship. An attempt to level all religions, and to make it a matter of state policy to hold all in utter indifference, would have created universal disapprobation, if not universal indignation. . . .

§ **1870.**   But the duty of supporting religion, and especially the Christian religion, is very different from the right to force the consciences of other men, or to punish them for worshipping God in the manner, which, they believe, their accountability to him requires. It has been truly said, that "religion, or the duty we owe to our Creator, and the manner of discharging it, can be dictated only by reason and conviction, not by force or violence." Mr. Locke himself, who did not doubt the right of government to interfere in matters of religion, and especially to encourage Christianity, at the same time has expressed his opinion of the right of private judgment, and liberty of conscience, in a manner becoming his character, as a sincere friend of civil and religious liberty. "No man, or society of men," says he, "have any authority to impose their opinions or interpretations on any other, the meanest Christian; since, in matters of religion, every man must know, and believe, and give an account for himself." The rights of conscience are, indeed, beyond the just reach of any human power. They are given by God, and cannot be encroached upon by human authority, without a criminal disobedience of the precepts of natural, as well as of revealed religion.

§ **1871.**   The real object of the amendment was, not to countenance, much less to advance Mahometanism, or Judaism, or infidelity, by prostrating Christianity; but to exclude all rivalry among Christian sects, and to prevent any national ecclesiastical establishment, which should give to an hierarchy the exclusive patronage of the national government. It thus cut off the means of religious persecution (the vice and pest of former ages) and of the subversion of the rights of conscience in matters of religion, which had been trampled upon almost from the days of the Apostles to the present age. The history of the parent country had afforded the most solemn warnings and melancholy instructions on this head; and even New England, the land of the persecuted puritans, as well as other colonies, where the Church of England had maintained its superiority, would furnish out a chapter, as full of the darkest bigotry and intolerance, as any, which could be found to disgrace the pages of foreign annals. Apostasy, heresy, and nonconformity had been standard crimes for public appeals, to kindle the flames of persecution, and apologize for the most atrocious triumphs over innocence and virtue.

15

Alexis de Tocqueville:
Democracy in America (1835)

Tocqueville, a French statesmen and political thinker, traveled to the United States during the early 1830s, keeping a detailed journal of his observations of democratic politics and culture. He organized his thoughts into a two-volume work, Democracy in America, *that sought to identify democracy's weaknesses and to explain how they could be corrected or curbed. Here Tocqueville contends that Americans believe that democracy needs religion because of its ability to impose moral restraints on the majority and thus protect the rights of individuals and minorities.*

I have just shown what the direct influence of religion upon politics is in the United States; but its indirect influence appears to me to be still more considerable, and it never instructs the Americans more fully in the art of being free than when it says nothing of freedom.

The sects that exist in the United States are innumerable. They all differ in respect to the worship which is due to the Creator; but they all agree in respect to the duties which are due from man to man. Each sect adores the Deity in its own peculiar manner, but all sects preach the same moral law in the name of God. If it be of the highest importance to man, as an individual, that his religion should be true, it is not so to society. Society has no future life to hope for or to fear; and provided the citizens profess a religion, the peculiar tenets of that religion are of little importance to its interests. Moreover, all the sects of the United States are comprised within the great unity of Christianity, and Christian morality is everywhere the same. . . .

In the United States the influence of religion is not confined to the manners, but it extends to the intelligence of the people. Among the Anglo-Americans some profess the doctrines of Christianity from a sincere belief in them, and others do the same because they fear to be suspected of unbelief. Christianity, therefore, reigns without obstacle, by universal consent; the consequence is, as I have before observed, that every principle of the moral world is fixed and determinate, although the political world is abandoned to the debates and the experiments of men. Thus the human mind is never left to wander over a boundless field; and whatever may be its pretensions, it is checked from time to time by barriers that it cannot surmount. Before it can innovate, certain primary principles are laid down, and the boldest conceptions are subjected to certain forms which retard and stop their completion.

The imagination of the Americans, even in its greatest flights, is circumspect and undecided; its impulses are checked and its works unfinished. These habits of restraint recur in political society and are singularly favorable both to the tranquility of the people and to the durability of the institutions they have established. Nature and circumstances have made the inhabitants of the United States bold, as is sufficiently attested by the enterprising spirit with which they seek for fortune. If the mind of the Americans were free from all hindrances, they would shortly become the most daring innovators and the most persistent disputants in the world. But the revolutionists of America are obliged to profess an ostensible respect for Christian morality and equity, which does not permit them to violate wantonly the laws that oppose their designs; nor would they find it easy to surmount the scruples of their partisans even if they were able to get over their own. Hitherto no one in the United States has dared to advance the maxim that everything is permissible for the interests of society, an impious adage which seems to have been invented in an age of freedom to shelter all future tyrants. Thus, while the law permits the Americans to do what they please, religion prevents them from conceiving, and forbids them to commit, what is rash or unjust.

Religion in America takes no direct part in the government of society, but it must be regarded as the first of their political institutions; for if it does not impart a taste for freedom, it facilitates the use of it. Indeed, it is in this same point of view that the inhabitants of the United States themselves look upon religious belief. I do not know whether all Americans have a sincere faith in their religion—for who can search the human heart?—but I am certain that they hold it to be indispensable to the maintenance of republican institutions. This opinion is not peculiar to a class of citizens or to a party, but it belongs to the whole nation and to every rank of society. . . .

I have known of societies formed by Americans to send out ministers of the Gospel into the new Western states, to found schools and churches there, lest religion should be allowed to die away in those remote settlements, and the rising states be less fitted to enjoy free institutions than the people from whom they came. I met with wealthy New Englanders who abandoned the country in which they were born in order to lay the foundations of Christianity and of freedom on the banks of the Missouri or in the prairies of Illinois. Thus religious zeal is perpetually warmed in the United States by the fires of patriotism. These men do not act exclusively from a consideration of a future life; eternity is only one motive of their devotion to the cause. If you converse with these missionaries of Christian civilization, you will be surprised to hear them speak so often of the goods of this world, and to meet a politician where you expected to find a priest. They will tell you that "all the American republics are collectively involved with each other; if the republics of the West were to fall into anarchy, or to be mastered by a despot, the republican institutions which now flourish upon the shores of the Atlantic Ocean would be in great peril. It is therefore our interest that the new states should be religious, in order that they may permit us to remain free." Such are the opinions of the Americans; and if any hold that the religious spirit which I admire is the very thing most amiss in America, and that the only element wanting to the freedom and happiness of the human race on the other side of the ocean is to believe with Spinoza in the eternity of the world, or with Cabanis that thought is secreted by the brain, I can only reply that those who hold this language have never been in America and that they have never seen a religious or a free nation.

16

Abraham Lincoln: Message to the Voters of the Seventh Congressional District (1846)

Lincoln's message supports Tocqueville's claim that the Americans of that period regarded religion as essential to the preservation of their democratic and free political institutions. Lincoln evidently believed that an unanswered accusation of hostility to Christianity would be deadly to his political ambitions. He moreover shares the popular view that open hostility to religion tends to "injure the morals" of the community.

A charge having got into circulation in some of the neighborhoods of this District, in substance that I am an open scoffer at Christianity, I have by the advice of some friends concluded to notice the subject in this form. That I am not a member of any Christian Church, is true; but I have never denied the truth of the Scriptures; and I have never spoken with intentional disrespect of religion in general, or any denomination of Christians in particular. It is true that in early life I was inclined to believe in what I understand is called the "Doctrine of Necessity"—that is, that the human mind is impelled to action, or held in rest by some power, over which the mind itself has no control; and I have sometimes (with one, two or three, but never publicly) tried to maintain this opinion in argument. The habit of arguing thus however, I have, entirely left off for more than five years. And I add here, I have always understood this same opinion to be held by several of the Christian denominations. The foregoing, is the whole truth, briefly stated, in relation to myself, upon this subject.

I do not think I could myself, be brought to support a man for office, whom I knew to be an open enemy of, and scoffer at, religion. Leaving the higher matter of eternal consequences, between him and his Maker, I still do not think any man has the right thus to insult the feelings, and injure the morals, of the community in which he may live. If, then, I was guilty of such conduct, I should blame no man who should condemn me for it; but I do blame those, whoever they may be, who falsely put such a charge in circulation against me.

17

Abraham Lincoln: Farewell Address at Springfield (1861)

Americans have turned to religion not only as a source of moral conviction, but also as a source of solace in difficult times. Readings 17 and 18 illustrate the common appeal to the notion that America is under God's providential protection.

My friends: No one, not in my situation, can appreciate my feeling of sadness at this parting. To this place, and the kindness of these people, I owe every thing. Here I have lived a quarter of a century, and have passed from a young to an old man. Here my children have been born, and one is buried. I now leave, not knowing when, or whether ever, I may return, with a task before me greater than that which rested upon Washington. Without the assistance of that Divine Being, who ever attended him, I cannot succeed. With that assistance, I cannot fail. Trusting in Him, who can go with me, and remain with you, and be every where for good, let us confidently hope that all will yet be well. To His care commending you, as I hope in your prayers you will commend me, I bid you an affectionate farewell.

18

Abraham Lincoln: Proclamation of Thanksgiving (1863)

The year that is drawing towards its close has been filled with the blessings of fruitful fields and healthful skies. To these bounties, which are so constantly enjoyed that we are prone to forget the source from which they come, others have been added which are of so extraordinary a nature that they cannot fail to penetrate and soften even the heart which is habitually insensible to the ever-watchful providence of Almighty God. In the midst of a civil war of unequalled magnitude and severity, which has sometimes seemed to invite and provoke the aggression of foreign states, peace has been preserved with all nations, order has been maintained, the laws have been respected and obeyed, and harmony has prevailed everywhere except in the theatre of military conflict, while that theatre has been greatly contracted by the advancing armies and navies of the Union. The needful diversion of wealth and strength from the fields of peaceful industry to the national defense has not arrested the plough, the shuttle, or the ship. The axe has enlarged the borders of our settlements, and the mines, as well as of iron and coal as of the precious metals, have yielded even more abundantly than heretofore. Population has steadily increased, notwithstanding the waste that has been made in the camp, the siege, and the battlefield; and the country, rejoicing in the consciousness of augmented strength and vigor, is permitted to expect a continuance of years, with large increase of freedom.

No human counsel hath devised, nor hath any mortal hand worked out these great things. They are the gracious gifts of the Most High God, who, while dealing with us in anger for our sins, hath nevertheless remembered mercy.

It has seemed to me fit and proper that they should be reverently, solemnly, and gratefully acknowledged, as with one heart and voice, by the whole American people. I do, therefore, invite my fellow-citizens in every part of the United States, and also those who are at sea, and those who are sojourning in foreign lands, to set apart and observe the last Thursday of November next as a day of thanksgiving and prayer to our beneficent Father who dwelleth in the heavens. And I recommend to them that, while offering up the ascriptions justly due to Him for such singular deliverances and blessings, they do also, with humble penitence for our national perverseness and disobedience, commend to His tender care all those who have become widows, orphans, mourners, or sufferers in the lamentable civil strife in which we are unavoidably engaged, and fervently implore the interposition of the Almighty hand to heal the wounds of the nation, and to restore it, as soon as may be consistent with divine purposes, to the full enjoyment of peace, harmony, tranquility, and union.

19

Abraham Lincoln: An Excerpt from the Second Inaugural Address (1865)

A God who both exercises a providential government of the world and cares about the morality of human actions might providentially punish individuals or nations for their injustice. Thus the American tradition includes the idea that the country is not only under God's protection but also under His judgment. Lincoln explores this possibility in both readings 18 and 19, suggesting that the Civil War might be a divine punishment for the nation's sins.

On the occasion corresponding to this four years ago all thoughts were anxiously directed to an impending civil war. All dreaded it, all sought to avert it. While the inaugural address was being delivered from this place, devoted altogether to saving the Union without war, insurgent agents were in the city seeking to destroy it without war—seeking to dissolve the Union and divide effects by negotiation. Both parties deprecated war, but one of them would make war rather than let the nation survive, and the other would accept war rather than let it perish, and the war came.

One-eighth of the whole population were colored slaves, not distributed generally over the Union, but localized in the southern part of it. These slaves constituted a peculiar and powerful interest. All knew that this interest was somehow the cause of the war. To strengthen, perpetuate, and extend this interest was the object for which the insurgents would rend the Union even by war, while the Government claimed no right to do more than to restrict the territorial enlargement of it. Neither party expected for the war the magnitude or the duration which it has already attained. Neither anticipated that the cause of the conflict might cease with or even before the conflict itself should cease. Each looked for an easier triumph, and a result less fundamental and astounding. Both read the same Bible and pray to the same God, and each invokes His aid against the other. It may seem strange that any men should dare to ask a just God's assistance in wringing their bread from the sweat of other men's faces, but let us judge not, that we be not judged. The prayers of both could not be answered. That of neither has been answered fully. The Almighty has His own purposes. "Woe unto the world because of offenses; for it must needs be that offenses come, but woe to that man by whom the offense cometh." If we shall suppose that American slavery is one of those offenses which, in the providence of God, must needs come, but which, having continued through His appointed time, He now wills to remove, and that He gives to both North and South this terrible war as the woe due to those by whom the offense came, shall we discern therein any departure from those divine attributes which the believers in a living God always ascribe to Him? Fondly do we hope, fervently do we pray, that this mighty scourge of war may speedily pass away. Yet, if God wills that it continue until all the wealth piled by the bondsman's two hundred and fifty years of unrequited toil shall be sunk, and until every drop of blood drawn with the lash shall be paid by another drawn with the sword, as was said three thousand years ago, so still it must be said "the judgments of the Lord are true and righteous altogether."

With malice toward none, with charity for all, with firmness in the right as God gives us to see the right, let us strive on to finish the work we are in, to bind up the nation's wounds, to care for him who shall have borne the battle and for his widow and his orphan, to do all which may achieve and cherish a just and lasting peace among ourselves and with all nations.

DISCUSSION QUESTIONS FOR CHAPTER 3

1. How does John Winthrop's understanding of the public role of religion differ from that held by John Adams, Benjamin Franklin, and George Washington? Is the glory of God a proper aim for a political community? Is widespread religious belief necessary to maintaining a decent and free society?

2. How does James Madison and Thomas Jefferson's understanding of the place of religion differ from that held by Adams, Franklin, and Washington? Is politicized religion a threat to public peace and freedom, and should religion therefore be confined to the private sphere?

3. How does Jefferson's understanding of the First Amendment differ from that of George Washington and Justice Joseph Story? Does the "establishment clause" of the First Amendment require a strict separation of church and state?

4. How does Mercy Warren understand the influence of republican government on religious belief? Does the freedom of inquiry characteristic of republican government undermine religious belief?

5. What benefits does Tocqueville think America derives from the religious beliefs of its citizens? Is religion necessary to restrain the possible tyranny of the majority?

6. How do the selections from Abraham Lincoln illustrate the role religious belief plays in America's public life?

CHAPTER 4

Education

1

Thomas Shephard: Letter to His Son at Harvard College (1637)

In the following reading, Puritan minister Thomas Shephard exhorts his son to maximize his educational opportunities while at the only postsecondary school in the American colonies at the time (the second, William and Mary, would not be founded until 1693). Although by the late seventeenth century Harvard tended to be more secular, note the strong religious references present in the letter, reflecting the fact that Harvard was then primarily an institution that trained future Puritan clergy members.

. . . Remember that in ordering your Studies you make them, as pleasant as may be, and as fruitfull as possibly you are able, that so you may not be weary in the work God setts you about: and for the End remember these Rules. . . .

   1. Single out two or three scholars most Godly, Learned and studious, and whom you can most love, and who love you best, to be helps to you in your Studies; Gett therefore into the acquaintance of some of your Equalls, to spend some time with them often in discoursing and disputing about the things you hear and read and learn; as also grow acquainted with some that are your Superiors, of whom you may often ask questions and from whom you may learn more than by your Equals only.

   2. Mark every man[']s Disputations and Conferences, and study to gett some Good by every thing: and if your memory be not very strong, committ every notion this way gained unto Paper as soon as you gett into your Study.

   3. Lett your studies be so ordered as to have variety of Studies before you, that when you are weary of one book, you may take pleasure (through this variety) in another: and for this End read some Histories

often, which (they Say) make men wise, as Poets make witty; both which are pleasant things in the midst of more difficult studies.

4. Lett not your Studies be prosecuted in an immethodicall or Disorderly way; but (for the Generality) keep a fixed order of Studies Suited to your own Genius, and Circumstances of things, which in each year, att least, notwithstanding, there will be occasion of some variation of: Fix your Course, and the season for each kind of Study, and suffer no other matters, or persons needlessly to interrupt you, or take you off therefrom.

5. Lett difficult studies have the strength and flower of your time and thoughts: and therein suffer no difficulty to pass unresolved, but either by your own labour, or by enquiry of others, or by both, master it before you pass from it; pass not cursorily or heedlessly over such things. . . .

6. Come to your Studies with an Appetite, and weary not your body, mind, or Eyes with long poreing on your book, but break off & meditate on what you have read, and then to it again; of (if it be in fitt season) recreate your Self a little, and so to your work afresh; let your recreation be such as may stir the Body chiefly, yet not violent, and whether such or sedentry, let it be never more than may Serve to make your Spirit the more free and lively in your Studies.

7. Such books, as it is proper to read over, if they are very choice and not overlarge, read them over oftener than once: if it be not your own and that you are not like to procure it, then collect out of such book what is worthy to be noted therein: in which Collections take these Directions,

   1. Write not in loose papers, but in a fair Paper-book paged thro'out.
   2. Write faithfully the words of your Author.
   3. Sett down in your Paper-book the name of your Author, with the title of his book, and the page, where you find the Collection.
   4. Allow a margin to your paper-book no broader than wherein you may write the letters a, b, c, d, e, f &c. [that] the beginning of each observable Collection, if you have more Collections than two or three in a side.
   5. When you have written out such a book being marked with some distinguishing character (as 1. 2. 3. 4. . . . .) prepare another of the same dimensions as near as you can, and improve that as the former, and so onwards. . . .

8. Choose rather to confess your Ignorance in any matter of Learning, that you may [be] instructed by your Tutor. . . .

9. Suffer not too much to be spent, and break away in visits (visiting, or being visited) let them be Such as may be a whett to you in your

studies, and for your profitt in Learning some way of other, so that you be imparting to others or imparted to from them, or both, in some notion of other, upon all Such occasions.

10. Study the art of reducing all you read to practice in your orations &c: turning and improving elegantly to words and notions, and fancy of your author to Sett of quite another subject. . . . [L]et not crude, lame, bungling Stuff come out of your Study: and for that end, see that you neither play nor sleep, nor idle away a moment[']s time within your Study door, but remember your Study is your work-house only, and place of prayer.

11. So frame an[d] order your Studies, that the one may be a furtherance to the other. . . .

12. Be sparing in your Diet, as to meat and drink, that so after any repast your body may be a servant to your mind, and not a Clogg and Burden.

13. Take pains in, and time for preparing in private for your recitations, declamations, disputations, and such other exercises as you are called to attend before your Tutor or others; do not hurry them off indigestly, no not under pretence of Studying some other matter first: but first (I Say in the first place) attend those (straiten not your self in time for the thorough dispatch thereof) and then afterwards you may apply yourself as aforesaid to your private and more proper Studies; In all which, mind that reading without med-itation will be in a great measure unprofitable, and rawness and forgetfulness will be the Event: but meditation without reading will be barren soon; therefore read much that so you may have plenty of matter for meditation to work upon, and here I would not have you forgett a speech of your precious Grandfather to a Scholar that complained to him of a bad memory, which did dis-courage him from reading much in History, or other books. . . . So I say to you read! read! Something will stick in the mind, be dili-gent and good will come of it. . . .

2

Regulations at Yale College (1745)

By the end of the seventeenth century, education in the colonies, though becoming more modern, was still influenced heavily by religious impulses. Founded at the turn of the eighteenth century primarily to combat the growing liberalism and movement toward secularism at Harvard, Yale College became the third institution of higher learning in the colonies. As evidenced in the following, Yale promoted a classical education with a very strong religious flavor—a combination that would still retain some appeal in the United States in the years immediately following the American Revolution.

CONCERNING ADMISSION INTO COLLEGE

That none may Expect to be admitted into this College unless upon Examination of the Praesident and Tutors, They shall be found able Extempore to Read, Construe and Parce Tully, Virgil and the Greek Testament: and to write True Latin Prose and to understand the Rules of Prosodia, and Common Arithmetic, and shall bring Sufficient Testamony of his Blameless and inoffensive Life.

That no Person shall be admitted a Freshman into this College who is more than Twenty one Years old, unless by the special allowance of [the] President and Fellows or their Committee.

That no Person shall be admitted Undergraduate in this College until his Father, Guardian or some proper Person hath given a Sufficient Bond to the Steward of the College, to pay the Quarter Bills of the [said] Scholar allowed by the authority of College from Time to Time as long as He shall continue a Member of [said] College. . . .

OF A RELIGIOUS AND VIRTUOUS LIFE

All Scholars Shall Live Religious, Godly and Blameless Lives according to the Rules of God[']s Word, diligently Reading the holy Scriptures the Fountain of Light and Truth; and constan[t]ly attend upon all the Duties of Religion both in Publick and Secret.

That the President, or in his absence One of the Tutors Shall constantly Pray in the College-Hall every morning and Evening: and Shall read a Chapter or Suitable Portion of the Holy Scriptures, unless there be Some other Theological Discourse or Religious Exercise: and Every Member of the College whether Graduates or Undergraduates, whether Residing in the College or in the Town of New-Haven Shall Seasonably Attend upon Penalty that every Undergraduate who Shall be absent (without Sufficient Excuse) Shall be Fined one Penny and for comeing Tardy after the Introductory Collect is made Shall be fin'd one half penny.

The President is hereby Desired as he hath Time & Opportunity to make and Exhibit in the Hall Such a publick Exposition, Sermon or Discourse as he shall think proper for the Instruction of [Yale's] Scholars, and when He Shall See cause So to do and Give public Notice thereof, Every Undergraduate Shall be Obliged to Attend upon the Same Penalty as aforesaid. . . .

No student of this College Shall attend upon any Religious Meetings either Public or Private on the Sabbath or any other Day but Such as are appointed by Public Authority or Approved by the President upon Penalty of a Fine, Public Admonition, Confession or Otherwise according to the Nature or Demerit of the Offence. That if any Student Shall Prophane the Sabbath by unnecessary Business, Diversion, Walking abroad, or making any Indecent Noise or Disorder on the Said Day, or on the Evening before or after, or Shall be Guilty of any Rude, Profane, or indecent Behaviour in the Time of Public

Worship, or at Prayer at any Time in the College Hall, He Shall be punished, Admonished, or otherwise according to the nature and Demerit of his Crime. . . .

CONCERNING SCHOLASTICAL EXERCISES

That the President and Each of the Tutors Shall according to the best of their Discretion Instruct and bring forward their respective Classes in the Knowledge of the Three Learned languages, and in the Liberal Arts and Sciences. In the first Year They Shall principally Study the Tongues & Logic, and Shall in Some measure pursue the Study of the Tongues the Two next Years. In the Second Year They Shall Recite Rhetoric, Geometry and Geography. In the Third Year Natural Philosophy, Astronomy and Other Parts of the Mathematicks. In the Fourth Year Metaphysics and Ethics. And the respective Classes Shall Recite Such Books, and in Such a manner as has been accustomed, or Such as the President upon the Consultation with the Tutors Shall think proper.

OF PENAL LAWS

If any Scholar Shall be Guilty of Blasphemy, Fornication, Robbery, Forgery, or any other such Great and Atrocious Crime he Shall be Expelled forthwith.

If any Scholar Shall deny the Holy Scriptures or any part of Them to be the Word of God: or be guilty of Heresy or any Error directly Tending to Subvert the Fundamentals of Christianity, and continuing Obstinate Therein after the first and Second Admonition, He shall be Expelled.

If any Scholar shall be Guilty of Profane Swearing, Cursing, Vowing, any Petty or Implicit Oath, Profane or Irreverent Use of the Names, Attributes, Ordinances or Word of God; Disobedient or Contumacious or Refractory Carriage toward his Superiours, Fighting, Striking, Quarrelling, Challenging, Turbulent Words or Behaviour, Drunkenness, Uncleanness, lascivious Words or Actions, wearing woman's Apparel, Defrauding, Injustice, Idleness, Lying, Defamation, Tale bareing or any other Such like immoralities, He Shall be Punished by Fine, Confession, Admonition or Expulsion, as the nature and Circumstances of the case may Require.

If any Person be Guilty of Stealing, He Shall besides the Fine Pay Trible Damage and in all other cases of Injustice Shall make full Restitution to the Party injured.

If any Scholar Shall break open any Other Scholar[']s Door or Open it with a Pick-Lock or a False Key, He Shall be Fined One Shilling for the first Offence: and Two Shillings for the Second: and for the Third publickly admonished, Degraded or Expelled.

If any Scholar Shall Play at Cards or Dice at all: or at any Lawfull Game upon a Wager: or Shall bring any Quantity of Run, Wine, Brandy or other

Strong Liquor into College or into his Chamber where he Resides without Liberty from the President or Tutors, or Shall Go into any Tavern within Two miles of College and call for any Strong Liquor, or Spend his Time idly there unless with his Parent or Guardian, he sall for the first Offence be Fined Two Shillings and Sixpence, or be admonished: and for the Second Offence be Fined Five Shillings and be Degraded: and for the Third Offence be Expelled: and if any Scholar Shall Play at swords, Files or Cudgels, He Shall be Fined not Exceeding One Shilling. . . .

3

Benjamin Franklin: *Proposals Relating to the Education of Youth in Pennsylvania* (1749)

One of the most egalitarian of the Founding Fathers, Benjamin Franklin rose from relative obscurity to become a prominent printer, politician, scientist, and author. A generation before the outbreak of the American Revolution, Franklin wrote the following, which wrestles with the topic of education and includes a detailed outline of the components he wished to incorporate within a successful school. The famed American included a broad range of topics for study, which became the foundation of the Academy of Philadelphia (eventually the University of Pennsylvania in 1791).

. . . As to their STUDIES, it would be well if they could be taught every Thing that is useful, and every Thing that is ornamental: But Art is long, and their Time is short. It is therefore propos'd that they learn those Things that are likely to be most useful and most ornamental. Regard being had to the several Professions for which they are intended.

All should be taught to write a fair Hand, and swift, as that is useful to All. And with it may be learnt something of Drawing, by Imitation of Prints, and some of the first Principles of Perspective.

Arithmetick, Accounts, and some of the first Principles of Geometry and Astronomy.

The English Language might be taught by Grammar; in which some of our best Writers, as Tillotson, Addison, Pope, Algernoon Sidney, Cato's Letters, &c. should be Classicks: The Stiles principally to be cultivated, being the clear and the concise. Reading should also be taught, and pronouncing, properly, distinctly, emphatically; not with an even Tone, which under-does, nor a theatrical, which over-does Nature. . . .

But if HISTORY be made a constant Part of their Reading, such as the Translations of the Greek and Roman Historians, and the modern Histories of antient Greece and Rome, &c. may not almost all Kinds of useful Knowledge be that Way introduc'd to Advantage, and with Pleasure to the Student?

GEOGRAPHY, by reading with Maps, and being required to point out the Places where the greatest Actions were done, to give their old and new Names, with the Bounds, Situation, Extent of the Countries concern'd. . . .

MORALITY, by descanting and making continual Observations on the Causes of the Rise or Fall of any Man's Character, Fortune, Power, &c. mention'd in History; the Advantages of Temperance, Order, Frugality, Industry, Perseverance, &c. &c. Indeed the general natural Tendency of Reading good History, must be, to fix in the Minds of Youth deep Impressions of the Beauty and Usefulness of Virtue of all Kinds, Publick Spirit, Fortitude, &c. History will show the wonderful Effects of ORATORY, in governing, turning and leading great Bodies of Mankind, Armies, Cities, Nations. When the Minds of Youth are struck with Admiration at this, then is the Time to give them the Principles of that Art, which they will study with Taste and Application. Then they may be made acquainted with the best Models among the Antients, their Beauties being particularly pointed out to them. Modern Political Oratory being chiefly performed by the Pen and Press, its Advantages over the Antient in some Respects are to be shown; as that its Effects are more extensive, more lasting, &c.

History will also afford frequent Opportunities of showing the Necessity of a Publick Religion, from its Usefulness to the Publick; the Advantage of a Religious Character among private Persons; the Mischiefs of Superstition, &c. and the Excellency of the CHRISTIAN RELIGION above all others antient or modern. History will also give Occasion to expatiate on the Advantage of Civil Orders and Constitutions, how Men and their Properties are protected by joining in Societies and establishing Government; their Industry encouraged and rewarded, Arts invented, and Life made more comfortable: The Advantages of Liberty, Mischiefs of Licentiousness, Benefits arising from good Laws and a due Execution of Justice, &c. Thus may the first Principles of sound Politicks be fix'd in the Minds of Youth. . . .

When Youth are told, that the Great Men whose Lives and Actions they read in History, spoke two of the best Languages that ever were, the most expressive, copious, beautiful; and that the finest Writings, the most correct Compositions, the most perfect Productions of human Wit and Wisdom, are in those Languages, which have endured Ages, and will endure while there are Men; that no Translation can do them Justice, or give the Pleasure found in Reading the Originals; that those Languages contain all Science; that one of them is become almost universal, being the Language of Learned Men in all Countries; that to understand them is a distinguishing Ornament, &c. they may be thereby made desirous of learning those Languages, and their Industry sharpen'd in the Acquisition of them. . . .

While they are reading Natural History, might not a little Gardening, Planting, Grafting, Inoculating, &c. be taught and practised; and now and then Excursions made to the neighbouring Plantations of the best Farmers, their Methods observ'd and reason'd upon for the Information of Youth. The Improvement of Agriculture being useful to all, and Skill in it no Disparagement to any. . . .

The Idea of what is true Merit, should also be often presented to Youth, explain'd and impress'd on their Minds, as consisting in an Inclination join'd with an Ability to serve Mankind, one's Country, Friends and Family; which Ability is (with the Blessing of God) to be acquir'd or greatly encreas'd by true Learning; and should indeed be the great Aim and End of all Learning.

4

The Alphabet in the New England Primer (1777)

The textbook used by many colonists and early Americans in learning basic reading and writing skills, various editions of the Primer proliferated throughout the seventeenth, eighteenth, and into the nineteenth centuries. Take notice of the overt religious references, indicative of the Puritanical region of the Primer's origin—Massachusetts.

A Wise son maketh a glad father, but a foolish son is the heaviness of his mother.

B etter is a little with the fear of the Lord, than great treasure & trouble therewith.

C ome unto Christ all ye that labor and are heavy laden and he will give you rest.

D o not the abominable thing which I hate saith the Lord.

E xcept a man be born again, he cannot see the kingdom of God.

F oolishness is bound up in the heart of a child, but the rod of correction shall drive it far from him.

G odliness is profitable unto all things, having the promise of the life that now is, and that which is to come.

H oliness becomes GOD's house for ever.

I t is good for me to draw near unto GOD.

K eep thy heart with all diligence, for out of it are the issues of life.

L iars shall have their part in the lake which burns with fire and brimstone.

M any are the afflictions of the righteous, but the LORD delivereth them out of them all.

N ow is the accepted time, now is the day of salvation.

O ut of the abundance of the heart the mouth speaketh.

P ray to thy Father which is in secret; and thy Father which sees in secret shall reward thee openly.

Q uit you like men, be strong, stand fast in the faith.

R emember thy Creator in the days of thy youth.

S eest thou a man wise in his own conceit, there is more hope of a fool than of him.

T rust in God at all times, ye people, pour out your hearts
　　before him.

U pon the wicked, God shall rain an horrible tempest.

W o to the wicked, it shall be ill with him, for the reward of
　　his hands shall be given him.

eX hort one another daily while it is called to day, lest any
　　of you be hardened thro' the deceitfulness of sin.

Y oung men ye have overcome the wicked one.

Z eal hath consumed me, because thy enemies have forgot-
　　ten the word of God.

5

Thomas Jefferson: *Notes on the State of Virginia* (1781)

*Of the Founding Fathers, Thomas Jefferson was arguably the most outspoken propo-
nent of a comprehensive and systematic educational system. As indicated in the following reading, Jefferson was primarily concerned with identifying talented young men,
regardless of class, to help lead the new American nation. The "Sage of Monticello"
envisioned a "natural aristocracy" in which individual talents were allowed to flourish
and were not subject to the whims of hereditary castes, as was the norm in Europe and
elsewhere during the late eighteenth century.*

Another object of the revisal is, to diffuse knowledge more generally through
the mass of the people. This bill proposes to lay off every county into small dis-
tricts of five or six miles square, called hundreds, and in each of them to establish
a school for teaching reading, writing, and arithmetic. The tutor to be supported
by the hundred, and every person in it entitled to send their children three years
gratis, and as much longer as they please, paying for it. These schools to be under
a visitor, who is annually to chuse the boy, of best genius in the school, of those
whose parents are too poor to give them further education, and to send him
forward to one of the grammar schools, of which twenty are proposed to be
erected in different parts of the country, for teaching Greek, Latin, geography,
and the higher branches of numerical arithmetic. Of the boys thus sent in any
one year, trial is to be made at the grammar schools one or two years, and the
best genius of the whole selected, and continued six years, and the residue dis-
missed. By this means twenty of the best geniusses will be raked from the rub-
bish annually, and be instructed, at the public expence, so far as the grammer
schools go. At the end of six years instruction, one half are to be discontinued
(from among whom the grammar schools will probably be supplied with future
masters); and the other half, who are to be chosen for the superiority of their
parts and disposition, are to be sent and continued three years in the study of
such sciences as they shall chuse, at William and Mary college, the plan of which

is proposed to be enlarged, as will be hereafter explained, and extended to all the useful sciences. The ultimate result of the whole scheme of education would be the teaching all the children of the state reading, writing, and common arithmetic: turning out ten annually of superior genius, well taught in Greek, Latin, geography, and the higher branches of arithmetic: turning out ten others annually, of still superior parts, who, to those branches of learning, shall have added such of the sciences as their genius shall have led them to: the furnishing to the wealthier part of the people convenient schools, at which their children may be educated, at their own expence.—The general objects of this law are to provide an education adapted to the years, to the capacity, and the condition of every one, and directed to their freedom and happiness. Specific details were not proper for the law. These must be the business of the visitors entrusted with its execution. The first stage of this education being the schools of the hundreds, wherein the great mass of the people will receive their instruction, the principal foundations of future order will be laid here. Instead therefore of putting the Bible and Testament into the hands of the children, at an age when their judgments are not sufficiently matured for religious enquiries, their memories may here be stored with the most useful facts from Grecian, Roman, European and American history. The first elements of morality too may be instilled into their minds; such as, when further developed as their judgments advance in strength, may teach them how to work out their own greatest happiness, by shewing them that it does not depend on the condition of life in which chance has placed them, but is always the result of a good conscience, good health, occupation, and freedom in all just pursuits.—Those whom either the wealth of their parents or the adoption of the state shall destine to higher degrees of learning, will go on to the grammar schools, which constitute the next stage, there to be instructed in the languages. The learning Greek and Latin, I am told, is going into disuse in Europe. I know not what their manners and occupations may call for: but it would be very ill-judged in us to follow their example in this instance. There is a certain period of life, say from eight to fifteen or sixteen years of age, when the mind, like the body, is not yet firm enough for laborious and close operations. If applied to such, it falls an early victim to premature exertion; exhibiting indeed at first, in these young and tender subjects, the flattering appearance of their being men while they are yet children, but ending in reducing them to be children when they should be men. The memory is then most susceptible and tenacious of impressions; and the learning of languages being chiefly a work of memory, it seems precisely fitted to the powers of this period, which is long enough too for acquiring the most useful languages antient and modern. I do not pretend that language is science. It is only an instrument for the attainment of science. But that time is not lost which is employed in providing tools for future operation: more especially as in this case the books put into the hands of the youth for this purpose may be such as will at the same time impress their minds with useful facts and good principles. If this period be suffered to pass in idleness, the mind becomes lethargic and impotent, as would the body it inhabits if unexercised during the same time. The sympathy between body and mind during their rise, progress and decline, is too strict and obvious to endanger our being misled while we reason from the one to the other.—As soon as they are of sufficient age, it is supposed they will be sent on from the grammar schools to the university, which constitutes our third and last stage, there to study those sciences which may be adapted to their views.—By that part of our plan which prescribes the selection of the youths of genius from among the classes of the poor, we hope to avail the state of those talents which nature has sown as liberally among the poor as the rich, but which perish without use, if not sought for and cultivated.—But of all the views of this law none is more important, none more legitimate, than that of rendering the people the safe, as they are the ultimate, guardians of their own liberty. For this purpose the reading in the first stage, where *they* will receive their whole education, is proposed, as has been said, to be chiefly historical. History by apprising them of the past will enable them to judge of the future; it will avail them of the experience of other times and other nations; it will qualify them as judges of the actions and designs of men; it will enable them to know ambition under every disguise it may assume; and knowing it, to defeat its views. In every government on earth is some trace of human weakness, some germ of corruption and degeneracy, which cunning will discover, and wickedness insensibly open, cultivate, and improve. Every government degenerates when trusted to the rulers of the people alone. The people themselves therefore are its only safe depositories. And to render even them safe their minds must be improved to a certain degree. This indeed is not all that is necessary, though it be essentially necessary. An amendment of our constitution must here come in aid of the public education. The influence over government must be shared among all the people. If every individual which composes their mass participates of the ultimate authority, the government will be safe; because the corrupting the whole mass will exceed any private resources of wealth: and public ones cannot be provided but by levies on the people. In this case every man would have to pay his own price. The government of Great-Britain has been corrupted, because but one man in ten has a right to vote for members of parliament. The sellers of the government therefore get nine-tenths of their price clear. It has been thought that corruption is restrained by confining the right of suffrage to a few of the wealthier of the people: but it would be more effectually restrained by an extension of that right to such numbers as would bid defiance to the means of corruption. . . .

6

George Washington:
Letter to George Chapman (1784)

Although not formally educated beyond his youth, the first President of the United States clearly understood the importance of an educated citizenry. Washington was a classical republican who believed that only a virtuous nation would be able to preserve its liberty and, thus, a strong educational system that promoted virtue was a necessity.

Here Washington corresponds with a friend and former Virginia schoolmaster, documenting his strong opinions on the topic of education.

Sir: Not until within a few days have I been honor'd with your favor of the 27th. of Septr. 1783, accompanying your treatise on Education.

My sentiments are perfectly in unison with yours sir, that the best means of forming a manly, virtuous and happy people, will be found in the right education of youth. Without *this* foundation, every other means, in my opinion, must fail; and it gives me pleasure to find that Gentlemen of your abilities are devoting their time and attention in pointing out the way. For your lucubrations on this subject which you have been so obliging as to send me, I pray you to accept my thanks, and an expression of the pleasure I felt at the declaration of your intention to devote a further portion of your time in so useful a study.

Of the importance of education our Assemblies, happily, seem fully impressed; they establishing new, and giving further endowments to the old Seminaries of learning, and I persuade myself will leave nothing unessayed to cultivate literature and useful knowledge, for the purpose of qualifying the rising generation for patrons of good government, virtue and happiness. I have the honor, etc.

7

Noah Webster: *On the Education of Youth in America* (1788)

Famous for his dictionary, new editions of which are still used today, Noah Webster was a visionary who wanted to reform the American educational system, whose curricula had been based on its European ancestor's. In the following reading, written several years before he began work on his dictionary, Webster illustrates that mimicking the educational practices from across the Atlantic is harmful to the collective American identity.

Another defect in our schools, which, since the revolution, is become inexcuseable, is the want of proper books. The collections which are now used consist of essays that respect foreign and ancient nations. The minds of youth are perpetually led to the history of Greece and Rome or to Great Britain; boys are constantly repeating the declamations of Demosthenes and Cicero, or debates upon some political question in the British Parliment. These are excellent specimens of good sense, polished stile and perfect oratory; but they are not interesting to children. They cannot be very useful, except to young gentlemen who want them as models of reasoning and eloquence, in the pulpit or at the bar.

But every child in America should be acquainted with his own country. He should read books that furnish him with ideas that will be useful to him in life and practice. As soon as he opens his lips, he should rehearse the history of his own country; he should lisp the praise of liberty, and of those illustrious heroes and statesmen, who have wrought a revolution in her favor.

A selection of essays, respecting the settlement and geography of America; the history of the late revolution and of the most remarkable characters and events that distinguished it, and a compendium of the principles of the federal and provincial governments, should be the principal school book in the United States. These are interesting objects to every man; they call home the minds of youth and fix them upon the interests of their own country, and they assist in forming attachments to it, as well as in enlarging the understanding.

"It is observed by the great Montesquieu, that the laws of education ought to be relative to the principles of the government."

In despotic governments, the people should have little or no education, except what tends to inspire them with a servile fear. Information is fatal to despotism.

In monarchies, education should be partial, and adapted to the rank of each class of citizens. But "in a republican government," says the same writer, "the whole power of education is required." Here every class of people should *know* and *love* the laws. This knowledge should be diffused by means of schools and newspapers; and an attachment to the laws may be formed by early impressions upon the mind.

Two regulations are essential to the continuance of republican governments: 1. Such a distribution of lands and such principles of descent and alienation, as shall give every citizen a power of acquiring what his industry merits. 2. Such a system of education as gives every citizen an opportunity of acquiring knowledge and fitting himself for places of trust. These are fundamental articles; the *sine qua non* of the existence of the American republics. Hence the absurdity of our copying the manners and adopting the institutions of Monarchies.

In several States, we find laws passed, establishing provision for colleges and academies, where people of property may educate their sons; but no provision is made for instructing the poorer rank of people, even in reading and writing. Yet in these same States, every citizen who is worth a few shillings annually, is entitled to vote for legislators. This appears to me a most glaring solecism in government. The constitutions are *republican,* and the laws of education are *monarchical.* The *former* extend civil rights to every honest industrious man; the *latter* deprive a large proportion of the citizens of a most valuable privilege.

In our American republics, where [government] is in the hands of the people, knowledge should be universally diffused by means of public schools. Of such consequence is it to society, that the people who make laws, should be well informed, that I conceive no Legislature can be justified in neglecting proper establishments for this purpose.

When I speak of a diffusion of knowledge, I do not mean merely a knowledge of spelling books, and the New Testament. An acquaintance with ethics, and with the general principles of law, commerce, money and government, is necessary for the yeomanry of a republican state. This acquaintance they might obtain by means of books calculated for schools, and read by the children, during the winter months, and by the circulation of public papers.

"In Rome it was the common exercise of boys at school, to learn the laws of the twelve tables by heart, as they did their poets and classic authors." What an excellent practice this in a free government!

It is said, indeed by many, that our common people are already too well informed. Strange paradox! The truth is, they have too much knowledge and spirit to resign their share in government, and are not sufficiently informed to govern themselves in all cases of difficulty.

There are some acts of the American legislatures which astonish men of information; and blunders in legislation are frequently ascribed to bad intentions. But if we examine the men who compose these legislatures, we shall find that wrong measures generally proceed from ignorance either in the men themselves, or in their constituents. They often mistake their own interest, because they do not foresee the remote consequences of a measure.

It may be true that all men cannot be legislators; but the more generally knowledge is diffused among the substantial yeomanry, the more perfect will be the laws of a republican state.

Every small district should be furnished with a school, at least four months in a year; when boys are not otherwise employed. This school should be kept by the most reputable and well informed man in the district. Here children should be taught the usual branches of learning; submission to superiors and to laws; the moral or social duties; the history and transactions of their own country; the principles of liberty and government. Here the rough manners of the wilderness should be softened, and the principles of virtue and good behaviour inculcated. The *virtues* of men are of more consequence to society than their *abilities;* and for this reason, the *heart* should be cultivated with more assiduity than the *head.*

Such a general system of education is neither impracticable nor difficult; and excepting the formation of a federal government that shall be efficient and permanent, it demands the first attention of American patriots. Until such a system shall be adopted and pursued; until the Statesman and Divine shall unite their efforts in *forming* the human mind, rather than in loping its excrescences, after it has been neglected; until Legislators discover that the only way to make good citizens and subjects, is to nourish them from infancy; and until parents shall be convinced that the *worst* of men are not the proper teachers to make the *best;* mankind cannot know to what a degree of perfection society and government may be carried. America affords the fairest opportunities for making the experiment, and opens the most encouraging prospect of success.

8

Benjamin Rush: Of the Mode of Education Proper in a Republic (1798)

Although he is best known as one of the nation's foremost physicians of the Revolutionary Era, Rush was also a strong supporter of education and believed that an effective system of schools could benefit society as a whole. Rush was also an intensely religious man, reflected in the following in his numerous references to Christianity. Note also that Rush briefly mentions female education—one of the few Founding Fathers to take an unsolicited interest in the subject.

The business of education has acquired a new complexion by the independence of our country. The form of government we have assumed, has created a new class of duties to every American. It becomes us, therefore, to examine our former habits upon this subject, and in laying the foundations for nurseries of wise and good men, to adapt our modes of teaching to the peculiar form of our government.

The first remark that I shall make upon this subject is, that an education in our own, is to be preferred to an education in a foreign country. The principle of patriotism stands in need of the reinforcement of prejudice, and it is well known that our strongest prejudices in favour of our country are formed in the first one and twenty years of our lives. . . .

I conceive the education of our youth in this country to be peculiarly necessary in Pennsylvania, while our citizens are composed of the natives of so many different kingdoms in Europe. Our schools of learning, by producing one general, and uniform system of education, will render the mass of the people more homogeneous, and thereby fit them more easily for uniform and peaceable government.

I proceed in the next place, to enquire, what mode of education we shall adopt so as to secure to the state all the advantages that are to be derived from the proper instruction of youth; and here I beg leave to remark, that the only foundation for a useful education in a republic is to be laid in Religion. Without this there can be no virtue, and without virtue there can be no liberty, and liberty is the object and life of all republican governments.

Such is my veneration for every religion that reveals the attributes of the Deity, or a future state of rewards and punishments, that I had rather see the opinions of Confucius or Mahomed inculcated upon our youth, than see them grow up wholly devoid of a system of religious principles. But the religion I mean to recommend in this place, is that of the New Testament.

It is foreign to my purpose to hint at the arguments which establish the truth of the Christian revelation. My only business is to declare, that all its doctrines and precepts are calculated to promote the happiness of society, and the safety and well being of civil government. A Christian cannot fail of being a republican. The history of the creation of man, and of the relation of our species to each other by birth, which is recorded in the Old Testament, is the best refutation that can be given to the divine right of kings, and the strongest argument that can be used in favor of the original and natural equality of all mankind. A Christian, I say again, cannot fail of being a republican, for every precept of the Gospel inculcates those degrees of humility, self-denial, and brotherly kindness, which are directly opposed to the pride of monarchy and the pageantry of a court. A Christian cannot fail of being useful to the republic, for his religion teacheth him, that no man "liveth to himself." And lastly, a Christian cannot fail of being wholly inoffensive, for his religion teacheth him, in all things to do to others what he would wish, in like circumstances, they should do to him.

From the observations that have been made it is plain, that I consider it is possible to convert men into republican machines. This must be done, if we expect them to perform their parts properly, in the great machine of the government of the state. That republic is sophisticated with monarchy or aristocracy that does not revolve upon the wills of the people, and these must be fitted to each other by means of education before they can be made to produce regularity and unison in government.

With the usual arts and sciences that are taught in our American colleges, I wish to see a regular course of lectures given upon History and Chronology. The science of government, whether it relates to constitutions or laws, can only be advanced by a careful selection of facts, and these are to be found chiefly in history. Above all, let our youth be instructed in the history of the ancient republics, and the progress of liberty and tyranny in the different states of Europe. I wish likewise to see the numerous facts that relate to the origin and present state of commerce, together with the nature and principles of money, reduced to such a system, as to be intelligible and agreeable to a young man. If we consider the commerce of our metropolis only as the avenue of the wealth of the state, the study of it merits a place in a young man's education; but, I consider commerce in a much higher light when I recommend the study of it in republican seminaries. I view it as the best security against the influence of hereditary monopolies of land, and, therefore, the surest protection against aristocracy. I consider its effects as next to those of religion in humanizing mankind, and lastly, I view it as the means of uniting the different nations of the world together by the ties of mutual wants and obligations.

I beg pardon for having delayed so long to say any thing of the separate and peculiar mode of education proper for women in a republic. I am sensible that they must concur in all our plans of education for young men, or no laws will ever render them effectual. To qualify our women for this purpose, they should not only be instructed in the usual branches of female education, but they should be taught the principles of liberty and government; and the obligations of patriotism should be inculcated upon them. The opinions and conduct of men are often regulated by the women in the most arduous enterprizes of life; and their approbation is frequently the principal reward of the hero's dangers, and the patriot's toils. Besides, the first impressions upon the minds of children are generally derived from the women. Of how much consequence, therefore, is it in a republic, that they should think justly upon the great subject of liberty and government! . . .

9

Thomas Jefferson: Letter to Nathaniel Burwell (1818)

As mentioned previously, Thomas Jefferson was the Founding Father arguably most concerned with education. However, one of Jefferson's glaring omissions in this area was his lack of concern about educational opportunities for women. In the following letter to his close friend Nathaniel Burwell, Jefferson ponders the topic, on which he had "not thought much" up to that late point in his life. Note his tendency to focus on areas of education for women that would inculcate primarily social graces and domestic expertise while ignoring the broader education he supported for men.

Your letter of February 17th found me suffering under an attack of rheumatism, which has but now left me at sufficient ease to attend to the letters I have received. A plan of female education has never been a subject of systematic contemplation with me. It has occupied my attention so far only as the education of my own daughters occasionally required. Considering that they would be placed in a country situation, where little aid could be obtained from abroad, I thought it essential to give them a solid education, which might enable them, when become mothers, to educate their own daughters, and even to direct the course for sons, should their fathers be lost, or incapable, or inattentive. My surviving daughter accordingly, the mother of many daughters as well as sons, has made their education the object of her life, and being a better judge of the practical part than myself, it is with her aid and that of one of her elves that I shall subjoin a catalogue of the books for such a course of reading as we have practiced.

A great obstacle to good education is the inordinate passion prevalent for novels, and the time lost in that reading which should be instructively employed. When this poison infects the mind, it destroys its tone and revolts it against wholesome reading. Reason and fact, plain and unadorned, are rejected. Nothing can engage attention unless dressed in all the figments of fancy, and nothing so bedecked comes amiss. The result is a bloated imagination, sickly judgment, and disgust towards all the real businesses of life. This mass of trash, however, is not without some distinction; some few modelling their narratives, although fictitious, on the incidents of real life, have been able to make them interesting and useful vehicles of sound morality. Such, I think, are Marmontel's new moral tales, but not his old ones, which are really immoral. Such are the writings of Miss Edgeworth, and some of those of Madame Genlis. For a like reason, too, much poetry should not be indulged. Some is useful for forming style and taste. Pope, Dryden, Thompson, Shakspeare, and of the French, Moliere, Racine, the Corneilles, may be read with pleasure and improvement.

The French language, become that of the general intercourse of nations, and from their extraordinary advances, now the depository of all science, is an indispensable part of education for both sexes. In the subjoined catalogue, therefore, I have placed the books of both languages indifferently, according as the one or the other offers what is best.

The ornaments too, and the amusements of life, are entitled to their portion of attention. These, for a female, are dancing, drawing, and music. The first is a healthy exercise, elegant and very attractive for young people. Every affectionate parent would be pleased to see his daughter qualified to participate with her companions, and without awkwardness at least, in the circles of festivity, of which she occasionally becomes a part. It is a necessary accomplishment, therefore, although of short use, for the French rule is wise, that no lady dances after marriage. This is founded in solid physical reasons, gestation and nursing leaving little time to a married lady when this exercise can be either safe or innocent. Drawing is thought less of in this country than in Europe. It is an innocent and engaging amusement, often useful, and a qualification not to be neglected in one who is to become a mother and an instructor. Music is invaluable where a person has an ear. Where they have not, it should not be attempted. It furnishes a delightful recreation for the hours of respite from the cares of the day, and lasts us through life. The taste of this country, too, calls for this accomplishment more strongly than for either of the others.

I need say nothing of household economy, in which the mothers of our country are generally skilled, and generally careful to instruct their daughters. We all know its value, and that diligence and dexterity in all its processes are inestimable treasures. The order and economy of a house are as honorable to the mistress as those of the farm to the master, and if either be neglected, ruin follows, and children destitute of the means of living. This, Sir, is offered as a summary sketch on a subject on which I have not thought much.

10

Emma Willard: *Improving Female Education* (1819)

By the turn of the nineteenth century an increasing chorus of Americans began to actively support expanded educational opportunities for women. The opening of institutions of higher learning to include women accelerated during the first half of the nineteenth century, and the systematic education of girls and women became increasingly common. The following two readings reflect a common theme in the promotion of female education— the positive impact that such an arrangement would have on society as a whole. Emma

Willard, who founded several schools for girls and women during her lifetime, promotes the role of women as the collective conscience of society, whereas Catharine Beecher, another active educator of the era, asserts the importance of physical education for women and the need for newly educated women to understand effective mechanisms for transferring their expanding knowledge to others.

If the improvement of the American female character, and that alone, could be effected by public liberality, employed in giving better means of instruction, such improvement of one half of society, and that half, which barbarous and despotic nations have ever degraded, would of itself be an object, worthy of the most liberal government on earth; but if the female character be raised, it must inevitably raise that of the other sex: and thus does the plan proposed, offer, as the object of legislative bounty, to elevate the whole character of the community.

As evidence that this statement does not exaggerate the female influence in society, our sex need but be considered in the single relation of mothers. In this character, we have the charge of the whole mass of individuals, who are to compose the succeeding generation; during that period of youth, when the pliant mind takes any direction, to which it is steadily guided by a forming hand. How important a power is given by this charge! Yet, little do too many of my sex know how, either to appreciate it or improve it. Unprovided with the means of acquiring that knowledge, which flows liberally to the other sex—having our times of education devoted to frivolous acquirements, how should we understand the nature of the mind so as to be aware of the importance of those early impressions, which we make upon the minds of our children?—or how should we be able to form enlarged and correct views, either of the character, to which we ought to mold them, or of the means most proper to form them aright?

Considered in this point of view, were the interests of male education alone to be consulted, that of females becomes of sufficient importance to engage the public attention. Would we rear the human plant to its perfection, we must fertilize the soil which produces it. If it acquire its first bent and texture upon a barren plain, it will avail comparatively little, should it be afterwards transplanted to a garden. . . .

Not only has there been a want of system concerning female education, but much of what has been done, has proceeded upon mistaken principles.

One of these is, that, without regard to the difference periods of life, proportionate to their importance, the education of females has been too exclusively directed, to fit them for displaying to advantage the charms of youth and beauty. Though it may be proper to adorn this period of life, yet, it is incomparably more important to prepare for the serious duties of maturer years. Though well to decorate the blossom, it is far better to prepare for the harvest. In the vegetable creation, nature seems but to sport, when she embellishes the flower; while all her serious cares are directed to perfect the fruit.

Another error is that it has been made the first object in educating our sex, to prepare then to please the other. But reason and religion teach, that we too are primary existences; that it is for us to move, in the orbit of our duty, around the Holy Center of perfection, the companions, not the satellites of men; else, instead of shedding around us in their proper course, we must accompany them in their wildest deviations. . . .

That nature designed for our sex the care of children, she has made manifest, by mental, as well as physical indications. She has given us, in a greater degree than men, the gentle arts of insinuation, to soften their minds, and fit them to receive impressions; a greater quickness of invention to vary modes of teaching to different dispositions; and more patience to make repeated efforts. There are many females of ability to whom the business of instructing children is highly acceptable, and who would devote all their faculties to their occupation. They would have no higher pecuniary object to engage their attention, and their reputation as instructors they would consider as important; whereas, whenever able and enterprising men, engage in this business, they considerate as merely temporary employment, to further some other object, to the attainment of which, their best thoughts and calculations are directed. If then women were properly fitted by instruction, they would be likely to teach children better than the other sex; they could afford to do it cheaper; and those men who would otherwise be engaged in this employment, might be at liberty to add to the wealth of the nation, by any of those thousand occupations, from which women are necessarily debarred. . . .

You are our natural guardians,—our brothers,—our fathers, and our rulers. You know that our ductile minds, readily take the impressions of education. Why then have you neglected our education? Why have you looked with lethargic indifference, on circumstances ruinous to the formation of our characters, which you might have controlled? . . .

1. Females, by having their understandings cultivated, their reasoning powers developed and strengthened, may be expected to act more from the dictates of reason and less from those of fashion and caprice.

2. With minds thus strengthened they would be taught systems of morality, enforced by sanctions of religion; and they might be expected to acquire juster and more enlarged views of their duty and stronger and higher motives to its performance.

3. This plan of education, offers all that can be done to preserve female youth from a contempt of useful labor. The pupils would become accustomed to it, in conjunction with the high objects of literature, and the elegant pursuits of the fine arts; and it is to be hoped that both from habit and association, they might in future life, regard it as respectable. . . .

In calling on my patriotic countrymen to effect so noble an object, the consideration of national glory, should not be overlooked. Ages have rolled away;—barbarians have trodden the weaker sex beneath their feet;—tyrant[s] have robbed us of the present light of heaven, and fain would take its future.

Nations calling themselves polite have made us the fancies idols of a ridiculous worship, and we have repaid them with ruin for their folly. But where is that wise and heroic country, which has considered that our rights are sacred, though we cannot defend them? that tho' a weaker, we are an essential part of the body politic, whose corruption or improvement must affect the whole? And which, having thus considered, has sought to give us by education, that rank in the scale of being, to which our importance entitles us? History shows not that country. It shows many, whose legislatures have sought to improve their various vegetable productions, and their breeds of useful brutes; but none whose public councils have made it an object of their deliberations, to improve the character of their women. Yet, though history lifts not her finger to such an one, anticipation does. She points to a nation, which having thrown off the shackles of authority and precedent, shrinks not from schemes of improvement, because other nations have never attempted them; but which, in its pride of independence, would rather lead than follow in the march of human improvement; a nation wise and magnanimous to plan, enterprising to undertake, and rich in resources to execute. Does not every American exult that this country is his own? And who knows how great and good a race of men may yet arise from the forming hand of mothers, enlightened by the bounty of that beloved country,—to defend her liberties,—to plan her future improvement,—and to raise her unparalleled glory?

11

Catharine Beecher: *Suggestions Respecting Improvements in Education* (1829)

It is to mothers and to teachers that the world is to look for the character which is to be enstamped on each succeeding generation, for it is to them that the great business of education is almost exclusively committed. And will it not appear by examination that neither mothers nor teachers have ever been properly educated for their profession? What is the *profession of a woman?* Is it not to form immortal minds, and to watch, to nurse, and to rear the bodily system, so fearfully and wonderfully made, and upon the order and regulation of which the health and well-being of the mind so greatly depends?

But let most of our sex, upon whom these arduous duties devolve, be asked: Have you ever devoted any time and study, in the course of your education, to any preparation for these duties? Have you been taught anything of the structure, the nature, and the laws of the body which you inhabit? Were you ever taught to understand the operation of diet, air, exercise, and modes of dress upon the human frame? Have the causes which are continually operating to prevent good health and the modes by which it might be perfected and preserved ever been made the subject of any *instruction?* Perhaps almost every voice would respond, no. We have attended to almost everything more than to this; we have been taught more concerning the structure of the earth, the laws of the heavenly bodies, the habits and formation of plants, the philosophy of languages—more of *almost anything* than the structure of the human frame and the laws of health and reason.

But is it not the business, the *profession* of a woman to guard the health and form the physical habits of the young? And is not the cradle of infancy and the chamber of sickness sacred to woman alone? And ought she not to know at least some of the *general principles* of that perfect and wonderful piece of mechanism committed to her preservation and care?

The *restoration* of health is the physician's profession, but the *preservation* of it falls to other hands, and it is believed that the time will come when woman will be taught to understand something respecting the construction of the human frame; the physical results which will naturally follow from restricted exercise, unhealthy modes of dress, improper diet, and many other causes which are continually operating to destroy the health and life of the young.

Again let our sex be asked respecting the instruction they have received in the course of their education on that still more arduous and difficult department of their profession which relates to the *intellect* and the *moral susceptibilities*. Have you been taught the powers and faculties of the human mind, and the laws by which it is regulated? Have you studied how to direct its several faculties; how to restore those that are overgrown, and strengthen and mature those that are deficient? Have you been taught the best modes of *communicating* knowledge as well as of *acquiring* it? Have you learned the best mode of correcting bad *moral* habits and forming good ones? Have you made it an object to find how a selfish disposition may be made generous; how a reserved temper may be made open and frank; how pettishness and ill humor may be changed to cheerfulness and kindness? Has any woman studied her profession in this respect?

It is feared the same answer must be returned, if not from all, at least from most of our sex. No; we have acquired wisdom from the observation and experience of others on almost all other subjects, but the philosophy of the direction and control of the human mind has not been an object of thought or study. And thus it appears that, though it is woman's *express business* to rear the body and form the mind, there is scarcely anything to which her attention has been less directed.

But this strange and irrational neglect, may be considered as the result, of an equal neglect as it respects those whose *exclusive* business it is, to form the mind and communicate knowledge. To the parents of a family there are many other cares committed besides the formation of the mental and moral habits of children. Indeed, the pecuniary circumstances of most parents will allow them to devote but little time to the discharge of such duties. . . . Another defect in education is that it has not been made a *definite object* with teachers *to prepare their pupils to instruct others*. For of how comparatively little value is knowledge laid up in the mind if it is never to be imparted to others, and yet how few have ever been taught to communicate their ideas with facility and propriety. That there is a best way of *teaching* as well as of doing everything else cannot be disputed, and this can no more be learned by *intuition* than can any of the mechanical arts. This can be made an object of instruction as much as any other art, and a woman, ordinarily, might be *taught* to converse with ease and fluency, and to communicate knowledge with accuracy and perspicuity, with far less time and effort than is now given to the acquisition of *music*.

If a teacher, in communicating ideas, should make it a part of the *duty* of a scholar to communicate the same to a third person, either to a child already ignorant or to some friend who would give a listening ear, much would be accomplished in this way. During many recitations it is desirable to induce the pupils to ask questions and express opinions with this object in view. Nothing aids more in this art than attempting to *teach others*, and all who become teachers will probably find that in this and various other ways they *receive* almost as much benefit as they *confer*.

If all females were not only well educated themselves but were prepared to communicate in an easy manner their stores of knowledge to others; if they not only knew how to regulate their own minds, tempers, and habits but how to effect improvements in those around them, the face of society would speedily be changed. The time *may* come when the world will look back with wonder to behold how much time and effort have been given to the mere cultivation of the memory, and how little mankind have been aware of what every teacher, parent, and friend could accomplish in forming the social, intellectual, and moral character of those by whom they are surrounded.

12

The Massachusetts Compulsory School Attendance Act (1836)

Although the Founding Fathers had virtually all supported an educational system that would allow the talented and intelligent to distinguish themselves, following the Revolution few states initiated movements to publicly fund schools and, most importantly, none required attendance. Always progressive in the field of education, Massachusetts began the trend of mandatory school attendance that burgeoned throughout the remainder of the nineteenth century and culminated with universal regulations in all states by the early part of the twentieth century. Although the following act does not explicitly state that all children were required to attend school for a predetermined number of years or even months, it was the first of its kind in attempting to eliminate the exploitation of child laborers by connecting their ability to work with their school attendance.

Be it enacted by the Senate and House of Representatives, in the General Court assembled and by the authority of the same, as follows:

Section 1. From and after the first day of April in the year eighteen hundred and thirty seven, no child under the age of fifteen years shall be employed to labor in any manufacturing establishment, unless such child shall have attended some public or private day school, where instruction is given by a teacher qualified . . . at least three months of the twelve months next preceding any and every year, in which such child shall be so employed.

Section 2. The owner, agent or superintendent of any manufacturing establishment contrary to the provisions of this act, shall forfeit the sum of fifty dollars for each offence, to be recovered by indictment, to the use of common schools in the towns respectively where said establishments may be situated.

13

Horace Mann: *Tenth Annual Report of the Secretary of the Massachusetts State Board of Education* (1846)

One of the great champions of education during the first half of the nineteenth century, Horace Mann was a successful lawyer and politician before being named the Secretary of Education in Massachusetts in 1837—a post he held until 1848. During his tenure in office Mann was extremely active in promoting education, eventually gaining support for the public funding of libraries, teacher training schools, and the strengthening of compulsory attendance laws. The following reading includes one of Mann's most famous annual reports while Secretary of Education, in which Mann connects education to a number of America's founding principles and asserts that education is a right of all citizens.

The Pilgrim Fathers amid all their privations and dangers conceived the magnificent idea, not only of a universal, but of a free education for the whole people. To find the time and the means to reduce this grand conception to practice, they stinted themselves, amid all their poverty, to a still scantier pittance; amid all their toils, they imposed upon themselves still more burdensome labors; and amid all their perils, they braved still greater dangers. Two divine ideas filled their great hearts,—their duty to God and society. For the one they built the church, for the other they opened the school. Religion and knowledge,—two attributes of the same glorious and eternal truth, and that truth the only one on which immortal or mortal happiness can be securely founded! . . .

[T]here is not at the present time, with the exception of the States of New England and a few small communities elsewhere, a country or a state in Christendom which maintains a system of free schools for the education of its children.

I believe that this amazing dereliction from duty, especially in our own country, originates more in the false notions which men entertain *respecting the nature of their right to property* than in any thing else. In the district school meeting, in the town meeting, in legislative halls, everywhere, the advocates for a more generous education could carry their respective audiences with them in behalf of increased privileges for our children, were it not instinctively foreseen that increased privileges must be followed by increased taxation. Against this obstacle, argument falls dead. The rich man who has no children declares that the exaction of a contribution from him to educate the children of his neighbor is an invasion of his rights of property. The man who has reared and educated a family of children denounces it as a double tax when he is called upon to assist in educating the children of others also; or, if he has reared in his own children without educating them, he thinks it peculiarly oppressive to be obliged to do for others what he refrained from doing even for himself. Another, having children, but disdaining to educate them with the common mass, withdraws them from the public school, puts them under what he calls "selecter influences," and then thinks it a grievance to be obliged to support a school which he contemns. Or, if these different parties so far yield to the force of traditionary sentiment and usage, and to the public opinion around them, as to consent to do something for the cause, they soon reach the limit of expenses at which their admitted obligation or their alleged charity terminates.

It seems not irrelevant, therefore, in this connection, and for the purpose of strengthening the foundation on which our free school system reposes, to inquire into the nature of a man's right to the property he possesses, and to satisfy ourselves respecting the question whether any man has such an indefeasible title to his estates or such an absolute ownership of them as renders it unjust in the government to assess upon him his share of the expenses of educating the children of the community up to such a point as the nature of the institutions under which he lives, and the well-being of society, require.

I believe in the existence of a great, immortal, immutable principle of natural law, or natural ethics,—a principle antecedent to all human institutions, and incapable of being abrogated by any ordinance of man,—a principle of divine origin, clearly legible in the ways of Providence as those ways are manifested in the order of nature and in the history of the race, which proves the *absolute right* to an education of every human being that comes into the world, and which, of course, proves the correlative duty of every government to see that the means of that education are provided for all.

In regard to the application of this principle of natural law,—that is, in regard to the extent of the education to be provided for all at the public expense,—some difference of opinion may fairly exist under different political organizations; but, under our republican government, it seems clear that the minimum of this education can never be less than such as is sufficient to qualify each citizen for the civil and social duties he will be called to discharge,— such an education as teaches the individual the great laws of bodily health, as qualifies for the fulfillment of parental duties, as is indispensable for the civil functions of a witness or a juror, as is necessary for the voter in municipal and in national affairs, and, finally, as is requisite for the faithful and conscientious discharge of all those duties which devolve upon the inheritor of a portion of the sovereignty of this great republic. . . .

In obedience to the laws of God and to the laws of all civilized communities, society is bound to protect the natural life of children; and this natural life cannot be protected without the appropriation and use of a portion of the property which society possesses. We prohibit infanticide under penalty of death. We practise a refinement in this particular. The life of an infant is inviolable, even before he is born; and he who feloniously takes it, even before birth, is as subject to the extreme penalty of the law as though he had struck down manhood in its vigor, or taken away a mother by violence from the sanctuary of home where she blesses her offspring. But why preserve the natural life of a child, why preserve unborn embryos of life, if we do not intend to watch over and to protect them, and to expand their subsequent existence into usefulness and happiness? As individuals, or as an organized community, we have no natural right, we can derive no authority or countenance from reason, we can cite no attribute or purpose of the divining nature, for giving birth to any human being, and then inflicting upon that being the curse of ignorance, of poverty, and of vice, with all their attendant calamities. We are brought, then, to this startling but inevitable alternative,— the natural life of an infant should be extinguished as soon as it is born, or the means should be provided to save that life from being a curse to its possessor; and, therefore, every State is morally bound to enact a code of laws legalizing and enforcing infanticide or a code of laws establishing free schools. . . .

14

Morrill Act (1862)

Although the majority of Americans by the latter half of the nineteenth century had access to basic forms of education, institutions of higher learning were still beyond the reach of most. Soon after the outbreak of the Civil War, Congress authorized the passage of the Morrill Act, which allocated, for every state then in the union, 30,000 acres of federal land for each senator and representative for the purpose of founding and supporting colleges. The land was to be used directly by the college or sold, with the proceeds providing an endowment for the permanent establishment of the institution. The 1862 Morrill Act, along with later versions, was responsible for the creation of most state universities across the country today and was a key factor in democratizing education in the United States.

Be it enacted by the Senate and House of Representatives of the United States of America in Congress as assembled, that there be granted to the several States, for the purposes hereinafter mentioned, an amount of public land, to be apportioned to each State a quantity equal to thirty thousand acres for each Senator and Representative in Congress to which the States are respectively entitled by the apportionment under the census of eighteen hundred and sixty; *Provided,* That no mineral lands shall be selected or purchased under the provisions of this act.

Sec. 2. *And be it further enacted,* That the land aforesaid, after being Surveyed, shall be apportioned to the several States in sections or subdivisions of sections, not less than one-quarter of a section; and whenever there are public lands in a State subject to sale at private entry at one dollar and twenty-five cents per acre, the quantity to which said State shall be entitled shall be selected from such lands within the limits of such State, and the Secretary of the Interior is hereby directed to issue to each of the States in which there is not the quantity of public lands subject to sale at private entry at one dollar and twenty-five cents per acre, to which said State may be entitled under the provisions of this act, land scrip to the amount in acres for the deficiency of its distributive share: said scrip to be sold by said States and the proceeds thereof applied to the uses and purposes prescribed in this act, and for no other use or purpose whatsoever: *Provided,* That in no case shall any State to which land scrip may thus be issued be allowed to locate the same within the limits of any other State, or of any Territory of the United States, but their assignees may thus locate said land scrip upon any of the unappropriated lands of the United States subject to sale at private entry at one dollar and twenty-five cents, or less, per acre: A*nd provided, further,* That not more than one million acres shall be located by such assignees in any one of the States: *And provided, further,* That no such location shall be made before one year from the passage of this act.

Sec. 3. *And be it further enacted,* That all expenses of management, superintendence, and taxes from date of selection of said lands, previous to their sales, and all expenses incurred in the management and disbursement of the moneys which may be received therefrom, shall be paid by the States to which they may belong, out of the treasury of said States, so that the entire proceeds of the sale of said lands shall be applied without any diminution whatever to the purposes hereinafter mentioned.

Sec. 4. *And be it further enacted,* That all moneys derived from the sale of the lands aforesaid by the States to which the lands are apportioned, and from the sales of land scrip hereinbefore provided for, shall be invested in stocks of the United States, or of the States, or some other safe stocks, yielding not less than five per centum upon the par value of said stocks; and that the moneys so invested shall constitute a perpetual fund, the capital of which shall remain forever undiminished, (except so far as may be provided in section fifth of this act,) and the interest of which shall be inviolably appropriated, by each State which may take and claim the benefit of this act, to the endowment, support, and maintenance of at least one college where the leading object shall be, without excluding other scientific and classical studies, and including military tactics, to teach such branches of learning as are related to agriculture and the mechanic arts, in such manner as the legislatures of the States may respectively prescribe, in order to promote the liberal and practical education of the industrial classes in the several pursuits and professions in life.

15

Harper's Weekly Editorial: "An Undoubted Right" (1874)

Following the conclusion of the Civil War, one of the most difficult situations involved the plight of the million of newly freed slaves. Some Americans advocated full and immediate equality, others encouraged a more gradual assimilation, whereas still others sought to keep them relegated to second-class citizens. Supporters of African American rights, white and black alike, recognized that education was a key component to the enduring success of African Americans. The following is an editorial published in one of the most progressive journals of the day, Harper's Weekly, *in which the author, George Curtis, urges support for an African American school in Georgia. Note the reference to the Ku Klux Klan and Curtis's mention of other Northern supporters for the venture.*

There is one kind of civil right which the strictest constitutional interpretation will not deny to the colored citizens of the Southern States, and that is the right of educating their own children at their own expense, assisted by the voluntary aid of others. This is what William Craft, whose story was very familiar during the Fugitive Slave Act excitement twenty-three years ago, proposes to do in South Georgia. His object is to give the poor country colored children a chance at the rudiments of education. Mr. Craft and his wife and son have bought a plantation or farm of 1800 acres about twenty miles from Savannah, to which families with children will remove, hiring part of the land and paying a portion of the crop toward the school, while the children will work upon the land to raise grain and vegetables for their own use. Mr. Craft in 1871 tried a similar experiment upon another spot, advanced the money, and secured a good crop; but the Ku-Klux destroyed the buildings and the harvest. Several gentlemen in Boston, in New York, and elsewhere have subscribed to further a project which is in such capable hands; and whoever is disposed may address Mr. Craft at 252 West Twenty-sixth Street, New York.

DISCUSSION QUESTIONS FOR CHAPTER 4

1. What similarities and differences do you notice about the characteristics of the educational experiences at Harvard, Yale, and Franklin's proposed academy? What dimension(s) does the New England Primer alphabet reflect regarding early American society?

2. Why did Jefferson and others of the founding generation believe that education was so important to the survival of the new nation? Is

Jefferson's proposal elitist or enlightened? Do you think Jefferson truly believed in equality of opportunity for white men?

3. Compare and contrast the views of Webster and Rush on their proposed models of education. What argument do they share in common? Why is Rush so insistent on religion permeating the curriculum in schools? Why do you think Webster seems less concerned about the implementation of religious instruction in schools?

4. Why was the topic of female education not of great concern for Jefferson and other founders? Why would many people, such as Emma Willard and Catharine Beecher, ultimately argue that female education was a vital component to a vibrant nation? What specific suggestions do Willard and Beecher promote regarding the education of girls and women?

5. Why did compulsory education eventually become a reality in the United States? What common theme is evident in the final four readings? What connections can you make between these readings and current student loan and grant programs?

CHAPTER 5

Republican Government

1

An Excerpt from the Declaration and Resolves of the Continental Congress (1774)

This reading illustrates the widely held understanding of the founding generation that political justice requires republican government—that is, government that represents the citizens and that derives its authority from their consent.

The good people of the several colonies of New Hampshire, Massachusetts Bay, Rhode Island and Providence Plantations, Connecticut, New York, New Jersey, Pennsylvania, Newcastle, Kent, and Sussex on Delaware, Maryland, Virginia, North Carolina, and South Carolina, justly alarmed at these arbitrary proceedings of parliament and administration, have severally elected, constituted, and appointed deputies to meet, and sit in general Congress, in the city of Philadelphia, in order to obtain such establishment, as that their religion, laws, and liberties, may not be subverted: Whereupon the deputies so appointed being now assembled, in a full and free representation of these colonies, taking into their most serious consideration, the best means of attaining the ends aforesaid, do, in the first place, as Englishmen, their ancestors in like cases have usually done, for asserting and vindicating their rights and liberties, *Declare,* That the inhabitants of the English colonies in North-America, by the immutable laws of nature, the principles of the English constitution, and the several charters or compacts, have the following RIGHTS: . . .

Resolved, 4. That the foundation of English liberty, and of all free government, is a right in the people to participate in their legislative council: and as the English colonists are not represented, and from their local and other circumstances, cannot properly be represented in the British parliament, they are entitled to a free and exclusive power of legislation in their several provincial legislatures, where their right of representation can alone be preserved, in all cases of taxation and internal polity, subject only to the negative of their sovereign, in such manner as has been heretofore used and accustomed: But, from the necessity of the case, and a regard to the mutual interest of both countries, we cheerfully consent to the operation of such acts of the British parliament, as are bona fide, restrained to the regulation of our external commerce, for the purpose of securing the commercial advantages of the whole empire to the mother country, and the commercial benefits of its respective members; excluding every idea of taxation internal or external, for raising a revenue on the subjects, in America, without their consent.

2

Alexander Hamilton: An Excerpt from "The Farmer Refuted" (1775)

In the following excerpt, a twenty-year-old Alexander Hamilton brings to light the theoretical foundations of the founders' commitment to republican government. By the laws of nature, he contends, just government must be based on the consent of the governed; and fundamental rights cannot be secure when such consent is not obtained.

Good and wise men, in all ages . . . have supposed that the deity, from the relations we stand in to himself and to each other, has constituted an eternal and immutable law, which is, indispensably, obligatory upon all mankind, prior to any human institution whatever.

This is what is called the law of nature, "which, being coeval with mankind, and dictated by God himself, is, of course, superior in obligation to any other. It is binding all over the globe, in all countries, and at all times. No human laws are of any validity if contrary to this; and such of them as are valid, derive all their authority, mediately or immediately, from this original" (Blackstone).

Upon this law depend the natural rights of mankind; the supreme being gave existence to man, together with the means of preserving and beatifying that existence. He endowed him with rational faculties, by the help of which to discern and pursue such things as were consistent with his duty and interest, and invested him with an inviolable right to personal liberty, and personal safety.

Hence, in a state of nature no man had any moral power to deprive another of his life, limbs, property, or liberty; nor the least authority to command or exact obedience from him, except that which arose from the ties of consanguinity.

Hence also the origin of all civil government, justly established, must be a voluntary compact between the rulers and the ruled, and must be liable to such limitations as are necessary for the security of the absolute rights of the latter; for what original title can any man or set of men have to govern others except their own consent? To usurp dominion over a people, in their own despite, or to grasp at a more extensive power than they are willing to entrust, is to violate that law of nature, which gives every man a right to his personal liberty, and can, therefore, confer no obligation to obedience. . . .

If we examine the pretensions of parliament by this criterion, which is evidently a good one, we shall presently detect their injustice. First, they are subversive of our natural liberty because an authority is assumed over us which we by no means assent to. And secondly, they divest us of that moral security for our lives and properties, which we are entitled to and which it is the primary end of society to bestow. For such security can never exist while we have no part in making the laws that are to bind us, and while it may be the interest of our uncontrolled legislators to oppress us as much as possible.

3

Jonathan Boucher: An Excerpt from *A View of the Causes and Consequences of the American Revolution* (1775)

Because the American Revolution succeeded and its leaders were able to institute a new and republican form of government, we often forget that a large number of Americans, known as Tories, rejected the Revolutionary position and preferred that the colonies remain a part of the British Empire. Boucher, an Anglican clergyman, was one such loyalist whose pro-British opinions were so controversial that he had to flee America and move to England in 1775. In 1797 he published as a book a number of his political sermons from the Revolutionary period in which he had argued against independence. In the following excerpt, from a sermon preached in 1775, he contradicts the Revolutionary opinion that the equality of human beings requires that government be based on the consent of the governed.

This popular notion, that government was originally formed by the consent or by a compact of the people, rests on, and is supported by . . . [the] notion . . . that the whole human race is born equal; and that no man is naturally inferior, or, in any respect, subjected to another; and that he can be made subject to another only by his own consent. The position is equally ill-founded and false both in its premises and conclusions. In hardly any sense that can be imagined is the position strictly true; but, as applied to the case under consideration, it is demonstrably not true. Man differs from man in everything that can be supposed to lead to supremacy and subjection, *as one star differs from another star in glory.* It was the purpose of the Creator that man should be social; but, without government, there can be no society; nor, without some relative inferiority and superiority, can there be any government. A musical instrument composed of chords, keys, or pipes, all perfectly equal in size and power, might as well be expected to produce harmony, as a society composed of members all perfectly equal to be productive of order and peace. If (according to the idea of the advocates of this chimerical scheme of equality) no man could rightfully *be compelled to come in* and be a member even of a government to be formed by a regular compact, but by his own individual consent, it clearly follows, from the same principles, that neither could he rightfully be made or compelled to submit to the ordinances of any government already formed, to which he has not individually or actually consented. On the principle of equality, neither his parents, nor even the vote of a majority of the society (however virtuously and honorably that vote might be obtained), can have any such authority over any man. Neither can it be maintained that acquiescence implies consent; because acquiescence may have been extorted from impotence or incapacity. Even an explicit consent can bind a man no longer than he chooses to be bound. The same principle of equality that exempts him from being governed without his own consent clearly entitles him to recall and resume that consent whenever he sees fit; and he alone has a right to judge when and for what reasons it may be resumed.

Any attempt, therefore, to introduce this fantastic system into practice would reduce the whole business of social life to the wearisome, confused, and useless task of mankind's first expressing, and then withdrawing, their consent to an endless succession of schemes of government. Governments, though always forming, would never be completely formed; for the majority today might be the minority tomorrow, and, of course, that which is now fixed might and would be soon unfixed.

4

Sam Adams: An Excerpt from a Letter to Noah Webster (1784)

The following selection shows the confidence many leading Americans felt that republican government would, through its responsibility to the people, lead automatically to sound policy and the security of individual rights.

I hope it will not be in the Power of any designing Men, by imposing upon credulous though well meaning Persons, to keep this Country, who may be happy if they will, long in a State of Discord and Animosity. We may see, from the present State of Great Britain, how rapidly such a Spirit will drive a Nation to destruction. It is prudent for the People to keep a watchful Eye over the Conduct of all those who are entrusted with Public Affairs. Such Attention is the People's great Security. But there is Decency and Respect due to Constitutional Authority, and those Men, who under any Pretence or by any Means whatever, would lessen the Weight of Government lawfully exercised, must be Enemies to our happy Revolution and the Common Liberty. County Conventions and popular Committees served an excellent Purpose when they were first in Practice. No one therefore needs to regret the Share he may then have had in them. But I candidly own it is my Opinion, with Deference to the

Opinions of other Men, that as we now have constitutional and regular Governments and all our Men in Authority depend upon the annual and free Elections of the People, we are safe without them. To say the least, they are become useless. Bodies of Men, under any Denomination whatever, who convene themselves for the Purpose of deliberating upon and adopting Measures which are cognizable by Legislatures only will, if continued, bring Legislatures to Contempt and Dissolution. If the public Affairs are illy conducted, if dishonest or incapable Men have crept unawares into Government, it is happy for us, that under our American Constitutions the Remedy is at hand, and in the Power of the great Body of the People. Due Circumspection and Wisdom at the next Elections will set all right, without the Aid of any self Created Conventions or Societies of Men whatever. While we retain those simple Democracies in all our Towns which are the Basis of our State Constitutions, and make a good Use of them, it appears to me we cannot be enslaved or materially injured. It must however be confessed, that Imperfection attends all human affairs.

5

James Madison: Excerpts from *Federalist* 10 (1787)

The founders' belief in the simple goodness of republican government did not last long. Indeed, their experience of republican institutions under the Articles of Confederation convinced many of them, as this selection indicates, that republicanism could be hostile to the common good and to the rights of minorities. This realization, however, led to a desire not to reject but to reform republicanism. Here Madison argues that the dangerous tendencies of republican government can be controlled by organizing it on a large scale. The resulting diversity of interests, he contends, will result in a moderate politics in which the rights of individuals and minorities will be relatively secure.

Among the numerous advantages promised by a well constructed Union, none deserves to be more accurately developed than its tendency to break and control the violence of faction. The friend of popular governments never finds himself so much alarmed for their character and fate, as when he contemplates their propensity to this dangerous vice. He will not fail, therefore, to set a due value on any plan which, without violating the principles to which he is attached, provides a proper cure for it. The instability, injustice, and confusion introduced into the public councils, have, in truth, been the mortal diseases under which popular governments have everywhere perished; as they continue to be the favorite and fruitful topics from which the adversaries to liberty derive their most specious declamations. The valuable improvements made by the American constitutions on the popular models, both ancient and modern, cannot certainly be too much admired; but it would be an unwarrantable partiality, to contend that they have as effectually obviated the danger on this side, as was wished and expected. Complaints are everywhere heard from our most considerate and virtuous citizens, equally the friends of public and private faith, and of public and personal liberty, that our governments are too unstable, that the public good is disregarded in the conflicts of rival parties, and that measures are too often decided, not according to the rules of justice and the rights of the minor party, but by the superior force of an interested and overbearing majority. . . .

By a faction, I understand a number of citizens, whether amounting to a majority or a minority of the whole, who are united and actuated by some common impulse of passion, or of interest, adverse to the rights of other citizens, or to the permanent and aggregate interests of the community.

There are two methods of curing the mischiefs of faction: the one, by removing its causes; the other, by controlling its effects.

There are again two methods of removing the causes of faction: the one, by destroying the liberty which is essential to its existence; the other, by giving to every citizen the same opinions, the same passions, and the same interests.

It could never be more truly said than of the first remedy, that it was worse than the disease. Liberty is to faction what air is to fire, an aliment without which it instantly expires. But it could not be less folly to abolish liberty, which is essential to political life, because it nourishes faction, than it would be to wish the annihilation of air, which is essential to animal life, because it imparts to fire its destructive agency.

The second expedient is as impracticable as the first would be unwise. As long as the reason of man continues fallible, and he is at liberty to exercise it, different opinions will be formed. As long as the connection subsists between his reason and his self-love, his opinions and his passions will have a reciprocal influence on each other; and the former will be objects to which the latter will attach themselves. The diversity in the faculties of men, from which the rights of property originate, is not less an insuperable obstacle to a uniformity of interests. The protection of these faculties is the first object of government. From the protection of different and unequal faculties of acquiring property, the possession of different degrees and kinds of property immediately results; and from the influence of these on the sentiments and views of the respective proprietors, ensues a division of the society into different interests and parties.

The latent causes of faction are thus sown in the nature of man; and we see them everywhere brought into different degrees of activity, according to the different circumstances of civil society. . . .

The inference to which we are brought is, that the *causes* of faction cannot be removed, and that relief is only to be sought in the means of controlling its *effects*.

If a faction consists of less than a majority, relief is supplied by the republican principle, which enables the majority to defeat its sinister views by regular vote. It may clog the administration, it may convulse the society; but it will be unable to execute and mask its violence under the forms of the Constitution. When a majority is included in a faction, the form of popular government, on the other hand, enables it to sacrifice to its ruling passion or interest both the public good and the rights of other citizens. To secure the public good and

private rights against the danger of such a faction, and at the same time to preserve the spirit and the form of popular government, is then the great object
to which our inquiries are directed. Let me add that it is the great desideratum
by which this form of government can be rescued from the opprobrium under
which it has so long labored, and be recommended to the esteem and adoption of mankind.

By what means is this object attainable? Evidently by one of two only. Either
the existence of the same passion or interest in a majority at the same time must
be prevented, or the majority, having such coexistent passion or interest, must be
rendered, by their number and local situation, unable to concert and carry into
effect schemes of oppression. If the impulse and the opportunity be suffered to
coincide, we well know that neither moral nor religious motives can be relied
on as an adequate control. They are not found to be such on the injustice and
violence of individuals, and lose their efficacy in proportion to the number combined together, that is, in proportion as their efficacy becomes needful.

From this view of the subject it may be concluded that a pure democracy,
by which I mean a society consisting of a small number of citizens, who assemble and administer the government in person, can admit of no cure for the
mischiefs of faction. A common passion or interest will, in almost every case,
be felt by a majority of the whole; a communication and concert result from
the form of government itself; and there is nothing to check the inducements
to sacrifice the weaker party or an obnoxious individual. Hence it is that such
democracies have ever been spectacles of turbulence and contention; have ever
been found incompatible with personal security or the rights of property; and
have in general been as short in their lives as they have been violent in their
deaths. Theoretic politicians, who have patronized this species of government,
have erroneously supposed that by reducing mankind to a perfect equality in
their political rights, they would, at the same time, be perfectly equalized and
assimilated in their possessions, their opinions, and their passions.

A republic, by which I mean a government in which the scheme of representation takes place, opens a different prospect, and promises the cure for
which we are seeking. Let us examine the points in which it varies from pure
democracy, and we shall comprehend both the nature of the cure and the efficacy which it must derive from the Union.

The two great points of difference between a democracy and a republic
are: first, the delegation of the government, in the latter, to a small number of
citizens elected by the rest; secondly, the greater number of citizens, and greater
sphere of country, over which the latter may be extended.

The effect of the first difference is, on the one hand, to refine and enlarge
the public views, by passing them through the medium of a chosen body of
citizens, whose wisdom may best discern the true interest of their country, and
whose patriotism and love of justice will be least likely to sacrifice it to temporary or partial considerations. . . .

The other point of difference is, the greater number of citizens and extent
of territory which may be brought within the compass of republican than of
democratic government; and it is this circumstance principally which renders

factious combinations less to be dreaded in the former than in the latter. The smaller the society, the fewer probably will be the distinct parties and interests composing it; the fewer the distinct parties and interests, the more frequently will a majority be found of the same party; and the smaller the number of individuals composing a majority, and the smaller the compass within which they are placed, the more easily will they concert and execute their plans of oppression. Extend the sphere, and you take in a greater variety of parties and interests; you make it less probable that a majority of the whole will have a common motive to invade the rights of other citizens; or if such a common motive exists, it will be more difficult for all who feel it to discover their own strength, and to act in unison with each other. Besides other impediments, it may be remarked that, where there is a consciousness of unjust or dishonorable purposes, communication is always checked by distrust in proportion to the number whose concurrence is necessary.

Hence, it clearly appears, that the same advantage which a republic has over a democracy, in controlling the effects of faction, is enjoyed by a large over a small republic—is enjoyed by the Union over the States composing it. . . .

In the extent and proper structure of the Union, therefore, we behold a republican remedy for the diseases most incident to republican government. And according to the degree of pleasure and pride we feel in being republicans, ought to be our zeal in cherishing the spirit and supporting the character of Federalists.

6

Robert Yates: An Excerpt from *Brutus* 1 (1787)

Not everyone at the time of the founding was convinced by Madison's argument that increasing the size of the society would control the deficiencies of republican government while still maintaining its spirit. In the following passage Yates in fact contends that, whatever the intentions of the Constitution's framers, in a large society the government will inevitably lose whatever republican character it might initially possess.

Let us now proceed to enquire . . . whether it be best the thirteen United States should be reduced to one great republic, or not? It is here taken for granted, that all agree in this, that whatever government we adopt, it ought to be a free one; that it should be so framed as to secure the liberty of the citizens of America, and such an one as to admit of a full, fair, and equal representation of the people. The question then will be, whether a government thus constituted, and founded on such principles, is practicable, and can be exercised over the whole United States, reduced into one state?

If respect is to be paid to the opinion of the greatest and wisest men who have ever thought or wrote on the science of government, we shall be constrained to conclude, that a free republic cannot succeed over a country of such immense extent, containing such a number of inhabitants, and these increasing in such rapid progression as that of the whole United States. . . .

History furnishes no example of a free republic, anything like the extent of the United States. The Grecian republics were of small extent; so also was that of the Romans. Both of these, it is true, in process of time, extended their conquests over large territories of country; and the consequence was, that their governments were changed from that of free governments to those of the most tyrannical that ever existed in the world.

Not only the opinion of the greatest men, and the experience of mankind, are against the idea of an extensive republic, but a variety of reasons may be drawn from the reason and nature of things, against it. In every government, the will of the sovereign is the law. In despotic governments, the supreme authority being lodged in one, his will is law, and can be as easily expressed to a large extensive territory as to a small one. In a pure democracy the people are the sovereign, and their will is declared by themselves; for this purpose they must all come together to deliberate, and decide. This kind of government cannot be exercised, therefore, over a country of any considerable extent; it must be confined to a single city, or at least limited to such bounds as that the people can conveniently assemble, be able to debate, understand the subject submitted to them, and declare their opinion concerning it.

In a free republic, although all laws are derived from the consent of the people, yet the people do not declare their consent by themselves in person, but by representatives, chosen by them, who are supposed to know the minds of their constituents, and to be possessed of integrity to declare this mind. In every free government, the people must give their assent to the laws by which they are governed. This is the true criterion between a free government and an arbitrary one. The former are ruled by the will of the whole, expressed in any manner they may agree upon; the latter by the will of one, or a few. If the people are to give their assent to the laws, by persons chosen and appointed by them, the manner of the choice and the number chosen, must be such, as to possess, be disposed, and consequently qualified to declare the sentiments of the people; for if they do not know, or are not disposed to speak the sentiments of the people, the people do not govern, but the sovereignty is in a few. Now, in a large extended country, it is impossible to have a representation, possessing the sentiments, and of integrity, to declare the minds of the people, without having it so numerous and unwieldy, as to be subject in great measure to the inconveniency of a democratic government.

The territory of the United States is of vast extent; it now contains near three millions of souls, and is capable of containing much more than ten times that number. Is it practicable for a country, so large and so numerous as they will soon become, to elect a representation, that will speak their sentiments, without their becoming so numerous as to be incapable of transacting public business? It certainly is not.

In a republic, the manners, sentiments, and interests of the people should be similar. If this be not the case, there will be a constant clashing of opinions; and the representatives of one part will be continually striving against those of the other. This will retard the operations of government, and prevent such conclusions as will promote the public good. If we apply this remark to the condition of the United States, we shall be convinced that it forbids that we should be one government. The United States includes a variety of climates. The productions of the different parts of the union are very variant, and their interests, of consequence, diverse. Their manners and habits differ as much as their climates and productions; and their sentiments are by no means coincident. The laws and customs of the several states are, in many respects, very diverse, and in some opposite; each would be in favor of its own interests and customs, and, of consequence, a legislature, formed of representatives from the respective parts, would not only be too numerous to act with any care or decision, but would be composed of such heterogeneous and discordant principles, as would constantly be contending with each other. . . .

A free republic will never keep a standing army to execute its laws. It must depend upon the support of its citizens. But when a government is to receive its support from the aid of the citizens, it must be so constructed as to have the confidence, respect, and affection of the people. Men who, upon the call of the magistrate, offer themselves to execute the laws, are influenced to do it either by affection to the government, or from fear; where a standing army is at hand to punish offenders, every man is actuated by the latter principle, and therefore, when the magistrate calls, will obey: but, where this is not the case, the government must rest for its support upon the confidence and respect which the people have for their government and laws. The body of the people being attached, the government will always be sufficient to support and execute its laws, and to operate upon the fears of any faction which may be opposed to it, not only to prevent an opposition to the execution of the laws themselves, but also to compel the most of them to aid the magistrate; but the people will not be likely to have such confidence in their rulers, in a republic so extensive as the United States, as necessary for these purposes. The confidence which the people have in their rulers, in a free republic, arises from their knowing them, from their being responsible to them for their conduct, and from the power they have of displacing them when they misbehave: but in a republic of the extent of this continent, the people in general would be acquainted with very few of their rulers: the people at large would know little of their proceedings, and it would be extremely difficult to change them. The people in Georgia and New Hampshire would not know one another's mind, and therefore could not act in concert to enable them to effect a general change of representatives. The different parts of so extensive a country could not possibly be made acquainted with the conduct of their representatives, nor be informed of the reasons upon which measures were founded. The consequence will be, they will have no confidence in their legislature, suspect them of ambitious views, be jealous of every measure they adopt, and will not support the laws they pass. Hence the government will be nerveless and inefficient, and no way will be left to render it otherwise, but by establishing an armed force to execute the laws at the point of the bayonet—a government of all others the most to be dreaded. . . .

In so extensive a republic, the great officers of government would soon become above the control of the people, and abuse their power to the purpose of aggrandizing themselves, and oppressing them. The trust committed to the executive offices, in a country of the extent of the United-States, must be various and of magnitude. The command of all the troops and navy of the republic, the appointment of officers, the power of pardoning offences, the collecting of all the public revenues, and the power of expending them, with a number of other powers, must be lodged and exercised in every state, in the hands of a few. When these are attended with great honor and emolument, as they always will be in large states, so as greatly to interest men to pursue them, and to be proper objects for ambitious and designing men, such men will be ever restless in their pursuit after them. They will use the power, when they have acquired it, to the purposes of gratifying their own interest and ambition, and it is scarcely possible, in a very large republic, to call them to account for their misconduct, or to prevent their abuse of power.

These are some of the reasons by which it appears, that a free republic cannot long subsist over a country of the great extent of these states. If then this new constitution is calculated to consolidate the thirteen states into one, as it evidently is, it ought not to be adopted. . . .

7

Samuel Bryan: An Excerpt from *Centinel* 1 (1787)

In the following excerpt from his series of Anti-Federalist essays, Bryan denies that the Constitution is sufficiently republican in spirit. Its institutional arrangements, he contends, tend toward the establishment of an aristocratic form of government.

I shall now examine the construction of the proposed general government.

Article 1, Section 1: "All legislative powers herein granted shall be vested in a Congress of the United States, which shall consist of a senate and house of representatives." By another section the president (the principal executive officer) has a conditional control over their proceedings.

Section 2: "The house of representatives shall be composed of members chosen every second year, by the people of the several states. The number of representatives shall not exceed one for every 30,000 inhabitants."

The senate, the other constituent branch of the legislature, is formed by the legislature of each state appointing two senators, for the term of six years.

The executive power by Article 2, Section 1 is to be vested in a president of the United States of America, elected for four years: Section 2 gives him "power, by and with the consent of the senate to make treaties, provided two thirds of the senators present concur; and he shall nominate, and by and with the advice and consent of the senate, shall appoint ambassadors, other public ministers and consuls, judges of the Supreme Court, and all other officers of the United States, whose appointments are not herein otherwise provided for, and which shall be established by law," etc. And by another section he has the absolute power of granting reprieves and pardons for treason and all other high crimes and misdemeanors, except in case of impeachment.

The foregoing are the outlines of the plan.

Thus we see, the house of representatives, are on the part of the people to balance the senate, who I suppose will be composed of the *better sort,* the *well born,* etc. The number of the representatives (being only one for every 30,000 inhabitants) appears to be too few, either to communicate the requisite information, of the wants, local circumstances and sentiments of so extensive an empire, or to prevent corruption and undue influence, in the exercise of such great powers; the term for which they are to be chosen, too long to preserve a due dependence and accountability to their constituents; and the mode and places of their election not sufficiently ascertained, for as Congress have the control over both, they may govern the choice, by ordering the *representatives* of a *whole* state, to be *elected* in *one* place, and that too may be the most *inconvenient.*

The senate, the great efficient body in this plan of government, is constituted on the most unequal principles. The smallest state in the union has equal weight with the great states of Virginia, Massachusetts, or Pennsylvania. The Senate, besides its legislative functions, has a very considerable share in the Executive; none of the principal appointments to office can be made without its advice and consent. The term and mode of its appointment, will lead to permanency; the members are chosen for six years, the mode is under the control of Congress, and as there is no exclusion by rotation, they may be continued for life, which, from their extensive means of influence, would follow of course. The President, who would be a mere pageant of state, unless he coincides with the views of the Senate, would either become the head of the aristocratic junta in that body, or its minion, besides, their influence being the most predominant, could the best secure his re-election to office. And from his power of granting pardons, he might screen from punishment the most treasonable attempts on liberties of the people, when instigated by the Senate.

From this investigation into the organization of this government, it appears that it is devoid of all responsibility or accountability to the great body of the people, and that so far from being a regular balanced government, it would be in practice *a permanent aristocracy.*

8

James Madison: An Excerpt from *Federalist* 39 (1788)

Like many later critics of the Constitution, some Anti-Federalists contended that it represented less an effort to reform popular government than a betrayal of popular government. These Anti-Federalists saw aristocratic tendencies in the institutions of government established by the Constitution, and especially in the Senate and the Presidency, which were designed to be somewhat insulated from public opinion. Here Madison defends the Constitution against such charges, arguing that under it all government power is ultimately derived in some way or another from the "great body of the people."

The first question that offers itself is, whether the general form and aspect of the government be strictly republican? It is evident that no other form would be reconcilable with the genius of the people of America; with the fundamental principles of the revolution; or with that honorable determination, which animates every votary of freedom, to rest all our political experiments on the capacity of mankind for self-government. If the plan of the Convention therefore be found to depart from the republican character, its advocates must abandon it as no longer defensible.

What then are the distinctive characters of the republican form? . . .

If we resort for a criterion, to the different principles on which different forms of government are established, we may define a republic to be, or at least may bestow that name on, a government which derives all its powers directly or indirectly from the great body of the people; and is administered by persons holding their offices during pleasure, for a limited period, or during good behavior. It is *essential* to such a government, that it be derived from the great body of the society, not from an inconsiderable proportion, or a favored class of it; otherwise a handful of tyrannical nobles, exercising their oppressions by a delegation of their powers, might aspire to the rank of republicans, and claim for their government the honorable title of republic. It is *sufficient* for such a government, that the persons administering it be appointed, either directly or indirectly, by the people; and that they hold their appointments by either of the tenures just specified; otherwise every government in the United States, as well as every other popular government that has been or can be well organized or well executed, would be degraded from the republican character. According to the Constitution of every State in the Union, some or other of the officers of government are appointed indirectly only by the people. According to most of them the chief magistrate himself is so appointed. And according to one, this mode of appointment is extended to one of the coordinate branches of the legislature. According to all the Constitutions also, the tenure of the highest offices is extended to a definite period, and in many instances, both within the legislative and executive departments, to a period of years. According to the provisions of most of the constitutions, again, as well as according to the most respectable and received opinions on the subject, the members of the judiciary department are to retain their offices by the firm tenure of good behavior.

On comparing the Constitution planned by the Convention, with the standard here fixed, we perceive at once that it is in the most rigid sense conformable to it. The House of Representatives, like that of one branch at least of all the State Legislatures, is elected immediately by the great body of the people. The Senate, like the present Congress, and the Senate of Maryland, derives its appointment indirectly from the people. The President is indirectly derived from the choice of the people, according to the example in most of the States. Even the judges, with all other officers of the Union, will, as in the several

States, be the choice, though a remote choice, of the people themselves. The duration of the appointments is equally conformable to the republican standard, and to the model of the State Constitutions. The House of Representatives is periodically elective as in all the States: and for the period of two years as in the State of South Carolina. The Senate is elective for the period of six years; which is but one year more than the period of the Senate of Maryland; and but two more than that of the Senates of New York and Virginia. The President is to continue in office for the period of four years; as in New York and Delaware, the chief magistrate is elected for three years, and in South Carolina for two years. In the other States the election is annual. In several of the States however, no constitutional provision is made for the impeachment of the Chief Magistrate. And in Delaware and Virginia, he is not impeachable till out of office. The President of the United States is impeachable at any time during his continuance in office. The tenure by which the Judges are to hold their places, is, as it unquestionably ought to be, that of good behavior. The tenure of the ministerial offices generally will be a subject of legal regulation, conformably to the reason of the case, and the example of the State Constitutions.

Could any further proof be required of the republican completion of this system, the most decisive one might be found in its absolute prohibition of titles of nobility, both under the Federal and the State Governments; and in its express guarantee of the republican form to each of the latter.

9

Alexander Hamilton: An Excerpt from *Federalist* 71 (1788)

Although Madison may be correct in asserting that all power under the Constitution derives from the people, it is also undeniable that parts of the Constitution were designed precisely to limit the political influence of popular opinion. In this passage Hamilton justifies such arrangements, contending that true republicanism requires only that the people's "deliberate sense," in contrast to their passing whims, prevails.

There are some who would be inclined to regard the servile pliancy of the Executive to a prevailing current, either in the community or in the legislature, as its best recommendation. But such men entertain very crude notions, as well of the purposes for which government was instituted, as of the true means by which the public happiness may be promoted. The republican principle demands that the deliberate sense of the community should govern the conduct of those to whom they entrust the management of their affairs; but it does not require an unqualified complaisance to every sudden breeze of passion, or to every transient impulse which the people may receive from the arts of men, who flatter their prejudices to betray their interests. It is a just observation, that the people commonly *intend* the public good. This often applies to their very errors. But their good sense would despise the adulator who should pretend that they always *reason right* about the *means* of promoting it. They know from experience that they sometimes err; and the wonder is that they so seldom err as they do, beset, as they continually are, by the wiles of parasites and sycophants, by the snares of the ambitious, the avaricious, the desperate, by the artifices of men who possess their confidence more than they deserve it, and of those who seek to possess rather than to deserve it. When occasions present themselves, in which the interests of the people are at variance with their inclinations, it is the duty of the persons whom they have appointed to be the guardians of those interests, to withstand the temporary delusion, in order to give them time and opportunity for more cool and sedate reflection. Instances might be cited in which a conduct of this kind has saved the people from very fatal consequences of their own mistakes, and has procured lasting monuments of their gratitude to the men who had courage and magnanimity enough to serve them at the peril of their displeasure.

10

James Madison: An Excerpt from *Federalist* 52 (1788)

Although the framers sought to create a republican form of government, the original Constitution does little to define the right to vote. The issue does not even arise with regard to the Senate, which was to be elected by members of the state legislatures, or the president, who was to be elected through an electoral college, with each state free to determine the method of choosing electors. Even in relation to the House of Representatives, which was to be directly elected by the people, the Constitution does not define the right to vote with the specificity that we might expect. Here Madison discusses the Constitution's provision for the right to vote and explains the considerations that led the Constitutional Convention to leave it somewhat undefined.

From the more general inquiries pursued in the four last papers, I pass on to a more particular examination of the several parts of the government. I shall begin with the House of Representatives. The first view to be taken of this part of the government relates to the qualifications of the electors and the elected. Those of the former are to be the same with those of the electors of the most numerous branch of the State legislatures. The definition of the right of suffrage is very justly regarded as a fundamental article of republican government. It was incumbent on the convention, therefore, to define and establish this right in the Constitution. To have left it open for the occasional regulation of the Congress, would have been improper for the reason just mentioned. To have submitted it to the legislative discretion of the States, would have been improper for the same reason; and for the additional reason that it would have rendered too dependent on the State governments that branch of the federal government which ought to be dependent on the people alone. To have reduced the different qualifications in the different States to one uniform rule, would probably have been as dissatisfactory to some of the States as it would have been difficult to the convention. The provision made by the convention appears, therefore, to be the best that lay within their option. It must be satisfactory to every State, because it is conformable to the standard already established, or which may be established, by the State itself. It will be safe to the United States, because, being fixed by the State constitutions, it is not alterable by the State governments, and it cannot be feared that the people of the States will alter this part of their constitutions in such a manner as to abridge the rights secured to them by the federal Constitution. . . .

11

Chancellor James Kent: Speech to the New York State Constitutional Convention (1821)

Although the founding generation believed, like Madison, that republican government had to be based on "the great body of the people," a number of states initially tied the right to vote to the ownership of a certain amount of property. In the following selection Chancellor Kent lays out the thinking behind such property qualifications, contending that universal suffrage, or the extension of the right to vote to all regardless of wealth, excessively empowers the poor and therefore threatens the security of property.

The senate has hitherto been elected by the farmers of the state—by the free and independent lords of the soil, worth at least $250 in freehold estate, over and above all debts charged thereon. The governor has been chosen by the same electors, and we have hitherto elected citizens of elevated rank and character. Our assembly has been chosen by freeholders, possessing a freehold of the value of $50, or by persons renting a tenement of the yearly value of $5, and who have been rated and actually paid taxes to the state. By the report before us, we propose to annihilate, at one stroke, all those property distinctions and to bow before the idol of universal suffrage. That extreme democratic principle, when applied to the legislative and executive departments of government, has been regarded with terror, by the wise men of every age, because in every European republic, ancient and modern, in which it has been tried, it has terminated disastrously, and been productive of corruption, injustice, violence, and tyranny. And dare we flatter ourselves that we are a peculiar people, who can run the career of history, exempted from the passions which have disturbed and corrupted the rest of mankind? If we are like other races of men, with similar follies and vices, then I greatly fear that our posterity will have reason to deplore in sackcloth and ashes, the delusion of the day. at present to interfere with the report of the committee, so far as respects the qualifications of electors for governor and members of assembly. I shall feel grateful if we may be permitted to retain the stability and security of a senate, bottomed upon the freehold property of the state. Such a body, so constituted, may prove a sheet anchor amidst the future factions and storms of the republic. . . .

Now, sir, I wish to preserve our senate as the representative of the landed interest. I wish those who have an interest in the soil, to retain the exclusive possession of a branch in the legislature, as a strong hold in which they may find safety through all the vicissitudes which the state may be destined, in the course of Providence, to experience. I wish them to be always enabled to say that their freeholds cannot be taxed without their consent. The men of no property, together with the crowds of dependants connected with great manufacturing and commercial establishments, and the motley and undefinable population of crowded ports, may, perhaps, at some future day, under skilful management, predominate in the assembly, and yet we should be perfectly safe if no laws could pass without the free consent of the owners of the soil. That security we at present enjoy; and it is that security which I wish to retain.

The apprehended danger from the experiment of universal suffrage applied to the whole legislative department, is no dream of the imagination. It is too mighty an excitement for the moral constitution of men to endure. The tendency of universal suffrage, is to jeopardize the rights of property, and the principles of liberty. There is a constant tendency in human society, and the history of every age proves it; there is a tendency in the poor to covet and to share the plunder of the rich; in the debtor to relax or avoid the obligation of contracts; in the majority to tyrannize over the minority, and trample down their rights; in the indolent and the profligate, to cast the whole burdens of society upon the industrious and the virtuous; and there is a tendency in ambitious and wicked men, to inflame these combustible materials. It requires a vigilant government, and a firm administration of justice, to counteract that tendency. . . .

The notion that every man that works a day on the road, or serves an idle hour in the militia, is entitled as of right to an equal participation in the whole power of the government, is most unreasonable, and has no foundation in justice. We had better at once discard from the report such a nominal test of merit. If such persons have an equal share in one branch of the legislature, it is surely as much as they can in justice or policy demand. Society is an association for the protection of property as well as of life, and the individual who contributes only one cent to the common stock, ought not to have the same power and influence in directing the property concerns of the partnership, as he who contributes his thousands. He will not have the same inducements to care, and diligence, and fidelity. His inducements and his temptation would be to divide the whole capital upon the principles of an agrarian law.

12

David Buel: Speech to the New York State Constitutional Convention (1821)

Here Buel responds to Kent's arguments in reading 11. He notes the trend toward the abolition of property qualifications and suggests that it is in the spirit of true republicanism. He also contends that given the widespread property ownership in America, no property qualification is necessary to protect the rights of property.

Of the twenty-four states which compose this union, twelve states require only a certain time of residence as a qualification to vote for all their elective offices—eight require in addition to residence the payment of taxes or the performance of militia duty—four states only require a freehold qualification, viz. New York, North Carolina, Virginia, and Rhode Island. . . .

The progressive extension of the right of suffrage by the reformations which have taken place in several of the state constitutions, adds to the force of the authority. By the original constitution of Maryland (made in 1776), a considerable property qualification was necessary to constitute an elector. By successive alterations in the years 1802, and 1810, the right has been extended to all the white citizens who have a permanent residence in the state. A similar alteration has been made in the constitution of South Carolina; and by the recent reformations in the constitutions of Connecticut and Massachusetts, property qualifications in the electors have been abolished; the right is extended in the former almost to universal suffrage, and in the latter to all the citizens who pay taxes. It is not in the smaller states only, that these liberal principles respecting suffrage, have been adopted. The constitution of Pennsylvania, adopted in the year 1790, extends the right of suffrage to all the citizens who pay taxes, and to their sons between the age of twenty-one and twenty-two years. . . .

It is said by those who contend that the right of voting for senators should be confined to the landholders, that the framers of our constitution were wise and practical men, and that they deemed this distinction essential to the security of the landed property; and that we have not encountered any evils from it during the forty years experience which we have had. To this I answer, that if the restriction of the right of suffrage has produced no positive evil, it cannot be shown to have produced any good results.

The qualifications for assembly voters, under the existing constitution, are as liberal as any which will probably be adopted by this Convention. Is it pretended that the assembly, during the forty-three years experience which we have enjoyed under our constitution, has been, in any respect, inferior to the senate? Has the senate, although elected exclusively by freeholders, been composed of men of more talents, or greater probity, than the assembly? Have the rights of property, generally, or of the landed interest in particular, been more vigilantly watched, and more carefully protected by the senate than by the assembly? I might appeal to the journals of the two houses, and to the recollections and information of the members of the committee on this subject; but it is unnecessary, as I understand the gentlemen who support the amendment, distinctly admit, that hitherto the assembly has been as safe a depository of the rights of the landed interest, as the senate. But it is supposed that the framers of our constitution must have had wise and cogent reasons for making such a distinction between the electors of the different branches of the government. May we not, however, without the least derogation from the wisdom and good intentions of the framers of our constitution, ascribe the provision in question to circumstances which then influenced them, but which no longer ought to have weight?

When our constitution was framed, the domain of the state was in the hands of a few. The proprietors of the great manors were almost the only men of great influence; and the landed property was deemed worthy of almost exclusive consideration. Before the revolution, freeholders only were allowed to exercise the right of suffrage. The notions of our ancestors, in regard to real property, were all derived from England. The feudal tenures were universally adopted. The law of primogeniture, by which estates descended to the eldest son, and the rule of descent by which the male branches inherited the paternal estate, to the exclusion of the female, entails, and many other provisions of feudal origin were in force. The tendency of this system, it is well understood, was to keep the lands of the state in few hands. But since that period, by the operation of wiser laws, and by the prevalence of juster principles, an entire revolution has taken place in regard to real property. Our laws for regulating descents, and for converting entailed estates into fee-simple, have gradually increased the number of landholders: Our territory has been rapidly divided and subdivided: And although the landed interest is no longer controlled by the influence of a few great proprietors, its aggregate importance is vastly increased, and almost the whole community have become interested in its protection. In New England, the inhabitants, from the earliest period, have enjoyed the system which we are progressively attaining to. There, the property of the soil has always been in the hands of the many. The great bulk of the population are farmers and freeholders, yet no provision is incorporated in their constitutions, excluding those who are not freeholders from a full participation in the right of suffrage. May we not trace the notions of the framers of our constitution, respecting the exclusive privilege of the freeholders, to the same source from whence they derived all their ideas of real property? . . .

It is conceded by my honorable friend, that the great landed estates must be cut up by the operation of our laws of descent; that we have already seen those laws effect a great change; and that it is the inevitable tendency of our rules of descent, to divide up our territory into farms of moderate size. The real property, therefore, will be in the hands of the many. But in England, and other European kingdoms, it is the policy of the aristocracy to keep the lands in few hands. The laws of primogeniture, the entailments and family settlements, all tend to give a confined direction to the course of descents. Hence we find in Europe, the landed estates possessed by a few rich men; and the great bulk of the population poor, and without that attachment to the government which is found among the owners of the soil. Hence, also, the poor envy and hate the rich, and mobs and insurrections sometimes render property insecure. Did I believe that our population would degenerate into such a state, I should, with the advocates for the amendment, hesitate in extending the right of suffrage; but I confess I have no such fears. I have heretofore had doubts respecting the safety of adopting the principles of a suffrage as extensive as that now contemplated. I have given to the subject the best reflection of which I am capable; and I have satisfied myself, that there is no danger in adopting those liberal principles which are incorporated in almost all the constitutions of these United States.

I contend, that by the true principle of our government, property, as such, is not the basis of representation. Our community is an association of persons—of human beings—not a partnership founded on property. The declared object of the people of this state in associating, was, to "establish such a government as they deemed best calculated to secure the rights and liberties of the good people of the state, and most conducive to their happiness and safety." Property, it is admitted, is one of the rights to be protected and secured; and although the protection of life and liberty is the highest object of attention, it is certainly true, that the security of property is a most interesting and important object in every free government. Property is essential to our temporal happiness; and is necessarily one of the most interesting subjects of legislation. The desire of acquiring property is a universal passion. I readily give to property the important place which has been assigned to it by the honorable member from Albany [Chancellor Kent]. To property we are indebted for most of our comforts, and for much of our temporal happiness. The numerous religious, moral, and benevolent institutions which are every where established, owe their existence to wealth; and it is wealth which enables us to make those great internal improvements which we have undertaken. Property is only one of the incidental rights of the person who possesses it; and, as such, it must be made secure; but it does not follow, that it must therefore be represented specifically in any branch of the government.

13

Alexis de Tocqueville: *Democracy in America* (1835)

Tocqueville believed that the democratic wave sweeping America and the world could not be turned back, and he therefore would have opposed any effort to reverse the trend toward universal suffrage. Nevertheless, his aim was to identify the defects of democratic political institutions with a view to correcting or moderating them. Thus in the following passage he articulates what he takes to be a serious defect of universal suffrage: its tendency to result in poor, or at best mediocre, political leadership.

Many people in Europe are apt to believe without saying it, or to say without believing it, that one of the great advantages of universal suffrage is that it entrusts the direction of affairs to men who are worthy of the public confidence. They admit that the people are unable to govern of themselves, but they aver that the people always wish the welfare of the state and instinctively designate those who are animated by the same good will and who are the most fit to wield the supreme authority. I confess that the observations I made in America by no means coincide with these opinions. On my arrival in the United States I was surprised to find so much distinguished talent among the citizens and so little among the heads of the government. It is a constant fact that at the present day the ablest men in the United States are rarely placed at the head of affairs; and it must be acknowledged that such has been the result in proportion as democracy has exceeded all its former limits. The race of American statesmen has evidently dwindled most remarkably in the course of the last fifty years.

Several causes may be assigned for this phenomenon. It is impossible, after the most strenuous exertions, to raise the intelligence of the people above a certain level. Whatever may be the facilities of acquiring information, whatever may be the profusion of easy methods and cheap science, the human mind can never be instructed and developed without devoting considerable time to these objects. The greater or lesser ease with which people can live without working is a sure index of intellectual progress. This boundary is more remote in some countries and more restricted in others, but it must exist somewhere as long as the people are forced to work in order to procure the means of subsistence; that is to say, as long as they continue to be the people. It is therefore quite as difficult to imagine a state in which all the citizens are very well informed as a state in which they are all wealthy; these two difficulties are correlative. I readily admit that the mass of the citizens sincerely wish to promote the welfare of the country; nay, more, I even grant that the lower classes mix fewer considerations of personal interest with their patriotism than the higher orders; but it is always more or less difficult for them to discern the best means of attaining the end which they sincerely desire. Long and patient observation and much acquired knowledge are requisite to form a just estimate of the character of a single individual. Men of the greatest genius often fail to do it, and can it be supposed that the common people will always succeed? The people have neither the time nor the means for an investigation of this kind. Their conclusions are hastily formed from a superficial inspection of the more prominent features of a question. Hence it often happens that mountebanks of all sorts are able to please the people, while their truest friends frequently fail to gain their confidence.

Moreover, democracy not only lacks that soundness of judgment which is necessary to select men really deserving of their confidence, but often have not the desire or the inclination to find them out. It cannot be denied that democratic institutions strongly tend to promote the feeling of envy in the human heart; not so much because they afford to everyone the means of rising to the same level with others as because those means perpetually disappoint the persons who employ them. Democratic institutions awaken and foster a passion for equality which they can never entirely satisfy. This complete equality eludes the grasp of the people at the very moment when they think they have grasped it, and "flies," as Pascal says, "with an eternal flight"; the people are excited in the pursuit of an advantage, which is more precious because it is not sufficiently remote to be unknown or sufficiently near to be enjoyed. The lower orders are agitated by the chance of success, they are irritated by its uncertainty; and they pass from the enthusiasm of pursuit to the exhaustion of ill success, and lastly to the acrimony of disappointment. Whatever transcends their own limitations appears to be an obstacle to their desires, and there is no superiority, however legitimate it may be, which is not irksome in their sight.

It has been supposed that the secret instinct which leads the lower orders to remove their superiors as much as possible from the direction of public affairs is peculiar to France. This is an error, however; the instinct to which I allude is not French, it is democratic; it may have been heightened by peculiar political circumstances, but it owes its origin to a higher cause.

In the United States the people do not hate the higher classes of society, but are not favorably inclined towards them and carefully exclude them from the exercise of authority. They do not fear distinguished talents, but are rarely fond of them. In general, everyone who rises without their aid seldom obtains their favor.

While the natural instincts of democracy induce the people to reject distinguished citizens as their rulers, an instinct not less strong induces able men to retire from the political arena, in which it is so difficult to retain their independence, or to advance without becoming servile. This opinion has been candidly expressed by Chancellor Kent, who says, in speaking with high praise of that part of the Constitution which empowers the executive to nominate the judges: "It is indeed probable that the men who are best fitted to discharge the duties of this high office would have too much reserve in their manners, and too much austerity in their principles, for them to be returned by the majority at an election where universal suffrage is adopted." Such were the opinions which were printed without contradiction in America in the year 1830!

I hold it to be sufficiently demonstrated that universal suffrage is by no means a guarantee of the wisdom of the popular choice. Whatever its advantages may be, this is not one of them.

14

Alexis de Tocqueville: *Democracy in America* (1835)

Here Tocqueville seeks the solutions to the problems addressed in the previous reading. He indicates what historical, cultural, and legal forces can moderate the tendency of universal suffrage to produce inferior political leadership.

If passing occurrences sometimes check the passions of democracy, the intelligence and the morals of the community exercise an influence on them which is not less powerful and far more permanent. This is very perceptible in the United States.

In New England, where education and liberty are the daughters of morality and religion, where society has acquired age and stability enough to enable it to form principles and hold fixed habits, the common people are accustomed to respect intellectual and moral superiority and to submit to it without complaint, although they set at naught all those privileges which wealth and birth have introduced among mankind. In New England, consequently, the democracy makes a more judicious choice than it does elsewhere.

But as we descend towards the South, to those states in which the constitution of society is more recent and less strong, where instruction is less general and the principles of morality, religion, and liberty are less happily combined, we perceive that talents and virtues become more rare among those who are in authority.

Lastly, when we arrive at the new Southwestern states, in which the constitution of society dates but from yesterday and presents only an agglomeration of adventurers and speculators, we are amazed at the persons who are invested with public authority, and we are led to ask by what force, independent of legislation and of the men who direct it, the state can be protected and society be made to flourish.

There are certain laws of a democratic nature which contribute, nevertheless, to correct in some measure these dangerous tendencies of democracy. On entering the House of Representatives at Washington, one is struck by the vulgar demeanor of that great assembly. Often there is not a distinguished man in the whole number. Its members are almost all obscure individuals, whose names bring no associations to mind. They are mostly village lawyers, men in trade, or even persons belonging to the lower classes of society. In a country in which education is very general, it is said that the representatives of the people do not always know how to write correctly.

At a few yards' distance is the door of the Senate, which contains within a small space a large proportion of the celebrated men of America. Scarcely an individual is to be seen in it who has not had an active and illustrious career: the Senate is composed of eloquent advocates, distinguished generals, wise magistrates, and statesmen of note, whose arguments would do honor to the most remarkable parliamentary debates of Europe.

How comes this strange contrast, and why are the ablest citizens found in one assembly rather than in the other? Why is the former body remarkable for its vulgar elements, while the latter seems to enjoy a monopoly of intelligence and talent? Both of these assemblies emanate from the people; both are chosen by universal suffrage; and no voice has hitherto been heard to assert in America that the Senate is hostile to the interests of the people. From what cause, then, does so startling a difference arise? The only reason which appears to me adequately to account for it is that the House of Representatives is elected by the people directly, while the Senate is elected by elected bodies. The whole body of the citizens name the legislature of each state, and the Federal Constitution converts these legislatures into so many electoral bodies, which return the members of the Senate. The Senators are elected by an indirect application of the popular vote; for the legislatures which appoint them are not aristocratic or privileged bodies, that elect in their own right, but they are chosen by the totality of the citizens; they are generally elected every year, and enough new members may be chosen every year to determine the senatorial appointments. But this transmission of the popular authority through an assembly of chosen men operates an important change in it by refining its discretion and improving its choice. Men who are chosen in this manner accurately represent the majority of the nation which governs them; but they represent only the elevated thoughts that are current in the community and the generous propensities that prompt its nobler actions rather than the petty passions that disturb or the vices that disgrace it.

The time must come when the American republics will be obliged more frequently to introduce the plan of election by an elected body into their system of representation or run the risk of perishing miserably among the shoals of democracy.

15

Senator William Stewart: Speech in Favor of the Fifteenth Amendment (1869)

In the following selection Senator Stewart, a Nevada Republican, urges the Senate to pass the proposal that would become the Fifteenth Amendment, which prohibited the United States or any state from denying anyone the right to vote on the basis of "race, color, or previous condition of servitude." He contends that extending the right to vote to the newly freed slaves is essential to the full realization of America's foundational commitment to political equality.

I do not propose to occupy the time of the Senate in discussing this great question at any length. It is the culmination of a contest which has lasted for thirty years. It is the logical result of the rebellion, of the abolition of slavery, and of the conflicts in this country during and before the war. Every person in the country has discussed it . . . and now we are to place the grand result, I hope, in the Constitution of the United States. . . . This amendment is a declaration to make all men, without regard to race or color, equal before the law. The arguments in favor of it are so numerous, so convincing, that they carry conviction to every mind. The proposition itself has been recognized by the good men of this nation; and it is important, as the new administration enters upon the charge of the affairs of this country, that it should start on this high and noble principle that all men are free and equal, that they are really equal before the law. We cannot stop short of this.

It must be done. It is the only measure that will really abolish slavery. It is the only guarantee against peon laws and against oppression. It is that guarantee which was put in the Constitution of the United States originally, the guarantee that each man shall have a right to protect his own liberty. It repudiates that arrogant, self-righteous assumption, that one man can be charged with the liberties and destinies of another. You may put this in the form of legislative enactment; you may empower Congress to legislate; you may empower the States to legislate, and they will agitate the question. Let it be made the immutable law of the land; let it be fixed; and then we shall have peace. Until then there is no peace. I cannot add to the many eloquent speeches that have been made on this great question in this House. I will not attempt it. I want a vote. I will not occupy time. The proposition itself is more eloquent than man can be. It is a declaration too high, too grand, too noble, too just, to be ornamented by oratory. . . .

16

Senator James Dixon: Speech Against the Fifteenth Amendment (1869)

Here Senator Dixon, a Connecticut Republican, argues against the Fifteenth Amendment on the grounds that it represents an impermissible deviation from American Federalism. Although the founders left the definition of the right to vote up to the state constitutions, the amendment would make it part of the federal Constitution. Thus it would deprive the states of the character of independent republics, each free to determine the scope of the franchise itself.

[I]t is not, perhaps, too much to say that this is the most important question in many of its bearings which has ever been presented to Congress in the shape of a proposed Constitutional Amendment.

What is the question? It is not merely a question of suffrage. . . . The question is not what shall be the qualification of the voter, but who shall create, establish, and prescribe those qualifications; not who shall be the voter, but who shall make the voter.

In considering that question we ought to remember that it is utterly impossible that any State should be an independent republic which does not entirely control its own laws with regard to the right of suffrage. Nor does it make the slightest difference with regard to this that any abdication of abnegation of its power is voluntary. It may be said that it is proposed that the States shall voluntarily relinquish their power to control the subject of suffrage within their respective limits. Sir, suppose a state should voluntarily assume upon itself a foreign yoke, or declare by a majority of its own people, or even by a unanimous vote, that it would prefer a monarchy, would the fact of its being voluntary at all affect the question whether it was still an independent republic?

Now, sir, it may be that the people of this country in their present condition of mind are ready to relinquish the power in the States of regulating their own laws with regard to suffrage; and if it should prove so, and the result should show that [the States] now consent that a central power should regulate that question, and should do this voluntarily and freely, nevertheless they would by that action lose their character as republican governments. And, sir, that is the reason why it was that in the formation of the Constitution of the United States there was an entire neglect to interfere in the slightest degree with the question of suffrage in the several states. Look through the Constitution as it was formed, and you find no allusions whatever to the question of suffrage, except by reference to existing laws and qualifications in the then existing States. . . . [W]hen it is proposed to amend the Constitution of the United States in this respect it is very questionable whether it is not an amendment which subverts the whole foundation and principle of the Government. . . .

There are . . . doubtless in all the States, many who are in favor of universal suffrage without distinction of race or color, who yet cling to the right of each State to decide as to the qualifications of its own voters. The pending constitutional amendment proposes to transfer this power from the States to the General Government by the consent of three-fourths of the States; but the character of the Government is no less changed by this mode of effecting the alteration than if it were done by act of Congress. All the States will not consent to the change, and those States which do not thus consent will be deprived by external power of the essential characteristic of self-government as completely as if the change were made by a mere law of Congress.

Furthermore, those States which consent to the amendment are merely the artificers of their own ruin as communities entitled to local self-government. They destroy freely and voluntarily, but yet they not the less destroy their character as independent States of the Union. Even the consent of a State, however freely rendered, would not prevent the necessary consequence, namely, the loss of the vital and essential element of self-government, consisting in the power of deciding freely, independently, and without appeal upon the qualifications of voters. Therefore it will be found that many advocates of negro suffrage will condemn and oppose this attempt to overthrow the State governments and reduce them to utter insignificance by the establishment of the principle involved in this amendment. They are unwilling to see the ancient Commonwealths which won our national independence and formed our national Government, together with their younger sisters who fill up the number of our United States, reduced from the proud position of independent, self-governing republics to the humble and helpless condition of subject provinces whose people exercise the right of suffrage under conditions and regulations imposed by a central power. . . .

17

Senator Willard Warner: Speech on the Fifteenth Amendment (1869)

Here Senator Warner, an Alaska Republican, criticizes the Fifteenth Amendment for not going far enough in the direction of universal suffrage. In the end, the amendment was passed by both houses of Congress. It was ratified by a sufficient number of States in 1870.

The Senator from Connecticut rightly states the question. The question before us is not one of negro suffrage. It is the question of suffrage itself. It is the broad question who shall be the voters of this country, in whose hands shall rest the political power. I take issue squarely with the Senator from Connecticut when he claims that Connecticut is a sovereign State, and that to her rightfully belongs the privilege of determining who of the citizens of the Republic shall have the right to vote and hold office. . . .

The theory of our Government is that power, the sovereign power, belongs to the people, not to a portion of the people, not to the learned, not to the ignorant, not to the rich, not to the poor, not to the great, not to the weak, but to all the people. We eschew in our system of government all aristocracies, whether of birth, of wealth, or of learning. Based as are our institutions on the idea that the right of self-government is inherent in manhood, we profess to give each individual an equal share of political power. . . .

I think it is a proposition too plain for argument that to the people, the whole people, the nation, belongs the decision of the question who shall exercise political power—in other and plainer words, who shall vote and hold office. And I think that it is equally clear that, to be true to our system and to the ideas upon which it is based, we must conclude that all men of sound mind are entitled to these rights.

To allow States to determine who of the citizens of the nation shall have political power is to give away the most essential and vital attribute of sovereignty—to concede a power which may be used to build up an aristocracy or to change and destroy our system of government. . . .

To propose to put into the Constitution any words which shall control the action of the States in this matter is to concede the great principle for which I argue, that to the nation belongs the determination of the question who shall have political power. Then the only question remaining is [does this Amendment] settle it aright? Let us examine the force and scope of this provision.

First, it does not determine who shall vote and hold office. Secondly, it does not protect any class of citizens against disfranchisement or disqualification. It simply and only provides that certain classes indicated shall not be disfranchised or disqualified for certain reasons, namely, race, color, or condition. For any other reason any State may deprive any portion of its citizens of all share in the Government. The animus of this amendment is a desire to protect and enfranchise the colored citizens of the country; yet, under it and without any violation of its letter or spirit, nine tenths of them might be prevented from voting . . . by the requirement on the part of the States or of the United States of an intelligence or property qualification.

Is this the Dead Sea fruit which we are to gather from the plantings of a hundred years? Is this to be the sum of the triumph of the grand struggle of a century past in this country for equal rights, a struggle whose pathway is marked by the graves of unnumbered martyrs, and whose culmination rocked the Republic to its base and reddened a thousand fields with the blood of its best sons?

Lame and impotent conclusion. You fail to protect the only classes of your citizens who need protection. Knowledge is power. Wealth is power. The learned and the rich scarcely need the ballot for their protection. . . . The millionaire in his money, and the man of education in his knowledge and his brain, have each a power in government greater than a hundred ballots, a power which the Constitution neither gives nor can take away. It is the poor, the unlearned man, who has nothing but the ballot, to whom it is a priceless heritage, a protection and a shield. . . .

I would admit woman, the most beautiful, the purest and best of God's creations, to an equal voice with us in the Government. As she is now the sharer of all our pleasures, the partner in all our joys, I would have her share with us the powers, the duties, and the responsibilities of government. . . .

But I know that woman's suffrage is not now attainable, and I would not, as a practical legislator, jeopardize the good which is attainable by linking with it that which is impossible. Besides, whenever the women of this country ask with anything like unanimity for the ballot they will get it.

DISCUSSION QUESTIONS FOR CHAPTER 5

1. Contrast the "patriot" view of the Continental Congress and Alexander Hamilton to the "Tory" view of Phillip Boucher. Does political justice require that government rule only with the consent of the governed?

2. Why is Samuel Adams confident that republican government will protect the rights of individuals? Why does James Madison not share that confidence? Does republican government, if unregulated, tend to turn into majority tyranny?

3. How does Robert Yates's understanding of the conditions necessary for republican government differ from that of Madison? Is republican government more likely to flourish in a large or in a small society?

4. Contrast the views of Samuel Bryan to those of Madison and Hamilton (in readings 8 and 9). Do the political arrangements of the Constitution

lead in the direction of aristocratic government, or are they simply prudent qualifications of republican rule?

5. How does James Kent differ from David Buel on the question of universal suffrage? Does extending the right to vote to all citizens regardless of their wealth jeopardize the right to private property?

6. Is Tocqueville correct that universal suffrage leads to mediocre political leadership? If so, can that tendency be restrained by the methods he advocates?

7. Compare the arguments of Senators Steward, Dixon, and Warner. In amending the Constitution to extend the suffrage to African American men, did the nation undermine the federal character of the Union? Or did the country not go far enough by failing to extend the vote to women?

CHAPTER 6

Limited Government

1

John Locke: An Excerpt from the *Second Treatise of Civil Government* (1690)

Locke's political philosophy profoundly influenced the American founders. In this passage he articulates the view that the natural rights of human beings require that government be limited in the scope of its powers.

The great end of men's entering into society, being the enjoyment of their properties in peace and safety, and the great instrument and means of that being the laws established in that society; the first and fundamental positive law of all commonwealths is the establishing of the legislative power; as the first and fundamental natural law, which is to govern even the legislative itself, is the preservation of the society, and (as far as will consist with the public good) of every person in it. . . .

Though the legislative, whether placed in one or more, whether it be always in being, or only by intervals, though it be the supreme power in every common-wealth; yet,

First, It is not, nor can possibly be absolutely arbitrary over the lives and fortunes of the people: for it being but the joint power of every member of the society given up to that person, or assembly, which is legislator; it can be no more than those persons had in a state of nature before they entered into society, and gave up to the community: for no body can transfer to another more power than he has in himself; and no body has an absolute arbitrary power over himself, or over any other, to destroy his own life, or take away the life or property of another. A man, as has been proved, cannot subject himself to the arbitrary power of another; and having in the state of nature no arbitrary power over the life, liberty, or possession of another, but only so much as the law of nature gave him for the preservation of himself, and the rest of mankind; this is all he doth, or can give up to the common-wealth, and by it to the legislative power, so that the legislative can have no more than this. Their power, in the utmost bounds of it, is limited to the public good of the society. It is a power, that hath no other end but preservation, and therefore can never have a right to destroy, enslave, or designedly to impoverish the subjects. The obligations of the law of nature cease not in society, but only in many cases are drawn closer, and have by human laws known penalties annexed to them, to enforce their observation. Thus the law of nature stands as an eternal rule to all men, legislators as well as others. The rules that they make for other men's actions, must, as well as their own and other men's actions, be conformable to the law of nature, i.e. to the will of God, of which that is a declaration, and the fundamental law of nature being the preservation of mankind, no human sanction can be good, or valid against it.

2

An Excerpt from "An Old Whig No. 2" (1787)

The "Old Whig" letters were published in Philadelphia's Independent Gazetteer. In this selection, the author, who remains unknown, contends that the "necessary and proper" clause of the Constitution makes impossible the maintenance of limited government.

[The] powers [of Congress] are very extensive, but I shall not stay at present to inquire whether these *express* powers were necessary to be given to Congress, whether they are too great or too small. My object is to consider that *undefined, unbounded and immense power* which is comprised in the following clause: "And, to make all laws which shall be necessary and proper for carrying into execution the *foregoing powers and all other powers* vested by this constitution in the government of the United States; or in any department or offices thereof." Under such a clause as this can any thing be said to be reserved and kept back from Congress? Can it be said that the Congress have no power but what *is expressed?* "To make all laws which shall be necessary and proper" is in other words to make all such laws which *the Congress shall think necessary and proper*— for who shall judge for the legislature what is necessary and proper? Who shall set themselves above the sovereign? What inferior legislature shall set itself above the supreme legislature? To me it appears that no other power on earth can dictate to them or control them, unless by force; and force either internal or external is one of those calamities which every good man would wish his country at all times to be delivered from. This generation in America have seen enough of war and its usual concomitants to prevent all of us from wishing to see any more of it—all except those who make a trade of war. But to the question: without force what can restrain the Congress from making such laws as they please? What limits are there to their authority? I fear none at all; for surely it cannot justly be said that they have no power but what is expressly given to them, where by the very terms of their creation they are vested with the powers of making laws in all cases necessary and proper; when from the nature of their power they must necessarily be the judges, what laws are necessary and proper. The British act of Parliament, declaring the power of Parliament to make laws to bind America in all cases whatsoever, was not more extensive; for it is as true as a maxim, that even the British Parliament neither could nor would pass any law in any case in which they did not either deem it necessary and proper to make such law or pretend to deem it so. And in such cases it is not of a farthing consequence whether they really are of opinion that the law is necessary and proper, or only *pretend to think so;* for who can overrule their pretensions? No one; unless we had a bill of rights to which we might appeal, and under which we might contend against any assumption of undue power and appeal to the judicial branch of the government to protect us by their judgments. This reasoning I fear . . . is but too just; and yet, if any man should doubt the truth of it; let me ask him one other question: what is the meaning of the latter part of the clause which vests the Congress with the authority of making all laws which shall be necessary and proper for carrying into execution *all other powers*—besides the foregoing powers vested, etc, etc. Was it thought that the foregoing powers might perhaps admit of some restraint in *their* construction as to what was necessary and proper to carry them into execution? Or was it deemed right to add still further that they should not be restrained to the powers already named? Besides the powers already mentioned, other powers may be assumed hereafter as contained by implication in this constitution. The Congress shall judge of what is necessary and proper in all these cases and in all other cases—in short in all cases whatsoever.

Where then is the restraint? How are Congress bound down to the powers expressly given? What is reserved or can be reserved?

3

James Madison: An Excerpt from *Federalist* 44 (1788)

In the following passage, Madison responds to the Anti-Federalist contention that the Constitution tends in the direction of unlimited government. The "necessary and proper" clause, he argues, is an essential component of the new government.

Few parts of the Constitution have been assailed with more intemperance than this; yet on a fair investigation of it, no part can appear more completely invulnerable. Without the *substance* of this power, the whole Constitution would be a dead letter. Those who object to the article therefore as a part of the Constitution, can only mean that the *form* of the provision is improper. But have they considered whether a better form could have been substituted?

There are four other possible methods which the Convention might have taken on this subject. They might have copied the second article of the existing confederation which would have prohibited the exercise of any power not *expressly* delegated; they might have attempted a positive enumeration of the powers comprehended under the general terms "necessary and proper"; they might have attempted a negative enumeration of them, by specifying the powers excepted from the general definition; they might have been altogether silent on the subject; leaving these necessary and proper powers, to construction and inference.

Had the Convention taken the first method of adopting the second article of confederation, it is evident that the new Congress would be continually exposed as their predecessors have been, to the alternative of construing the term "*expressly*" with so much rigor as to disarm the government of all real authority whatever, or with so much latitude as to destroy altogether the force of the restriction. It would be easy to show if it were necessary, that no important power, delegated by the Articles of Confederation, has been or can be executed by Congress, without recurring more or less to the doctrine of *construction* or *implication*. As the powers delegated under the new system are more extensive, the government which is to administer it would find itself still more distressed with the alternative of betraying the public interest by doing nothing; or of violating the Constitution by exercising powers, indispensably necessary and proper, but at the same time, not *expressly* granted.

Had the convention attempted a positive enumeration of the powers necessary and proper for carrying their other powers into effect; the attempt would have involved a complete digest of laws on every subject to which the Constitution relates; accommodated too not only to the existing state of things, but to all the possible changes which futurity may produce: For in every new application of a general power, the *particular powers,* which are the means of attaining the *object* of the general power, must always necessarily vary with that object; and be often properly varied whilst the object remains the same.

Had they attempted to enumerate the particular powers or means, not necessary or proper for carrying the general powers into execution, the task would have been no less chimerical; and would have been liable to this further objection; that every defect in the enumeration, would have been equivalent to a positive grant of authority. If to avoid this consequence they had attempted a partial enumeration of the exceptions, and described the residue by the general terms, *not necessary or proper:* It must have happened that the enumeration would comprehend a few of the excepted powers only; that these would be such as would be least likely to be assumed or tolerated, because the enumeration would of course select such as would be least necessary or proper, and that the unnecessary and improper powers included in the residuum, would be less forcibly excepted, than if no partial enumeration had been made.

Had the Constitution been silent on this head, there can be no doubt that all the particular powers, requisite as means of executing the general powers, would have resulted to the government, by unavoidable implication. No axiom is more clearly established in law, or in reason, than that wherever the end is required, the means are authorized; wherever a general power to do a thing is given, every particular power necessary for doing it, is included. Had this last method therefore been pursued by the Convention, every objection now urged against their plan, would remain in all its plausibility; and the real inconveniency would be incurred, of not removing a pretext which may be seized on critical occasions for drawing into question the essential powers of the Union.

If it be asked, what is to be the consequence, in case the Congress shall misconstrue this part of the Constitution, and exercise powers not warranted by its true meaning, I answer the same as if they should misconstrue or enlarge any other power vested in them, as if the general power had been reduced to particulars, and any one of these were to be violated; the same in short, as if the State Legislatures should violate their respective constitutional authorities. In the first instance, the success of the usurpation will depend on the executive and judiciary departments, which are to expound and give effect to the legislative acts; and in the last resort, a remedy must be obtained from the people, who can by the election of more faithful representatives, annul the acts of the usurpers. The truth is, that this ultimate redress may be more confided in against unconstitutional acts of the federal than of the State Legislatures, for this plain reason, that as every such act of the former, will be an invasion of the rights of the latter, these will be ever ready to mark the innovation, to sound the alarm to the people, and to exert their local influence in effecting a change of federal representatives. There being no such intermediate body between the State Legislatures and the people, interested in watching the conduct of the former, violations of the State Constitutions are more likely to remain unnoticed and unredressed.

4

James Madison: An Excerpt from *Federalist* 39 (1788)

In this selection Madison describes one of the Constitution's fundamental principles of limited government: Federalism, or the division of power between the federal government and the states. According to Madison, in the American system the power of the federal government is limited by the Constitution to "certain enumerated objects only," whereas the remaining governmental authority is left to the states.

"But it was not sufficient," say the adversaries of the proposed Constitution, "for the convention to adhere to the republican form. They ought, with equal care, to have preserved the *federal* form, which regards the Union as a *confederacy* of sovereign states; instead of which, they have framed a *national* government, which regards the Union as a *consolidation* of the States." And it is asked by what authority this bold and radical innovation was undertaken? The handle which has been made of this objection requires that it should be examined with some precision. . . .

The difference between a federal and national government, as it relates to the *operation of the government*, is supposed to consist in this, that in the former the powers operate on the political bodies composing the Confederacy, in their political capacities; in the latter, on the individual citizens composing the nation, in their individual capacities. On trying the Constitution by this criterion, it falls under the *national*, not the *federal* character. . . .

But if the government be national with regard to the *operation* of its powers, it changes its aspect again when we contemplate it in relation to the *extent* of its powers. The idea of a national government involves in it, not only an authority over the individual citizens, but an indefinite supremacy over all persons and things, so far as they are objects of lawful government. Among a people consolidated into one nation, this supremacy is completely vested in the national legislature. Among communities united for particular purposes, it is vested partly in the general and partly in the municipal legislatures. In the former case, all local authorities are subordinate to the supreme; and may be controlled, directed, or abolished by it at pleasure. In the latter, the local or municipal authorities form distinct and independent portions of the supremacy, no more subject, within their respective spheres, to the general authority, than the general authority is subject to them, within its own sphere. In this relation, then, the proposed government cannot be deemed a *national* one; since its jurisdiction extends to certain enumerated objects only, and leaves to the several States a residuary and inviolable sovereignty over all other objects. . . .

The proposed Constitution, therefore, is, in strictness, neither a national nor a federal Constitution, but a composition of both.

5

Robert Yates: An Excerpt from *Brutus* 1 (1787)

In this selection Yates, a prominent Anti-Federalist writer, offers a view of the Constitution's division of powers very different from Madison's. He contends that the Constitution does not adequately secure limited government because it tends to consolidate all power in the federal government and leaves nothing of importance to the states.

The first question that presents itself on the subject is, whether a confederated government be the best for the United States or not? Or in other words, whether the thirteen United States should be reduced to one great republic, governed by one legislature, and under the direction of one executive and judicial; or whether they should continue thirteen confederated republics, under the direction and control of a supreme federal head for certain defined national purposes only?

This enquiry is important, because, although the government reported by the convention does not go to a perfect and entire consolidation, yet it approaches so near to it, that it must, if executed, certainly and infallibly terminate in it.

This government is to possess absolute and uncontrollable power, legislative, executive and judicial, with respect to every object to which it extends, for by the last clause of section 8th, article 1st, it is declared "that the Congress shall have power to make all laws which shall be necessary and proper for carrying into execution the foregoing powers, and all other powers vested by this constitution, in the government of the United States; or in any department or office thereof." And by the 6th article, it is declared "that this constitution, and the laws of the United States, which shall be made in pursuance thereof, and the treaties made, or which shall be made, under the authority of the United States, shall be the supreme law of the land; and the judges in every state shall be bound thereby, any thing in the constitution, or law of any state to the contrary notwithstanding." It appears from these articles that there is no need of any intervention of the state governments, between the Congress and the people, to execute any one power vested in the general government, and that the constitution and laws of every state are nullified and declared void, so far as they are or shall be inconsistent with this constitution, or the laws made in pursuance of it, or with treaties made under the authority of the United States. The government then, so far as it extends, is a complete one, and not a confederation.

It is true this government is limited to certain objects, or to speak more properly, some small degree of power is still left to the states, but a little attention to the powers vested in the general government, will convince every candid man, that if it is capable of being executed, all that is reserved for the individual states must very soon be annihilated, except so far as they are barely necessary to the organization of the general government. The powers of the general legislature extend to every case that is of the least importance—there is nothing valuable to human nature, nothing dear to freemen, but what is within its power. It has authority to make laws which will affect the lives, the liberty, and property of every man in the United States; nor can the constitution or laws of any state, in any way prevent or impede the full and complete execution of every power given.

6

Robert Yates: An Excerpt from *Brutus* 2 (1787)

The Constitution as it was originally proposed by the Philadelphia convention contained no bill of rights—that is, no list of individual liberties to be protected from government infringement. The Anti-Federalists regarded this as a serious defect. In this selection Yates argues that limited government and the protection of individual freedom are not adequately secured in the absence of a bill of rights in the Constitution.

If we may collect the sentiments of the people of America, from their own most solemn declarations, they hold this truth as self evident, that all men are by nature free. No one man, therefore, or any class of men, have a right, by the law of nature, or of God, to assume or exercise authority over their fellows. The origin of society then is to be sought, not in any natural right which one man has to exercise authority over another, but in the united consent of those who associate. The mutual wants of men, at first dictated the propriety of forming societies; and when they were established, protection and defense pointed out the necessity of instituting government. In a state of nature every individual pursues his own interest; in this pursuit it frequently happened, that the possessions or enjoyments of one were sacrificed to the views and designs of another; thus the weak were a prey to the strong, the simple and unwary were subject to impositions from those who were more crafty and designing. In this state of things, every individual was insecure; common interest therefore directed, that government should be established, in which the force of the whole community should be collected, and under such directions, as to protect and defend every one who composed it. The common good, therefore, is the end of civil government, and common consent, the foundation on which it is established. To effect this end, it was necessary that a certain portion of natural liberty should be surrendered, in order, that what remained should be preserved: how great a proportion of natural freedom is necessary to be yielded by individuals, when they submit to government, I shall not now enquire. So much, however, must be given up, as will be sufficient to enable those, to whom the administration of the government is committed, to establish laws for the promoting the happiness of the community, and to carry those laws into effect. But it is not necessary, for this purpose, that individuals should relinquish all their natural rights. Some are of such a nature that they cannot be surrendered. Of this kind are the rights of conscience, the right of enjoying and defending life, etc. Others are not necessary to be resigned, in order to attain the end for which government is instituted, these therefore ought not to be given up. To surrender them, would counteract the very end of government, to wit, the common good. From these observations it appears, that in forming a government on its true principles, the foundation should be laid in the manner I before stated, by expressly reserving to the people such of their essential natural rights, as are not necessary to be parted with. The same reasons which at first induced mankind to associate and institute government, will operate to influence them to observe this precaution. If they had been disposed to conform themselves to the rule of immutable righteousness, government would not have been requisite. It was because one part exercised fraud, oppression, and violence on the other, that men came together, and agreed that certain rules should be formed, to regulate the conduct of all, and the power of the whole community lodged in the hands of rulers to enforce an obedience to them. But rulers have the same propensities as other men; they are as likely to use the power with which they are vested for private purposes, and to the injury and oppression of those over whom they are placed, as individuals in a state of nature are to injure and oppress one another. It is therefore as proper that bounds should be set to their authority, as that government should have at first been instituted to restrain private injuries.

This principle, which seems so evidently founded in the reason and nature of things, is confirmed by universal experience. Those who have governed, have been found in all ages ever active to enlarge their powers and abridge the public liberty. This has induced the people in all countries, where any sense of freedom remained, to fix barriers against the encroachments of their rulers. The country from which we have derived our origin, is an eminent example of this. Their magna charta and bill of rights have long been the boast, as well as the security, of that nation. I need say no more, I presume, to an American, than, that this principle is a fundamental one, in all the constitutions of our own states; there is not one of them but what is either founded on a declaration or bill of rights, or has certain express reservation of rights interwoven in the body of them. From this it appears, that at a time when the pulse of liberty beat high and when an appeal was made to the people to form constitutions for the government of themselves, it was their universal sense, that such declarations should make a part of their frames of government. It is therefore the more astonishing, that this grand security, to the rights of the people, is not to be found in this constitution.

It has been said, in answer to this objection, that such declaration[s] of rights, however requisite they might be in the constitutions of the states, are not necessary in the general constitution, because, "in the former case, every thing which is not reserved is given, but in the latter the reverse of the proposition prevails, and every thing which is not given is reserved." It requires but little attention to discover, that this mode of reasoning is rather specious than solid. The powers, rights, and authority, granted to the general government by this constitution, are as complete, with respect to every object to which they extend, as that of any state government. It reaches to every thing which concerns human happiness. Life, liberty, and property, are under its control. There is the same reason, therefore, that the exercise of power, in this case, should be restrained within proper limits, as in that of the state governments. To set this matter in a clear light, permit me to instance some of the articles of the bills of rights of the individual states, and apply them to the case in question.

For the security of life, in criminal prosecutions, the bills of rights of most of the states have declared, that no man shall be held to answer for a crime until he is made fully acquainted with the charge brought against him; he shall not be compelled to accuse, or furnish evidence against himself. The witnesses against him shall be brought face to face, and he shall be fully heard by himself or counsel. That it is essential to the security of life and liberty, that trial of facts be in the vicinity where they happen. Are not provisions of this kind as necessary in the general government, as in that of a particular state? The powers vested in the new Congress extend in many cases to life; they are authorized to provide for the punishment of a variety of capital crimes, and no restraint is laid upon them in its exercise, save only, that "the trial of all crimes, except in cases of impeachment, shall be by jury; and such trial shall be in the state where the said crimes shall have been committed." No man is secure of a trial in the county where he is charged to have committed a crime; he may be brought from Niagara to New York, or carried from Kentucky to Richmond for trial for an offence, supposed to be committed. What security is there, that a man shall be furnished with a full and plain description of the charges against him? That he shall be allowed to produce all proof he can in his favor? That he shall see the witnesses against him face to face, or that he shall be fully heard in his own defense by himself or counsel? . . .

I might proceed to instance a number of other rights, which were as necessary to be reserved, such as, that elections should be free, that the liberty of the press should be held sacred; but the instances adduced, are sufficient to prove, that this argument is without foundation. Besides, it is evident, that the reason here assigned was not the true one, why the framers of this constitution omitted a bill of rights; if it had been, they would not have made certain reservations, while they totally omitted others of more importance. We find they have, in the 9th section of the 1st article, declared, that the writ of habeas corpus shall not be suspended, unless in cases of rebellion, that no bill of attainder, or ex post facto law, shall be passed, that no title of nobility shall be granted by the United States, etc. If everything which is not given is reserved, what propriety is there in these exceptions? Does this constitution anywhere grant the power of suspending the habeas corpus, to make ex post facto laws, pass bills of attainder, or grant titles of nobility? It certainly does not in express terms. The only answer that can be given is, that these are implied in the general powers granted. With equal truth it may be said, that all the powers, which the bills of right, guard against the abuse of, are contained or implied in the general ones granted by this constitution.

7

Alexander Hamilton: An Excerpt from
Federalist 84 (1788)

Here Hamilton responds to the Anti-Federalist concern that the Constitution lacks a bill of rights. He contends that the Constitution adequately secures limited government without a bill of rights and even that the addition of a bill of rights would endanger limited government. Nevertheless, the Federalists were able to secure ratification of the Constitution only on the understanding that amendments adding a bill of rights would be considered once the new government was operational. This understanding was honored, and the First Congress proposed a bill of rights in the form of the first ten amendments to the Constitution, amendments that were quickly ratified by the states.

It has been several times truly remarked that bills of rights are, in their origin, stipulations between kings and their subjects, abridgements of prerogative in favor of privilege, reservations of rights not surrendered to the prince. Such was Magna Charta, obtained by the barons, sword in hand, from King John. Such were the subsequent confirmations of that charter by succeeding princes. Such was the *Petition of Right* assented to by Charles the First, in the beginning of his reign. Such, also, was the Declaration of Right presented by the Lords and Commons to the Prince of Orange in 1688, and afterwards thrown into the form of an act of parliament called the Bill of Rights. It is evident, therefore, that, according to their primitive signification, they have no application to constitutions professedly founded upon the power of the people, and executed by their immediate representatives and servants. Here, in strictness, the people surrender nothing; and as they retain every thing they have no need of particular reservations. "We, the People of the United States, to secure the blessings of liberty to ourselves and our posterity, do *ordain* and *establish* this Constitution for the United States of America." Here is a better recognition of popular rights, than volumes of those aphorisms which make the principal figure in several of our State bills of rights, and which would sound much better in a treatise of ethics than in a constitution of government.

But a minute detail of particular rights is certainly far less applicable to a Constitution like that under consideration, which is merely intended to regulate the general political interests of the nation, than to a constitution which has the regulation of every species of personal and private concerns. If, therefore, the loud clamors against the plan of the convention, on this score, are well founded, no epithets of reprobation will be too strong for the constitution of this State. But the truth is, that both of them contain all which, in relation to their objects, is reasonably to be desired.

I go further, and affirm that bills of rights, in the sense and to the extent in which they are contended for, are not only unnecessary in the proposed Constitution, but would even be dangerous. They would contain various exceptions to powers not granted; and, on this very account, would afford a colorable pretext to claim more than were granted. For why declare that things shall not be done which there is no power to do? Why, for instance, should it be said that the liberty of the press shall not be restrained, when no power is given by which restrictions may be imposed? I will not contend that such a provision would confer a regulating power; but it is evident that it would furnish, to men disposed to usurp, a plausible pretense for claiming that power. They might urge with a semblance of reason, that the Constitution ought not to be charged with the absurdity of providing against the abuse of an authority which was not given, and that the provision against restraining the liberty of the press afforded a clear implication, that a power to prescribe proper regulations concerning it was intended to be vested in the national government. This may serve as a specimen of the numerous handles which would be given to the doctrine of constructive powers, by the indulgence of an injudicious zeal for bills of rights.

On the subject of the liberty of the press, as much as has been said, I cannot forbear adding a remark or two: in the first place, I observe, that there is not a syllable concerning it in the constitution of this State; in the next, I contend, that whatever has been said about it in that of any other State, amounts to nothing. What signifies a declaration, that "the liberty of the press shall be inviolably preserved"? What is the liberty of the press? Who can give it any definition which would not leave the utmost latitude for evasion? I hold it to be impracticable; and from this I infer, that its security, whatever fine declarations may be inserted in any constitution respecting it, must altogether depend on public opinion, and on the general spirit of the people and of the government. And here, after all, as is intimated upon another occasion, must we seek for the only solid basis of all our rights.

8

James Madison: The Virginia Resolutions (1798)

During the Presidency of John Adams, the Federalist-controlled Congress passed the Alien and Sedition Acts, the latter of which criminalized untruthful and libelous statements about the government of the United States. Many Americans believed that these measures violated the limits on government power established by the Constitution and that the theory underlying the Constitution allowed the states to oppose such unconstitutional federal acts. Among those who advanced this argument were Thomas Jefferson, in the Kentucky Resolutions, and James Madison, in the Virginia Resolutions reproduced here.

Resolved. . . .

That this assembly most solemnly declares a warm attachment to the Union of the States, to maintain which it pledges all its powers; and that for this end, it is their duty to watch over and oppose every infraction of those principles which constitute the only basis of that Union, because a faithful observance of them, can alone secure its existence and the public happiness.

That this Assembly doth explicitly and peremptorily declare, that it views the powers of the federal government, as resulting from the compact, to which the states are parties; as limited by the plain sense and intention of the instrument constituting the compact; as no further valid than they are authorized by the grants enumerated in that compact; and that in case of a deliberate, palpable, and dangerous exercise of other powers, not granted by the said compact, the states who are parties thereto, have the right, and are in duty bound, to interpose for arresting the progress of the evil, and for maintaining within their respective limits, the authorities, rights and liberties appertaining to them.

That the General Assembly doth also express its deep regret, that a spirit has in sundry instances, been manifested by the federal government, to enlarge its powers by forced constructions of the constitutional charter which defines them; and that implications have appeared of a design to expound certain general phrases (which having been copied from the very limited grant of power, in the former articles of confederation were the less liable to be misconstrued) so as to destroy the meaning and effect, of the particular enumeration which necessarily explains and limits the general phrases; and so as to consolidate the states by degrees, into one sovereignty, the obvious tendency and inevitable consequence of which would be, to transform the present republican system of the United States, into an absolute, or at best a mixed monarchy.

That the General Assembly doth particularly protest against the palpable and alarming infractions of the Constitution, in the two late cases of the "Alien and Sedition Acts" passed at the last session of Congress; the first of which exercises a power nowhere delegated to the federal government, and which by uniting legislative and judicial powers to those of executive, subverts the general principles of free government; as well as the particular organization, and positive provisions of the federal constitution; and the other of which acts, exercises in like manner, a power not delegated by the constitution, but on the contrary, expressly and positively forbidden by one of the amendments thereto; a power, which more than any other, ought to produce universal alarm, because it is leveled against that right of freely examining public characters and measures, and of free communication among the people thereon, which has ever been justly deemed, the only effectual guardian of every other right. . . .

That the Governor be desired, to transmit a copy of the foregoing Resolutions to the executive authority of each of the other states, with a request that the same may be communicated to the Legislature thereof; and that a copy be furnished to each of the Senators and Representatives representing this state in the Congress of the United States.

9

Rhode Island's Response to the Virginia Resolutions (1799)

The Virginia Resolutions called forth the following response from the state of Rhode Island. The legislature argues, in effect, that the states must rely on the Supreme Court to enforce limited government and that the Virginia theory threatens anarchy. The practical issues posed by the Alien and Sedition Acts were resolved by the election of 1800, in which the Democratic Republicans, led by Thomas Jefferson, took control of the Congress and the presidency. The new Congress repealed the acts, and Jefferson as president pardoned those who had been previously convicted under them. Nevertheless, Madison's compact theory of the Constitution, which seems to presuppose the sovereignty of the states, proved influential in later constitutional controversies. It was invoked by South Carolina when it sought to stop the enforcement of federal tariffs in 1832, and again by it and the other southern States that attempted to secede in 1860 (see reading 13 in this chapter).

Certain resolutions of the Legislature of Virginia, passed on the 21st of December last, being communicated to the Assembly,

1. *Resolved,* That, in the opinion of this legislature, the second section of the third article of the Constitution of the United States, in these words, to wit—"The judicial power shall extend to all cases arising under the laws of the United States"—vests in the Federal Courts, exclusively, and in the Supreme Court of the United States, ultimately, the authority of deciding on the constitutionality of any act or law of the Congress of the United States.

2. *Resolved,* That for any state legislature to assume that authority would be: first, blending together legislative and judicial powers; second, hazarding an interruption of the peace of the states by civil discord, in case of a diversity of opinions among the state legislatures; each state

having, in that case, no resort, for vindicating its own opinions, but the strength of its own arm; third, submitting most important questions of law to less competent tribunals; and, fourth an infraction of the Constitution of the United States, expressed in plain terms.

3. *Resolved,* That, although, for the above reasons, this legislature, in their public capacity, do not feel themselves authorized to consider and decide on the constitutionality of the Sedition and Alien laws, (so called) yet they are called upon, by the exigency of this occasion, to declare that in their private opinions, these laws are within the powers delegated to Congress, and promotive of the welfare of the United States.

4. *Resolved,* That the governor communicate these resolutions to the supreme executive of the state of Virginia, and at the same time express to him that this legislature cannot contemplate, without extreme concern and regret, the many evil and fatal consequences which may flow from the very unwarrantable resolutions aforesaid, of the legislature of Virginia, passed on the twenty-first day of December last.

10

Chief Justice John Marshall: Opinion of the Court in *Marbury* v. *Madison* (1803)

Marshall, the fourth chief justice and probably the most influential, served from 1801 to 1835. This very important case established the Supreme Court's power of judicial review—that is, its authority to rule on the constitutionality of the acts of the other branches of government and of the States. Marshall contends that the Constitution was intended to establish limited government, but that without judicial review it would do so only in theory and not in practice.

The question, whether an act, repugnant to the constitution, can become the law of the land, is a question deeply interesting to the United States; but, happily, not of an intricacy proportioned to its interest. It seems only necessary to recognize certain principles, supposed to have been long and well established, to decide it.

That the people have an original right to establish, for their future government, such principles as, in their opinion, shall most conduce to their own happiness, is the basis on which the whole American fabric has been erected. The exercise of this original right is a very great exertion; nor can it nor ought it to be frequently repeated. The principles, therefore, so established are deemed fundamental. And as the authority, from which they proceed, is supreme, and can seldom act, they are designed to be permanent. This original and supreme will organizes the government, and assigns to different departments their respective powers. It may either stop here; or establish certain limits not to be transcended by those departments.

The government of the United States is of the latter description. The powers of the legislature are defined and limited; and that those limits may not be mistaken or forgotten, the constitution is written. To what purpose are powers limited, and to what purpose is that limitation committed to writing; if these limits may, at any time, be passed by those intended to be restrained? The distinction between a government with limited and unlimited powers is abolished, if those limits do not confine the persons on whom they are imposed, and if acts prohibited and acts allowed are of equal obligation. It is a proposition too plain to be contested, that the constitution controls any legislative act repugnant to it; or, that the legislature may alter the constitution by an ordinary act.

Between these alternatives there is no middle ground. The constitution is either a superior, paramount law, unchangeable by ordinary means, or it is on a level with ordinary legislative acts, and like other acts, is alterable when the legislature shall please to alter it.

If the former part of the alternative be true, then a legislative act contrary to the constitution is not law: if the latter part be true, then written constitutions are absurd attempts, on the part of the people, to limit a power in its own nature illimitable.

Certainly all those who have framed written constitutions contemplate them as forming the fundamental and paramount law of the nation, and consequently the theory of every such government must be, that an act of the legislature repugnant to the constitution is void.

This theory is essentially attached to a written constitution, and is consequently to be considered by this court as one of the fundamental principles of our society. It is not therefore to be lost sight of in the further consideration of this subject.

If an act of the legislature, repugnant to the constitution, is void, does it, notwithstanding its invalidity, bind the courts and oblige them to give it effect? Or, in other words, though it be not law, does it constitute a rule as operative as if it was a law? This would be to overthrow in fact what was established in theory; and would seem, at first view, an absurdity too gross to be insisted on. It shall, however, receive a more attentive consideration.

It is emphatically the province and duty of the judicial department to say what the law is. Those who apply the rule to particular cases, must of necessity expound and interpret that rule. If two laws conflict with each other, the courts must decide on the operation of each. So if a law be in opposition to the constitution: if both the law and the constitution apply to a particular case, so that the court must either decide that case conformably to the law, disregarding the constitution; or conformably to the constitution, disregarding the law: the court must determine which of these conflicting rules governs the case. This is of the very essence of judicial duty.

If then the courts are to regard the constitution; and the constitution is superior to any ordinary act of the legislature; the constitution, and not such ordinary act, must govern the case to which they both apply.

Those then who controvert the principle that the constitution is to be considered, in court, as a paramount law, are reduced to the necessity of maintaining that courts must close their eyes on the constitution, and see only the law.

This doctrine would subvert the very foundation of all written constitutions. It would declare that an act, which, according to the principles and theory of our government, is entirely void, is yet, in practice, completely obligatory. It would declare, that if the legislature shall do what is expressly forbidden, such act, notwithstanding the express prohibition, is in reality effectual. It would be giving to the legislature a practical and real omnipotence with the same breath which professes to restrict their powers within narrow limits. It is prescribing limits, and declaring that those limits may be passed at pleasure.

That it thus reduces to nothing what we have deemed the greatest improvement on political institutions—a written constitution—would of itself be sufficient, in America where written constitutions have been viewed with so much reverence, for rejecting the construction. But the peculiar expressions of the constitution of the United States furnish additional arguments in favor of its rejection.

The judicial power of the United States is extended to all cases arising under the constitution. Could it be the intention of those who gave this power, to say that, in using it, the constitution should not be looked into? That a case arising under the constitution should be decided without examining the instrument under which it arises?

This is too extravagant to be maintained.

In some cases then, the constitution must be looked into by the judges. And if they can open it at all, what part of it are they forbidden to read, or to obey? . . .

11

Chief Justice John Marshall: Opinion of the Court in *McCulloch* v. *Maryland* (1819)

Although Americans in the early republic agreed on the principles of limited government and Federalism, they did not always agree on how they were to be applied in particular circumstances. The following case illustrates an early conflict over the application of those principles.

In 1816 Congress incorporated the Second Bank of the United States. In 1818 the Maryland legislature enacted a tax on all banks operating within the state but not charted by the state government. James McCulloch, the cashier of the Baltimore branch of the Bank of the United States, refused to pay the state's tax, and consequently the State of Maryland brought suit against him in the state's courts to compel payment. The Maryland courts found for the state, and McCulloch appealed to the Supreme Court of the United States.

The case raised two questions: whether the powers of the federal government should be understood to include the power of incorporating a bank, and whether a state could exercise its legitimate powers in such a way as to impede the operations of the federal government. In the Court's opinion here, Chief Justice Marshall argues for a broad interpretation of the powers of the government of the United States and for the supremacy of the laws of the United States over those of the particular state governments.

The first question made in the cause is, has Congress power to incorporate a bank? . . .

This government is acknowledged by all to be one of enumerated powers. The principle, that it can exercise only the powers granted to it, would seem too apparent to have required to be enforced by all those arguments which its enlightened friends, while it was depending before the people, found it necessary to urge. That principle is now universally admitted. But the question respecting the extent of the powers actually granted, is perpetually arising, and will probably continue to arise, as long as our system shall exist. . . .

Among the enumerated powers, we do not find that of establishing a bank or creating a corporation. But there is no phrase in the instrument which, like the articles of confederation, excludes incidental or implied powers; and which requires that every thing granted shall be expressly and minutely described. Even the 10th amendment, which was framed for the purpose of quieting the excessive jealousies which had been excited, omits the word "expressly," and declares only that the powers "not delegated to the United States, nor prohibited to the States, are reserved to the States or to the people;" thus leaving the question, whether the particular power which may become the subject of contest has been delegated to the one government, or prohibited to the other, to depend on a fair construction of the whole instrument. The men who drew and adopted this amendment had experienced the embarrassments resulting from the insertion of this word in the articles of confederation, and probably omitted it to avoid those embarrassments. A constitution, to contain an accurate detail of all the subdivisions of which its great powers will admit, and of all the means by which they may be carried into execution, would partake of the prolixity of a legal code, and could scarcely be embraced by the human mind. It would probably never be understood by the public. Its nature, therefore, requires, that only its great outlines should be marked, its important objects designated, and the minor ingredients which compose those objects be deduced from the nature of the objects themselves. . . .

Although, among the enumerated powers of government, we do not find the word "bank" or "incorporation," we find the great powers to lay and collect taxes; to borrow money; to regulate commerce; to declare and conduct a war; and to raise and support armies and navies. The sword and the purse, all the external relations, and no inconsiderable portion of the industry of the nation, are entrusted to its government. It can never be pretended that these vast powers draw after them others of inferior importance, merely because they are inferior. Such an idea can never be advanced. But it may with great reason be contended, that a government, entrusted with such ample powers, on the due execution of which the happiness and prosperity of the nation so vitally depends, must also be entrusted with ample means for their execution. The power being given, it is the interest of the nation to facilitate its execution. It can never be their interest, and cannot be presumed to have been their intention, to clog and embarrass its execution by withholding the most appropriate means. Throughout this vast republic, from the St. Croix to the Gulf of Mexico, from the Atlantic to the Pacific, revenue is to be collected and expended, armies are to be marched and supported. The exigencies of the nation may require that the treasure raised in the north should be transported to the south, that raised in the east conveyed to the west, or that this order should be reversed. Is that construction of the constitution to be preferred which would render these operations difficult, hazardous, and expensive? Can we adopt that construction, (unless the words imperiously require it,) which would impute to the framers of that instrument, when granting these powers for the public good, the intention of impeding their exercise by withholding a choice of means? If, indeed, such be the mandate of the constitution, we have only to obey; but that instrument does not profess to enumerate the means by which the powers it confers may be executed; nor does it prohibit the creation of a corporation, if the existence of such a being be essential to the beneficial exercise of those powers. It is, then, the subject of fair inquiry, how far such means may be employed. . . .

The constitution of the United States has not left the right of Congress to employ the necessary means, for the execution of the powers conferred on the government, to general reasoning. To its enumeration of powers is added that of making "all laws which shall be necessary and proper, for carrying into execution the foregoing powers, and all other powers vested by this constitution, in the government of the United States, or in any department thereof." . . .

We admit, as all must admit, that the powers of the government are limited, and that its limits are not to be transcended. But we think the sound construction of the constitution must allow to the national legislature that discretion, with respect to the means by which the powers it confers are to be carried into execution, which will enable that body to perform the high duties assigned to it, in the manner most beneficial to the people. Let the end be legitimate, let it be within the scope of the constitution, and all means which are appropriate, which are plainly adapted to that end, which are not prohibited, but consist with the letter and spirit of the constitution, are constitutional. . . .

It being the opinion of the Court, that the act incorporating the bank is constitutional; and that the power of establishing a branch in the State of Maryland might be properly exercised by the bank itself, we proceed to inquire—

. . . Whether the State of Maryland may, without violating the constitution, tax that branch?

That the power of taxation is one of vital importance; that it is retained by the States; that it is not abridged by the grant of a similar power to the government of the Union; that it is to be concurrently exercised by the two governments: are truths which have never been denied. But, such is the paramount character of the constitution, that its capacity to withdraw any subject from the action of even this power, is admitted. The States are expressly forbidden to lay any duties on imports or exports, except what may be absolutely necessary for executing their inspection laws. If the obligation of this prohibition must be conceded—if it may restrain a State from the exercise of its taxing power on imports and exports; the same paramount character would seem to restrain, as it certainly may restrain, a State from such other exercise of this power, as is in its nature incompatible with, and repugnant to, the constitutional laws of the Union. A law, absolutely repugnant to another, as entirely repeals that other as if express terms of repeal were used.

On this ground the counsel for the bank place its claim to be exempted from the power of a State to tax its operations. There is no express provision for the case, but the claim has been sustained on a principle which so entirely pervades the constitution, is so intermixed with the materials which compose it, so interwoven with its web, so blended with its texture, as to be incapable of being separated from it, without rending it into shreds.

This great principle is, that the constitution and the laws made in pursuance thereof are supreme; that they control the constitution and laws of the respective States, and cannot be controlled by them. From this, which may be almost termed an axiom, other propositions are deduced as corollaries, on the truth or error of which, and on their application to this case, the cause has been supposed to depend. These are, 1st. that a power to create implies a power to preserve. 2nd. That a power to destroy, if wielded by a different hand, is hostile to, and incompatible with these powers to create and to preserve. 3rd. That where this repugnancy exists, that authority which is supreme must control, not yield to that over which it is supreme. . . .

That the power to tax involves the power to destroy; that the power to destroy may defeat and render useless the power to create; that there is a plain repugnance, in conferring on one government a power to control the constitutional measures of another, which other, with respect to those very measures, is declared to be supreme over that which exerts the control, are propositions not to be denied. But all inconsistencies are to be reconciled by the magic of the word *confidence*. Taxation, it is said, does not necessarily and unavoidably destroy. To carry it to the excess of destruction would be an abuse, to presume which, would banish that confidence which is essential to all government.

But is this a case of confidence? Would the people of any one State trust those of another with a power to control the most insignificant operations of their State government? We know they would not. Why, then, should we suppose that the people of any one State should be willing to trust those of another with a power to control the operations of a government to which they have confided their most important and most valuable interests? In the legislature of the Union alone, are all represented. The legislature of the Union alone, therefore, can be trusted by the people with the power of controlling measures which concern all, in the confidence that it will not be abused. This, then, is not a case of confidence, and we must consider it as it really is.

If we apply the principle for which the State of Maryland contends, to the constitution generally, we shall find it capable of changing totally the character of that instrument. We shall find it capable of arresting all the measures of the government, and of prostrating it at the foot of the States. The American people have declared their constitution, and the laws made in pursuance thereof, to be supreme; but this principle would transfer the supremacy, in fact, to the States. . . .

The Court has bestowed on this subject its most deliberate consideration. The result is a conviction that the States have no power, by taxation or otherwise, to retard, impede, burden, or in any manner control, the operations of the constitutional laws enacted by Congress to carry into execution the powers vested in the general government. This is, we think, the unavoidable consequence of that supremacy which the constitution has declared.

We are unanimously of opinion, that the law passed by the legislature of Maryland, imposing a tax on the Bank of the United States, is unconstitutional and void.

12

Chief Justice John Marshall: Opinion of the Court in *Barron* v. *Baltimore* (1833)

When actions taken by the city of Baltimore rendered some of his property useless, Barron sued, claiming a violation of the Fifth Amendment, which forbids the taking of private property for public use without just compensation. The Supreme Court, however, ruled against Barron on the argument that the protections found in the Bill of Rights were intended to restrain the federal government only, and not the states. On this early understanding, then, the insistence on limits applied primarily to the federal government, whereas the states were understood to have broad powers to define, at their own discretion, the rights of their citizens. This remained the accepted understanding until after the addition of the Fourteenth Amendment, which, according to later Supreme Court decisions, applied many of the provisions of the Bill of Rights to the states.

The question thus presented is, we think, of great importance, but not of much difficulty. The constitution was ordained and established by the people of the United States for themselves, for their own government, and not for the government of the individual states. Each state established a constitution for itself, and in that constitution, provided such limitations and restrictions on the powers of its particular government, as its judgment dictated. The people of the United States framed such a government for the United States as they supposed best adapted to their situation and best calculated to promote their interests. The powers they conferred on this government were to be exercised by itself; and the limitations on power, if expressed in general terms, are naturally, and, we think, necessarily, applicable to the government created by the instrument. They are limitations of power granted in the instrument itself; not of distinct governments, framed by different persons and for different purposes.

If these propositions be correct, the fifth amendment must be understood as restraining the power of the general government, not as applicable to the states. In their several constitutions, they have imposed such restrictions on their respective governments, as their own wisdom suggested; such as they deemed most proper for themselves. It is a subject on which they judge exclusively, and with which others interfere no further than they are supposed to have a common interest. . . .

Had the people of the several states, or any of them, required changes in their constitutions; had they required additional safeguards to liberty from the apprehended encroachments of their particular governments; the remedy was in their own hands, and could have been applied by themselves. A convention could have been assembled by the discontented state, and the required improvements could have been made by itself. The unwieldy and cumbrous machinery of procuring a recommendation from two-thirds of congress, and the assent of three-fourths of their sister states, could never have occurred to any human being, as a mode of doing that which might be effected by the state itself. Had the framers of these amendments intended them to be limitations on the powers of the state governments, they would have imitated the framers of the original constitution, and have expressed that intention. Had congress engaged in the extraordinary occupation of improving the constitutions of the several states, by affording the people additional protection from the exercise of power by their own governments, in matters which concerned themselves alone, they would have declared this purpose in plain and intelligible language. . . .

In almost every convention by which the constitution was adopted, amendments to guard against the abuse of power were recommended. These amendments demanded security against the apprehended encroachments of the general government—not against those of the local governments. In compliance with a sentiment thus generally expressed, to quiet fears thus extensively entertained, amendments were proposed by the required majority in congress, and adopted by the states. These amendments contain no expression indicating an intention to apply them to the state governments. This court cannot so apply them. We are of opinion, that the provision in the fifth amendment to the constitution, declaring that private property shall not be taken for public use, without just compensation, is intended solely as a limitation on the exercise of power by the government of the United States, and is not applicable to the legislation of the states. We are, therefore, of opinion, that there is no repugnancy between the several acts of the general assembly of Maryland, given in evidence by the defendants at the trial of this cause, in the court of that state, and the constitution of the United States.

13

South Carolina Declaration of the Causes of Secession (1860)

Upon Abraham Lincoln's election to the presidency, the legislature of South Carolina called for a convention to consider the possibility of secession from the Union. Members of the convention, chosen by a popular election, voted unanimously in favor of the Ordinance of Secession on December 20, 1860. On December 24 the convention adopted the following declaration to explain why it thought it was justified in severing the state's ties to the Union. According to South Carolina, the northern states had violated the Constitution by refusing to cooperate in the execution of those provisions intended to protect slave property and by electing a president determined to halt the spread of slavery. The "compact" theory on which the argument is based, according to which each state may enforce the limits imposed by the Constitution by deciding for itself whether they have been violated, is similar to that advanced by Madison in the Virginia Resolutions sixty-two years earlier.

[T]he State of South Carolina having resumed her separate and equal place among nations, deems it due to herself, to the remaining United States of America, and to the nations of the world, that she should declare the immediate causes which have led to this act.

In 1787, Deputies were appointed by the States to revise the articles of Confederation; and on 17th September, 1787, these Deputies recommended, for the adoption of the States, the Articles of Union, known as the Constitution of the United States. . . .

Thus was established by compact between the States, a government with defined objects and powers, limited to the express words of the grant. . . . We hold that the government thus established is subject to the two great principles asserted in the Declaration of Independence; and we hold further, that the mode of its formation subjects it to a third fundamental principle, namely, the law of compact. We maintain that in every compact between two or more parties, the obligation is mutual; that the failure of one of the contracting parties to perform a material part of the agreement, entirely releases the obligation of the other; and that, where no arbiter is provided, each party is remitted to his own judgment to determine the fact of failure, with all its consequences.

In the present case, that fact is established with certainty. We assert that fourteen of the States have deliberately refused for years past to fulfill their constitutional obligations, and we refer to their own statutes for the proof.

The Constitution of the United States, in its fourth Article, provides as follows:

"No person held to service or labor in one State under the laws thereof, escaping into another, shall, in consequence of any law or regulation therein, be discharged from such service or labor, but shall be delivered up, or claim of the party to whom such service or labor may be due."

This stipulation was so material to the compact that without it that compact would not have been made. The greater number of the contracting parties held slaves, and they had preciously evinced their estimate of the value of such a stipulation by making it a condition in the Ordinance for the government of the territory ceded by Virginia, which obligations, and the laws of the General Government, have ceased to effect the objects of the Constitution. The States of Maine, New Hampshire, Vermont, Massachusetts, Connecticut, Rhode Island, New York, Pennsylvania, Illinois, Indiana, Michigan, Wisconsin, and Iowa, have enacted laws which either nullify the acts of Congress, or render useless any attempt to execute them. . . . Thus the constitutional compact has been deliberately broken and disregarded by the non-slaveholding States; and the consequence follows that South Carolina is released from her obligation. . . .

We affirm that these ends for which this Government was instituted have been defeated, and the Government itself has been destructive of them by the action of the non-slaveholding States. Those States have assumed the right of deciding upon the propriety of our domestic institutions; and have denied the rights of property established in fifteen of the states and recognized by the Constitution; they have denounced as sinful the institution of Slavery; they have permitted the open establishment among them of societies, whose avowed object is to disturb the peace of and eloin the property of the citizens of other States. They have encouraged and assisted thousands of our slaves to leave their homes; and those who remain, have been incited by emissaries, books and pictures, to servile insurrection.

For twenty-five years this agitation has been steadily increasing, until it has now secured to its aid the power of the common Government. Observing the *forms* of the Constitution, a sectional party has found within that article establishing the Executive Department, the means of subverting the Constitution itself. A geographical line has been drawn across the Union, all the States north of that line have united in the election of a man to the high office of President of the United States whose opinions and purposes are hostile to Slavery. He is to be entrusted with the administration of the common Government, because he has declared "government cannot endure permanently half slave, half free," and that the public mind must rest in the belief that Slavery is in the course of ultimate extinction. . . .

On the 4th of March next this party will take possession of the Government. It has announced that the South shall be excluded from the common territory, that the Judicial tribunal shall be made sectional, and that a war must be waged against Slavery until it shall cease throughout the United States.

The guarantees of the Constitution will then no longer exist; the equal rights of the States will be lost. The Slaveholding States will no longer have the power of self-government, or self-protection, and the Federal Government will have become their enemy.

Sectional interest and animosity will deepen the irritation; and all hope of remedy is rendered vain, by the fact that the public opinion at the North has invested a great political error with the sanctions of a more erroneous religious belief.

We, therefore, the people of South Carolina, by our delegates in Convention assembled, appealing to the Supreme Judge of the world for the rectitude of our intentions, have solemnly declared that the Union heretofore existing between this State and the other State of North America is dissolved, and that the State of South Carolina has resumed her position among the nations of the world, as a separate and independent state, with full power to levy war, conclude peace, contract alliances, establish commerce, and to do all other acts and things which independent States may of right do.

14

Abraham Lincoln: An Excerpt from the Message to Congress in Special Session (1861)

In this message to Congress Lincoln denies the contention of South Carolina and other states that the Constitution's principles of limited government and Federalism extend so far as to justify secession from the Union. Lincoln argues that the "compact" theory of the "sovereignty" of the states is historically false, and he holds that secession is not so much a principle of limited government as of anarchy or the destruction of government.

It might seem, at first thought, to be of little difference whether the present movement at the South be called "secession" or "rebellion." The movers, however, well understand the difference. At the beginning, they knew they could never raise their treason to any respectable magnitude, by any name which implies violation of law. They knew their people possessed as much of moral sense, as much of devotion to law and order, and as much pride in, and reverence for, the history, and government, of their common country, as any other civilized, and patriotic people. They knew they could make no advancement directly in the teeth of these strong and noble sentiments. Accordingly they commenced by an insidious debauching of the public mind. They invented an ingenious sophism, which, if conceded, was followed by perfectly logical steps, through all the incidents, to the complete destruction of the Union. The sophism itself is, that any state of the Union may, consistently with the national Constitution, and therefore lawfully, and peacefully, withdraw from the Union, without the consent of the Union, or of any other state. The little disguise that the supposed right is to be exercised only for just cause, themselves to be the sole judge of its justice, is too thin to merit any notice.

With rebellion thus sugar-coated, they have been drugging the public mind of their section for more than thirty years; and, until at length, they have brought many good men to a willingness to take up arms against the government the day after some assemblage of men have enacted the farcical pretence of taking their State out of the Union, who could have been brought to no such thing the day before.

This sophism derives much—perhaps the whole—of its currency, from the assumption, that there is some omnipotent, and sacred supremacy, pertaining to a State—to each State of our Federal Union. Our States have neither more, nor less power, than that reserved to them, in the Union, by the Constitution— no one of them ever having been a State out of the Union. The original ones passed into the Union even before they cast off their British colonial dependence; and the new ones each came into the Union directly from a condition of dependence, excepting Texas. And even Texas, in its temporary independence, was never designated a State. The new ones only took the designation of States, on coming into the Union, while that name was first adopted for the old ones, in, and by, the Declaration of Independence. Therein the "United Colonies" were declared to be "Free and Independent States"; but, even then, the object plainly was not to declare their independence of one another, or of the Union; but directly the contrary, as their mutual pledge, and their mutual action, before, at the time, and afterwards, abundantly show. The express plighting of faith, by each and all of the original thirteen, in the Articles of Confederation, two years later, that the Union shall be perpetual, is most conclusive. Having never been States, either in substance, or in name, outside of the Union, whence this magical omnipotence of "State rights," asserting a claim of power to lawfully destroy the Union itself? Much is said about the "sovereignty" of the States; but the word, even, is not in the national Constitution; nor, as is believed, in any of the State constitutions. What is a "sovereignty," in the political sense of the term? Would it be far wrong to define it "A political community, without a political superior"? Tested by this, no one of our States, except Texas, ever was a sovereignty. And even Texas gave up the character on coming into the Union; by which act, she acknowledged the Constitution of the United States, and the laws and treaties of the United States made in pursuance of the Constitution, to be, for her, the supreme law of the land. The States have their status *in* the Union, and they have no other legal status. If they break from this, they can only do so against law, and by revolution. The Union, and not themselves separately, procured their independence, and their liberty. By conquest, or purchase, the Union gave each of them, whatever of independence, and liberty, it has. The Union is older than any of the States; and, in fact, it created them as States. Originally, some dependent colonies made the Union; and, in turn, the Union threw off their old dependence, for them, and made them States, such as they are. Not one of them ever had a State constitution, independent of the Union. Of course, it is not forgotten that all the new States framed their constitutions, before they entered the Union; nevertheless, dependent upon, and preparatory to, coming into the Union. . . .

The seceders insist that our Constitution admits of secession. They have assumed to make a National Constitution of their own, in which, of necessity, they have either discarded, or retained, the right of secession, as they insist, it exists in ours. If they have discarded it, they thereby admit that, on principle, it ought not to be in ours. If they have retained it, by their own construction of ours they show that to be consistent they must secede from one another, whenever they shall find it the easiest way of settling their debts, or effecting any other selfish, or unjust object. The principle itself is one of disintegration, and upon which no government can possibly endure.

If all the States, save one, should assert the power to drive that one out of the Union, it is presumed the whole class of seceder politicians would at once deny the power, and denounce the act as the greatest outrage upon State rights. But suppose that precisely the same act, instead of being called "driving the one out," should be called "the seceding of the others from that one," it would be exactly what the seceders claim to do; unless, indeed, they make the point, that the one, because it is a minority, may rightfully do, what the others, because they are a majority, may not rightfully do. These politicians are subtle, and profound, on the rights of minorities. They are not partial to that power which made the Constitution, and speaks from the preamble, calling itself "We, the People."

15

Justice David Davis: Opinion of the Court in *Ex Parte Milligan* (1866)

During the Civil War President Lincoln authorized military tribunals to try citizens charged with impeding the Union's war efforts. In this case the Supreme Court rejected such proceedings and insisted on strict compliance with the Constitution even in time of war and rebellion. It contended that the government could not constitutionally subject civilians to such tribunals, at least in an area of the country where the civil courts were open.

The controlling question in the case is this: Upon the facts stated in Milligan's petition, and the exhibits filed, had the military commission mentioned in it jurisdiction, legally, to try and sentence him? Milligan, not a resident of one of the rebellious states, or a prisoner of war, but a citizen of Indiana for twenty years past, and never in the military or naval service, is, while at his home, arrested by the military power of the United States, imprisoned, and, on certain criminal charges preferred against him, tried, convicted, and sentenced to be hanged by a military commission, organized under the direction of the military commander of the military district of Indiana. Had this tribunal the legal power and authority to try and punish this man?

No graver question was ever considered by this court, nor one which more nearly concerns the rights of the whole people; for it is the birthright of every American citizen when charged with crime, to be tried and punished according to law. . . .

The Constitution of the United States is a law for rulers and people, equally in war and in peace, and covers with the shield of its protection all classes of men, at all times, and under all circumstances. No doctrine, involving more pernicious consequences, was ever invented by the wit of man than that any of its provisions can be suspended during any of the great exigencies of government. Such a doctrine leads directly to anarchy or despotism, but the theory of necessity on which it is based is false; for the government, within the Constitution, has all the powers granted to it, which are necessary to preserve its existence; as has been happily proved by the result of the great effort to throw off its just authority.

Have any of the rights guaranteed by the Constitution been violated in the case of Milligan? and if so, what are they?

Every trial involves the exercise of judicial power; and from what source did the military commission that tried him derive their authority? Certainly no part of judicial power of the country was conferred on them; because the Constitution expressly vests it "in one supreme court and such inferior courts as the Congress may from time to time ordain and establish," and it is not pretended that the commission was a court ordained and established by Congress. They cannot justify on the mandate of the President; because he is controlled by law, and has his appropriate sphere of duty, which is to execute, not to make, the laws; and there is "no unwritten criminal code to which resort can be had as a source of jurisdiction."

But it is said that the jurisdiction is complete under the "laws and usages of war."

It can serve no useful purpose to inquire what those laws and usages are, whence they originated, where found, and on whom they operate; they can never be applied to citizens in states which have upheld the authority of the government, and where the courts are open and their process unobstructed. This court has judicial knowledge that in Indiana the Federal authority was always unopposed, and its courts always open to hear criminal accusations and redress grievances; and no usage of war could sanction a military trial there for any offence whatever of a citizen in civil life, in nowise connected with the military service. Congress could grant no such power; and to the honor of our national legislature be it said, it has never been provoked by the state of the country even to attempt its exercise. One of the plainest constitutional provisions was, therefore, infringed when Milligan was tried by a court not ordained and established by Congress, and not composed of judges appointed during good behavior. . . .

Another guarantee of freedom was broken when Milligan was denied a trial by jury. The great minds of the country have differed on the correct interpretation to be given to various provisions of the Federal Constitution; and judicial decision has been often invoked to settle their true meaning; but until recently no one ever doubted that the right of trial by jury was fortified in the organic law against the power of attack. It is now assailed; but if ideas can be expressed in words, and language has any meaning, this right—one of the most valuable in a free country—is preserved to every one accused of crime who is not attached to the army, or navy, or militia in actual service. The sixth amendment affirms that "in all criminal prosecutions the accused shall enjoy the right to a speedy and public trial by an impartial jury," language broad enough to embrace all persons and cases; but the fifth, recognizing the necessity of an indictment, or presentment, before any one can be held to answer for high crimes, "excepts cases arising in the land or naval forces, or in the militia, when in actual service, in time of war or public danger;" and the framers of the Constitution, doubtless, meant to limit the right of trial by jury, in the sixth amendment, to those persons who were subject to indictment or presentment in the fifth.

The discipline necessary to the efficiency of the army and navy, required other and swifter modes of trial than are furnished by the common law courts; and, in pursuance of the power conferred by the Constitution, Congress has declared the kinds of trial, and the manner in which they shall be conducted, for offences committed while the party is in the military or naval service. Every one connected with these branches of the public service is amenable to the jurisdiction which Congress has created for their government, and, while thus serving, surrenders his right to be tried by the civil courts. All other persons, citizens of states where the courts are open, if charged with crime, are guaranteed the inestimable privilege of trial by jury. This privilege is a vital principle, underlying the whole administration of criminal justice; it is not held by sufferance, and cannot be frittered away on any plea of state or political necessity. . . .

It is claimed that martial law covers with its broad mantle the proceedings of this military commission. The proposition is this: that in a time of war the commander of an armed force (if in his opinion the exigencies of the country demand it, and of which he is to judge), has the power, within the lines of his military district, to suspend all civil rights and their remedies, and subject citizens as well as soldiers to the rule of his will; and in the exercise of his lawful authority cannot be restrained, except by his superior officer or the President of the United States.

If this position is sound to the extent claimed, then when war exists, foreign or domestic, and the country is subdivided into military departments for mere convenience, the commander of one of them can, if he chooses, within his limits, on the plea of necessity, with the approval of the Executive, substitute military force for and to the exclusion of the laws, and punish all persons, as he thinks right and proper, without fixed or certain rules.

The statement of this proposition shows its importance; for, if true, republican government is a failure, and there is an end of liberty regulated by law. Martial law, established on such a basis, destroys every guarantee of the Constitution, and effectually renders the "military independent of and superior to the civil power"—the attempt to do which by the King of Great Britain was deemed by our fathers such an offence, that they assigned it to the world as one of the causes which impelled them to declare their independence. Civil liberty and this kind of martial law cannot endure together; the antagonism is irreconcilable; and, in the conflict, one or the other must perish. . . .

There are occasions when martial rule can be properly applied. If, in foreign invasion or civil war, the courts are actually closed, and it is impossible to administer criminal justice according to law, then, on the theatre of active military operations, where war really prevails, there is a necessity to furnish a substitute for the civil authority, thus overthrown, to preserve the safety of the army and society; and as no power is left but the military, it is allowed to govern by martial rule until the laws can have their free course. As necessity creates the rule, so it limits its duration; for, if this government is continued after the courts are reinstated, it is a gross usurpation of power. Martial rule can never exist where the courts are open, and in the proper and unobstructed exercise of their jurisdiction. It is also confined to the locality of actual war. Because, during the late Rebellion it could have been enforced in Virginia, where the national authority was overturned and the courts driven out, it does not follow that it should obtain in Indiana, where that authority was never disputed, and justice was always administered.

16

Chief Justice Salmon P. Chase: Concurring Opinion in *Ex Parte Milligan* (1866)

Although the entire Supreme Court agreed in striking down the trial of Milligan by a military tribunal, the Court split on the reasoning supporting the decision. The majority held that such procedures were not authorized by Congress, only ordered by the president, but continued and also held that it would be beyond the constitutional power of Congress to have authorized them. Four members, including the Chief Justice, disagreed. They contended that Congress could have authorized such trials if it had wanted, and they therefore supported a broader understanding of the government's war power than the majority was willing to concede.

[T]he opinion which has just been read . . . asserts not only that the military commission held in Indiana was not authorized by Congress, but that it was not in the power of Congress to authorize it. . . . We cannot agree to this. . . .

We think that Congress had power, though not exercised, to authorize the military commission which was held in Indiana.

We do not think it necessary to discuss at large the grounds of our conclusions. We will briefly indicate some of them.

The Constitution itself provides for military government as well as for civil government. And we do not understand it to be claimed that the civil safeguards of the Constitution have application in cases within the proper sphere of the former.

What, then, is that proper sphere? Congress has power to raise and support armies; to provide and maintain a navy; to make rules for the government and regulation of the land and naval forces; and to provide for governing such part of the militia as may be in the service of the United States.

It is not denied that the power to make rules for the government of the army and navy is a power to provide for trial and punishment by military courts without a jury. It has been so understood and exercised from the adoption of the Constitution to the present time.

Nor, in our judgment, does the fifth, or any other amendment, abridge that power. "Cases arising in the land and naval forces, or in the militia in actual service in time of war or public danger," are expressly excepted from the fifth amendment, "that no person shall be held to answer for a capital or otherwise infamous crime, unless on a presentment or indictment of a grand jury," and it is admitted that the exception applies to the other amendments as well as to the fifth. . . .

We think . . . that the power of Congress, in the government of the land and naval forces and of the militia, is not at all affected by the fifth or any other amendment. It is not necessary to attempt any precise definition of the boundaries of this power. But may it not be said that government includes protection and defense as well as the regulation of internal administration? And is it impossible to imagine cases in which citizens conspiring or attempting the destruction or great injury of the national forces may be subjected by Congress to military trial and punishment in the just exercise of this undoubted constitutional power? Congress is but the agent of the nation, and does not the security of individuals against the abuse of this, as of every other power, depend on the intelligence and virtue of the people, on their zeal for public and private liberty, upon official responsibility secured by law, and upon the frequency of elections, rather than upon doubtful constructions of legislative powers?

But we do not put our opinion, that Congress might authorize such a military commission as was held in Indiana, upon the power to provide for the government of the national forces.

Congress has the power not only to raise and support and govern armies but to declare war. It has, therefore, the power to provide by law for carrying on war. This power necessarily extends to all legislation essential to the prosecution of war with vigor and success, except such as interferes with the command of the forces and the conduct of campaigns. That power and duty belong to the President as commander-in-chief. Both these powers are derived from the Constitution, but neither is defined by that instrument. Their extent must be determined by their nature, and by the principles of our institutions. . . .

We by no means assert that Congress can establish and apply the laws of war where no war has been declared or exists.

Where peace exists the laws of peace must prevail. What we do maintain is, that when the nation is involved in war, and some portions of the country are invaded, and all are exposed to invasion, it is within the power of Congress to determine in what states or district such great and imminent public danger exists as justifies the authorization of military tribunals for the trial of crimes and offences against the discipline or security of the army or against the public safety.

In Indiana, for example, at the time of the arrest of Milligan and his co-conspirators, it is established by the papers in the record, that the state was a military district, was the theatre of military operations, had been actually invaded, and was constantly threatened with invasion. It appears, also, that a powerful secret association, composed of citizens and others, existed within the state, under military organization, conspiring against the draft, and plotting insurrection, the liberation of the prisoners of war at various depots, the seizure of the state and national arsenals, armed cooperation with the enemy, and war against the national government.

We cannot doubt that, in such a time of public danger, Congress had power, under the Constitution, to provide for the organization of a military commission, and for trial by that commission of persons engaged in this conspiracy. The fact that the Federal courts were open was regarded by Congress as a sufficient reason for not exercising the power; but that fact could not deprive Congress of the right to exercise it. Those courts might be open and undisturbed in the execution of their functions, and yet wholly incompetent to avert threatened danger, or to punish, with adequate promptitude and certainty, the guilty conspirators.

In Indiana, the judges and officers of the courts were loyal to the government. But it might have been otherwise. In times of rebellion and civil war it may often happen, indeed, that judges and marshals will be in active sympathy with the rebels, and courts their most efficient allies.

We have confined ourselves to the question of power. It was for Congress to determine the question of expediency. And Congress did determine it. That body did not see fit to authorize trials by military commission in Indiana, but by the strongest implication prohibited them. With that prohibition we are satisfied, and should have remained silent if the answers to the questions certified had been put on that ground, without denial of the existence of a power which we believe to be constitutional and important to the public safety.

DISCUSSION QUESTIONS FOR CHAPTER 6

1. Contrast the positions of "An Old Whig" and James Madison (in reading 3). Is the "necessary and proper" clause essential to an effective government, or does it simply create a state of unlimited powers?

2. Contrast Madison's position (in reading 4) with Robert Yates's (in reading 5). Does the Constitution provide adequately for a system of Federalism, or does it tend to consolidate all power in the hands of the central government?

3. How does the view of Robert Yates (in reading 6) differ from that of Alexander Hamilton (in reading 7)? Is a bill of rights unnecessary and dangerous, or is it required to protect individuals from a powerful national government?

4. Explain the differences between Madison's Virginia resolutions and the argument advanced in Rhode Island's response. Does limited government

require that states be able to resist unconstitutional laws, or does this violate the Constitution and invite anarchy?

5. What is the contribution of Chief Justice John Marshall to the American understanding and practice of limited government? Does limited government require a Supreme Court with the power of judicial review? Is limited government compatible with the understanding that the powers of the federal government are broad and supreme over those of the states? Why did Marshall not think that the Bill of Rights applied to the states?

6. Contrast South Carolina's declaration of secession with Abraham Lincoln's message to Congress. Does American Federalism include a right of states to leave the Union in response to measures they think unconstitutional?

7. Contrast Justice Davis's and Chief Justice Chase's views of the issues in *Ex Parte Milligan*. Does war require the suspension of ordinary constitutional limits on government power over individual rights?

CHAPTER 7

Economic Liberty

1

Gabriel Thomas: An Account of West Jersey and Pennsylvania (1698)

Gabriel Thomas was a resident of Pennsylvania and western New Jersey during the latter part of the seventeenth century. He describes quite clearly what will emerge as a common theme during the colonial era and the years immediately following the American Revolution—America as a great "poor man's" haven. Note especially Gabriel's reference to the availability of land and the religious tolerance that was indicative of Quaker communities.

. . . I must needs say, even the present Encouragements are very great and inviting, for Poor People (both Men and Women) of all kinds, can here get three times the Wages for their Labour they can in England or Wales. . . .

Labouring-Men have commonly here, between 14 and 15 Pounds a Year, and their Meat, Drink, Washing and Lodging; and by the Day their Wages is generally between Eighteen Pence and a Half a Crown, and Diet also; But in Harvest they have usually between Three and Four Shillings each Day, and Diet. The Maid Servants Wages is commonly betwixt Six and Ten Pounds per Annum, with very good Accommodation. And for the Women who get their Livelihood by their own Industry, their Labour is very dear. . . .

Corn and Flesh, and what else serves Man for Drink, Food and [fine clothing], is much cheaper here than in England, or elsewhere; but the chief reason why Wages of Servants of all sorts is much higher here than there, arises from the great Fertility and Produce of the Place; besides, if these large Stipends were refused them, they would quickly set up for themselves, for they can have Provision very cheap, and Land for a very small matter, or next to nothing in comparison of the Purchase of Lands in England; and the Farmers there, can better afford to give that great Wages than the Farmers in England can, for several Reasons very obvious.

As First, their Land costs them (as I said but just now) little or nothing in comparison, of which the Farmers commonly will get twice the encrease of

Corn for every Bushel they sow, that the Farmers in England can from the richest Land they have.

In the Second place, they have constantly good price for their Corn, by reason of the great and quick vent [trade] into Barbadoes and other Islands; through which means Silver is become more plentiful than here in England, considering the Number of People, and that causes a quick Trade for both Corn and Cattle; and that is the reason that Corn differs now from the Price formerly, else it would be at half the Price it was at then; for a Brother of mine (to my own particular knowledge) sold within the compass of one Week, about One Hundred and Twenty fat Beasts, most of them good handsom large Oxen.

Thirdly, They pay no Tithes, and their Taxes are inconsiderable; the Place is free for all Persuasions, in a Sober and Civil way; for the Church of England and the Quakers bear equal Share in the Government. They live Friendly and Well together; there is no Persecution for Religion, nor ever like to be; 'tis this that knocks all Commerce on the Head, together with high Imposts, strict Laws, and cramping Orders. Before I end this Paragraph, I shall add another Reason why Women[']s Wages are so exorbitant; they are not yet very numerous, which makes them stand upon high Terms for their several Services. . . .

Reader, what I have here written, is not a Fiction, Flam, Whim, or any sinister Design, either to impose upon the Ignorant, or Credulous, or to curry Favour with the Rich and Mighty, but in mere Pity and pure Compassion to the Numbers of Poor Labouring Men, Women, and Children in England, half starv'd, visible in their meagre looks, that are continually wandering up and down looking for Employment without finding any, who here need not lie idle a moment, nor want due Encouragement or Reward for their Work, much less Vagabond or Drone it about. Here are no Beggars to be seen (it is a Shame and Disgrace to the State that there are so many in England) nor indeed have any here the least Occasion or Temptation to take up that Scandalous Lazy Life.

Jealousie among Men is here very rare, and Barrenness among Women hardly to be heard of, nor are old Maids to be met with; for all commonly Marry before they are Twenty Years of Age, and seldom any young Married Women but hath a Child in her Belly, or one upon her Lap.

2

John Dickinson: Letter from a Farmer (1767)

A participant in the Constitutional Convention later in his career, Dickinson here argues during the initial stages of colonial reaction to British tax policy that levying duties on goods that Americans were obligated to purchase from Great Britain was a threat to American liberty. Although he argues strongly for American rights, note the measured tone that Dickinson displays throughout, indicative of his enduring reluctance to support a formal break between the colonies and Great Britain.

There is another late act of parliament, which appears to me to be unconstitutional, and as destructive to the liberty of these colonies, as that mentioned in my last letter; that is, the [Townshend Acts] for granting the duties on paper, glass, etc. . . .

Here we may observe an authority *expressly* claimed and exerted to impose duties on these colonies; not for the regulation of trade; not for the preservation or promotion of a mutually beneficial intercourse between the several constituent parts of the empire, heretofore the *sole objects* of parliamentary institutions; *but for the single purpose of levying money upon us.*

This I call an innovation; and a most dangerous innovation. . . .

Here then, my dear countrymen, rouse yourselves, and behold the ruin hanging over your heads. If you ONCE admit, that *Great Britain* may lay duties upon her exportations to us, *for the purpose of levying money on us only,* she then will have nothing to do, but to lay those duties on the articles which she prohibits us to manufacture—and the tragedy of *American* liberty is finished. We have been prohibited from procuring manufactures, in all cases, any where but from *Great Britain* (excepting linens, which we are permitted to import directly from *Ireland*). We have been prohibited, in some cases, from manufacturing for ourselves; and may be prohibited in others. We are therefore exactly in the situation of a city besieged, which is surrounded by the works of the besiegers in every part *but one.* If *that* is closed up, no step can be taken, *but to surrender at discretion.* If *Great Britain* can order us to come to her for necessaries we want, and can order us to pay what taxes she pleases before we take them away, or when we land them here, we are as abject slaves as *France* and *Poland* can show in wooden shoes and with uncombed hair. . . .

From what has been said, I think this uncontrovertible conclusion may be deduced, that when a ruling state obliges a dependent state to take certain commodities from her alone, it is implied in the nature of that obligation; is essentially requisite to give it the least degree of justice; and is inseparably united with it, in order to preserve any share of freedom to the dependent state; *that those commodities should never be loaded with duties,* for the sole purpose of levying money on the dependent state.

Upon the whole, the single question is, whether the parliament can legally impose duties to be paid *by the people of these colonies only,* for the sole purpose of raising a revenue, *on commodities which she obliges us to take from her alone,* or, in other words, whether the parliament can legally take money out of our pockets, without our consent. If they can, our boasted liberty is but

Vox et praeterea nihil.
A sound and nothing else.
A Farmer

3

William Manning: Observations on Shays' Rebellion (1799)

By 1786 a series of economic crises struck the United States as the newly created nation struggled to repay wartime debts with little access to hard currency. In this environment rural Americans were impacted most by the desire for specie and had difficulty satisfying creditors. In the summer of 1786 a Revolutionary War veteran, Daniel Shays, organized a small uprising primarily for the purpose of protesting what he felt was the unfair burden farmers were bearing during the unstable situation. In this reading, part of a larger collection of posthumously published pieces, the relatively unknown William Manning recounts Shays' Rebellion and offers advice throughout to his fellow "laborers." Note especially Manning's connection between participating in the electoral process and preserving one's economic liberty.

. . . At the close of the British war, although our paper money died away and left the people greatly in debt by it, and a great public debt was on us by the war, yet there was a large quantity of hard money among us sufficient for a medium. But for want of the proper regulation of trade and with the prices of labor and produce being higher here than in other countries, our merchants shipped the hard money off, load after load, by the hundred thousand dollars together to Britain for trifling gewgaws and things that were of no service to us, until there was but little left. Taxes were extremely high. Some counties were two or three years behind. And with the prices of labor and produce falling very fast, creditors began calling for old debts and saying that they would not take payment in paper money. Those who had money demanded forty or fifty percent for it. And fee office officers demanded three or four times so much fees as the law allowed them, and were so crowded with business that sometimes it was hard to get any done. Property was selling almost every day by execution for less than half its value. The jails were crowded with debtors. And with the people being ignorant that all their help lay in being fully and fairly represented in the legislature, many small towns neglected to send representatives in order to save the cost—so that the few only were represented at court [that is, the Massachusetts state legislature, known as the General Court], with an aristocratic Bowdoin as governor at their head.

Under all these circumstances, the people were driven to the greatest extremity. Many counties took to conventions remonstrances, and petitions to a court where they were not half represented. But not being heard, and in some instances charged with seditious meetings and intentions, under all these circumstances, some counties were so foolish as to stop the courts of justice by force of arms. This shook the government to its foundation. For instead of fatherly counsels and admonitions, the dog of war let loose upon them, and they were declared in a state of insurrection and rebellion.

In these circumstances, the few were all alive for the support of the government, and all those who would not be continually crying, "Government, Government," or who dared to say a word against their measures, were called Shaysites and rebels threatened with prosecutions, etc. But with a large majority of the people thinking that there was blame on both sides, or viewing one side as knaves and the other as fools, it was with great difficulty and delay before a sufficient number could be raised and sent to suppress those who had closed the courts.

But the suppression was done with the loss of but few lives. This put the people in the most zealous searches after a remedy for their grievances. Thousands and thousands of miles were ridden to consult each other on the affair, and they happily effected it in a few months only by using their privileges as electors. Bowdoin was turned out from being governor and Hancock was almost unanimously elected in his place. Many of the old representatives shared the same fate, and a full representation was from every part of the state, which soon found out means redress the grievances of the people, though they were attended with the most difficult circumstances, so that everything appeared like the clear and pleasant sunshine after a most tremendous storm.

This is a striking demonstration of the advantages of an elective government and shows how a people may run themselves into the greatest difficulties by inattention in elections, and how they can retrieve their circumstances by attending to them again. This Shays affair never would have happened if there had then been such a society as I now propose. Many people then would have sacrificed half their interest to have been possessed of such means of knowledge.

This affair, too, is a striking demonstration of the madness and folly of rising up against a government of our own choice when we have constitutional means of redress in our own hands. For although it was supposed by many that if Hancock had been governor at that time—even after the courts were stopped—that the whole affair might have been settled with less than a thousand dollars cost; yet it was so managed that it cost the state (in time and money) near a million dollars, and it almost entirely ruined hundreds of honest, well-meaning men that only needed the means of knowledge I have described.

Thus, my friends, I have freely given you my opinion of the causes that destroy free governments and of a remedy against them, not in the language and style of the learned (for I am not able), but in as plain a manner as I am capable. And I have done it from a conviction that it was my duty, and for the happiness of mankind. If I have misrepresented anything or used any unbecoming language, it is for the want of knowledge and learning. For I am a true friend to all orders of men and individuals I are friends to true liberty and the rights of man. The remedy I have described is not a costly one, for confident I am that penny laid out in it would soon save pounds in other needless expenses. Therefore, unless you see more difficulty in applying it, or less need of it than I do, you will immediately put it on foot and never give over until such a society is established on such a lasting foundation that the gates of hell will not prevail against it—which may the Almighty grant is the sincere desire of a Laborer.

4

Thomas Jefferson: Notes on the State of Virginia (1784)

Thomas Jefferson was the most visible and outspoken proponent of the "yeoman farmer" ideal, in which independent, vigorous, and virtuous farmers would form the foundation a new and progressive American nation. In the following reading, the author of the Declaration of Independence affirms his affinity for agricultural pursuits and expresses his disdain with merchants, whom he considers "panderers of vice." Jefferson even goes so far as to suggest that manufacturing was so dangerous to public virtue that the United States should consider outsourcing such occupations to foreign nations.

The political economists of Europe have established it as a principle that every state should endeavour to manufacture for itself: and this principle, like many others, we transfer to America, without calculating the difference of circumstance which should often produce a difference of result. In Europe the lands are either cultivated, or locked up against the cultivator. Manufacture must therefore be resorted to of necessity not of choice, to support the surplus of their people. But we have an immensity of land courting the industry of the husbandman. Is it best then that all our citizens should be employed in its improvement, or that one half should be called off from that to exercise manufactures and handicraft arts for the other? Those who labour in the earth are the chosen people of God, if ever he had a chosen people, whose breasts he has made his peculiar deposit for substantial and genuine virtue. It is the focus in which he keeps alive that sacred fire, which otherwise might escape from the face of the earth. Corruption of morals in the mass of cultivators is a phaenomenon of which no age nor nation has furnished an example. It is the mark set on those, who not looking up to heaven, to their own soil and industry, as does the husbandman, for their subsistance, depend for it on the casualties and caprice of customers. Dependance begets subservience and venality, suffocates the germ of virtue, and prepares fit tools for the designs of ambition. This, the natural progress and consequence of the arts, has sometimes perhaps been retarded by accidental circumstances: but, generally speaking, the proportion which the aggregate of the other classes of citizens bears in any state to that of its husbandmen, is the proportion of its unsound to its healthy parts, and is a good-enough barometer whereby to measure its degree of corruption. While we have land to labour then, let us never wish to see our citizens occupied at a work-bench, or twirling a distaff. Carpenters, masons, smiths, are wanting in husbandry: but, for the general operations of manufacture, let our work-shops remain in Europe. It is better to carry provisions and materials to workmen there, than bring them to the provisions and materials, and with them their manners and principles. The loss by the transportation of commodities across the Atlantic will be made up in happiness and permanence of government. The mobs of great cities add just so much to the support of pure government, as sores do to the strength of the human body. It is the manners and spirit of a people which preserve a republic in vigour. A degeneracy in these is a canker which soon eats to the heart of its laws and constitution.

5

Alexander Hamilton: Report on Manufactures (1791)

As the first secretary of treasury, Alexander Hamilton maintained an inordinate impact on the economic direction of the United States during the first decade of the country's existence. Arguably the most modern of the founders in his economic views, Hamilton envisioned an urban, currency-driven economy in direct contrast to the more agrarian ideal proposed by Thomas Jefferson and many other early American leaders. In the following reading, Hamilton argues for the fluid exchange of currency, both private and public, and insists that agricultural and merchant interests are not mutually exclusive but, in fact, complement one another.

... It is not uncommon to meet with an opinion that though the promoting of manufactures may be the interest of a part of the Union, it is contrary to that of another part. The Northern & southern regions are sometimes represented as having adverse interests in this respect. Those are called Manufacturing, these Agricultural states; and a species of opposition is imagined to subsist between the Manufacturing and Agricultural interests.

This idea of an opposition between those two interests is the common error of the early periods of every country, but experience gradually dissipates it. Indeed they are perceived so often to succour and to befriend each other, that they come at length to be considered as one: a supposition which has been frequently abused and is not universally true. Particular encouragements of particular manufactures may be of a Nature to sacrifice the interests of land-holders to those of manufacturers; But it is nevertheless a maxim well established by experience, and generally acknowledged, where there has been sufficient experience, that the *aggregate* prosperity of manufactures, and the *aggregate* prosperity of Agriculture are intimately connected. In the Course of the discussion, which has had place, various weighty considerations have been adduced operating in support of that maxim. Perhaps the superior steadiness of the demand of a domestic market for the surplus produce of the soil is alone a convincing argument of its truth.

Ideas of a contrariety of interests between the Northern and southern regions of the Union, are in the Main as unfounded as they are mischievous. The diversity of Circumstances on which such contrariety is usually predicated, authorises a directly contrary conclusion. Mutual wants constitute one of the strongest links of political connection, and the extent of these bears a natural proportion to the diversity in the means of mutual supply.

Suggestions of an opposite complexion are ever to be deplored, as unfriendly to the steady pursuit of one great common cause, and to the perfect harmony of all the parts.

In proportion as the mind is accustomed to trace the intimate connexion of interest, which subsists between all the parts of a Society united under the *same* government—the infinite variety of channels which serve to Circulate the prosperity of each to and through the rest—in that proportion will it be little apt to be disturbed by solicitudes and Apprehensions which originate in local discriminations. It is a truth as important as it is agreeable, and one to which it is not easy to imagine exceptions, that every thing tending to establish *substantial* and *permanent order*, in the affairs of a Country, to increase the total mass of industry and opulence, is ultimately beneficial to every part of it. On the Credit of this great truth, an acquiescence may safely be accorded, from every quarter, to all institutions & arrangements, which promise a confirmation of public order, and an augmentation of National Resource.

But there are more particular considerations, which serve to fortify the idea, that the encouragement of manufactures is the interest of all parts of the Union. If the Northern and middle states should be the principal scenes of such establishments, they would immediately benefit the more southern, by creating a demand for productions; some of which they have in common with the other states, and others of which are either peculiar to them, or more abundant, or of better quality, than elsewhere.

6

Alexander Hamilton: Remarks on the Constitutionality of the First National Bank of the United States (1791)

The following two pieces refer to the founding of the controversial First National Bank of the United States, which lasted until 1811. The two works also reflect one of the most enduring debates in American politics—broad versus strict interpretations of the Constitution. In the first reading, Hamilton proclaims that effectively governing and protecting a nation requires an active federal government with vast financial resources at its disposal. Jefferson, however, refutes Hamilton's claim based on the "necessary and proper" clause of the Constitution and maintains that Hamilton's vision of a national bank is only "convenient" and not "necessary."

. . . The proposed bank is to consist of an association of persons, for the purpose of creating a joint capital, to be employed chiefly and essentially in loans. So far the object is not only lawful, but it is the mere exercise of a right, which the law allows to every individual. The Bank of New York, which is not incorporated, is an example of such an association. The bill proposed ill addition that the government shall become a joint proprietor in this undertaking, and that it shall permit the bills of the company, payable on demand, to be receivable in its revenues; and stipulates that it shall not grant privileges, similar to those which are to be allowed to this company, to any others. All this is incontrovertibly within the compass of the discretion of the government. The only question is, whether it has a right to incorporate this company, in order to enable it the more effectually to accomplish ends, which are in themselves lawful.

To establish such a right, it remains to show the relation of such an institution to one or more of the specified powers of the government. Accordingly it is affirmed that it has a relation, more or less direct, to the power of collecting taxes, to that of borrowing money, to that of regulating trade between the States, and to those of raising and maintaining fleets and armies. To the two former the relation Nay be said to be immediate; and in the last place it will be argued, that it is clearly within the provision which authorizes the making of all needful rules and regulations concerning the property of the United States, as the same has been practiced upon by the government.

A bank relates to the collection of taxes in two ways indirectly, by increasing the quantity of circulating medium and quickening circulation, which facilitates the means of paying. . . .

A bank has a direct relation to the power of borrowing money, because it is an usual, and in sudden emergencies an essential, instrument in the obtaining of loans to government.

A nation is threatened with a war, large sums are wanted on a sudden to make the requisite preparations. Taxes are laid for the purpose, but it requires tine to obtain the benefit of them. Anticipation is indispensable. If there be a bank the supply can at once be had. If there be none, loans from individuals must be sought. The progress of these is often too slow for the exigency ill some situations they are not practicable at all. Frequently when they are, it is of great consequence to be able to anticipate the product of them by advance from a bank.

The essentiality of such an institution as an instrument of loans is exemplified at this very moment. An Indian expedition is to be prosecuted. The only fund, out of which the money can arise, consistently with the public engagements, is a tax, which only begins to be collected in July next. The preparations, however, are instantly to be made. The money must, therefore, be borrowed and of whom could it be borrowed if there were no public banks? . . .

Can it be believed that a compliance with this proposition would be unconstitutional? Does not this alone evince the contrary? It is a necessary part of a power to borrow, to be able to stipulate the consideration or conditions of a loan. It is efficient as has been remarked elsewhere, that this is not confined to the mere stipulation of a franchise. If it may, and it is not perceived why it may not, then the grant of a corporate capacity may be stipulated as a consideration of the loan. There seems to be nothing unfit or foreign from the nature of the thing in giving individuality, or a corporate capacity to a number of persons, who are willing to lend a sum of money to the government, the better to enable them to do it, and make them an ordinary instrument of loans in future emergencies of the state. But the more general view of the subject is still more satisfactory. The legislative power of borrowing money, and of making all laws necessary and proper for carrying into execution that power, seems obviously competent to the appointment of the organ, through which the abilities and wills of individuals may be roost efficaciously exerted for the accommodation of the government by loans. . . .

7

Thomas Jefferson: Views on the First National Bank of the United States (1791)

. . . I consider the foundation of the Constitution as laid on this ground: That "all powers not delegated to the United States, by the Constitution, nor prohibited by it to the States, are reserved to the States or to the people" [Twelfth Amendment]. To take a single step beyond the boundaries thus specially drawn around the powers of Congress, is to take possession of a boundless field of power, no longer susceptible of any definition.

The incorporation of a bank, and the powers assumed by this bill, have not, in my opinion, been delegated to the United States, by the Constitution. . . .

If has been urged that a bank will give great facility or convenience in the collection of taxes, Suppose this were true: yet the Constitution allows only the means which are "*necessary*," not those which are merely "convenient" for effecting the enumerated powers. If such a latitude of construction be allowed to this phrase as to give any non-enumerated power, it will go to everyone, for there is not one which ingenuity may not torture into a *convenience* in some instance *or other*, to *some one* of so long a list of enumerated powers. It would swallow up all the delegated powers, and reduce the whole to one power, as before observed. Therefore it was that the Constitution restrained them to the *necessary* means, that is to say, to those means without which the grant of power would be nugatory.

But let us examine this convenience and see what it is. The report on this subject . . . states the only *general* convenience to be, the preventing the transportation and re-transportation of money between the States and the treasury, (for I pass over the increase of circulating medium, ascribed to it as a want, and which, according to my ideas of paper money, is clearly a demerit.) Every State will have to pay a sum of tax money into the treasury; and the treasury will have to pay, in every State, a part of the interest on the public debt, and salaries to the officers of government resident in that State. In most of the States there will still be a surplus of tax money to come up to the seat of government for the officers residing there. The payments of interest and salary in each State may he made by treasury orders on the State collector. This will take up the greater part of the money he has collected in his State, and consequently prevent the great mass of it from being drawn out of the State. If there be a balance of commerce in favor of that State against the one in which the government resides, the surplus of taxes will be remitted by the bills of exchange drawn for that commercial balance. And so it must be if there was a bank. But if there be no balance of commerce, either direct or circuitous, all the banks in the world could not bring up the surplus of taxes, but in the form of money. Treasury orders then, and bills of exchange may prevent the displacement of the main mass of the money collected, without the aid of any bank; and where these fail, it cannot be prevented even with that aid.

Perhaps, indeed, bank bills may be a more *convenient* vehicle than treasury orders. But a little *difference* in the degree of *convenience* cannot constitute the necessity, which the Constitution makes the ground for assuming any non-enumerated power.

Besides, the existing banks will, without a doubt, enter into arrangements for lending their agency, and the more favorable, as there will be a competition among them for it; whereas the bill delivers us up bound to the national bank, who are free to refuse all arrangement, but on their own terms, and the public not free, on such refusal, to employ any other bank. That of Philadelphia I believe, now does this business, by their post-notes, which, by an arrangement with the treasury, are paid by any State collector to whom they are presented. This expedient alone suffices to prevent the existence of that *necessity* which may justify the assumption of a non-enumerated power as a means for carrying into effect an enumerated one. The thing may be done, and has been done, and well done, without this assumption, therefore it does not stand on that degree of *necessity*, which can honestly justify it. It may be said that a bank whose bills would have a currency all over the States, would be more convenient than one whose currency is limited to a single State. So it would be still more convenient that there should be a bank, whose bills should have a currency all over the world. But it does not follow from this superior conveniency, that there exists anywhere a power to establish such a bank; or that the world may not go on very well without it.

Can it be thought that the Constitution intended that for a shade or two of *convenience*, more or less, Congress should be authorized to break down the most ancient and fundamental laws of the several States; such as those against Mortmain, the laws of Alienage, the rules of descent, the acts of distribution, the laws of escheat and forfeiture, the laws of monopoly? Nothing but a necessity invincible by any other means, can justify such a prostitution of laws, which constitute the pillars of our whole system of jurisprudence. Will Congress be too strait-laced to carry the Constitution into honest effect, unless they may pass over the foundation-laws of the State government for the slightest convenience of theirs? . . .

8

Andrew Jackson: Veto Message Regarding the Bank of the United States (1832)

Upon unseating John Quincy Adams for the presidency in the 1828 election, Andrew Jackson became a symbol for the democratization of America. He championed rural over urban interests and believed that the best way to ensure liberty for all Americans was to limit the influence of the merchant classes. The rechartering of the Second Bank of the United States became the focal point for heated debate as evidenced by the following two readings. Some, such as Jackson, argued that the bank was a tool for the wealthy and powerful to obtain more money and power, whereas supporters of the bank, such as Massachusetts Senator Daniel Webster, reiterated what Alexander Hamilton had stated forty years before, that although a national bank might technically not be necessary, it was obviously prudent. Note especially Jackson's populist support of American liberty and Webster's response to those concerns. Also, the following two readings again illustrate the fundamental debate on the nature of the Constitution: Is it a document to be interpreted literally or broadly?

. . . A bank of the United States is in many respects convenient for the Government and useful to the people. Entertaining this opinion, and deeply impressed with the belief that some of the powers and privileges possessed by the existing bank are unauthorized by the Constitution, subversive of the rights of the States, and dangerous to the liberties of the people, I felt it my duty at an early period of my Administration to call the attention of Congress to the practicability of organizing an institution combining all its advantages and obviating these objections. I sincerely regret that in the act before me I can perceive none of those modifications of the bank charter which are necessary, in my opinion, to make it compatible with justice, with sound policy, or with the Constitution of our country.

The present corporate body, denominated the president, directors, and company of the Bank of the United States, will have existed at the time this act is intended to take effect twenty years. It enjoys an exclusive privilege of banking under the authority of the General Government, a monopoly of its favor and support, and, as a necessary consequence, almost a monopoly of the foreign and domestic exchange. The powers, privileges, and favors bestowed upon it in the original charter, by increasing the value of the stock far above its par value, operated as a gratuity of many millions to the stockholders. . . .

The modifications of the existing charter proposed by this act are not such, in my view, as make it consistent with the rights of the States or the liberties of the people. The qualification of the right of the bank to hold real estate, the limitation of its power to establish branches, and the power reserved to Congress to forbid the circulation of small notes are restrictions comparatively of little value or importance. All the objectionable principles of the existing corporation, and most of its odious features, are retained without alleviation. . . .

To appreciate the effects which this state of things will produce, we must take a brief review of the operations and present condition of the Bank of the United States. . . . As little stock is held in the West, it is obvious that the debt of the people in that section to the bank is principally a debt to the Eastern and foreign stockholders; that the interest they pay upon it is carried into the Eastern States and into Europe, and that it is a burden upon their industry and a drain of their currency, which no country can bear without inconvenience and occasional distress. . . .

In another of its bearings this provision is fraught with danger. Of the twenty-five directors of this bank five are chosen by the Government and twenty by the citizen stockholders. From all voice in these elections the foreign stockholders are excluded by the charter. In proportion, therefore, as the stock is transferred to foreign holders the extent of suffrage in the choice of directors is curtailed. Already is almost a third of the stock in foreign hands and not represented in elections. It is constantly passing out of the country, and this act will accelerate its departure. The entire control of the institution would necessarily fall into the hands of a few citizen stockholders, and the ease with which the object would be accomplished would be a temptation to designing men to secure that control in their own hands by monopolizing the remaining stock. There is danger that a president and directors would then be able to elect themselves from year to year, and without responsibility or control manage the whole concerns of the bank during the existence of its charter. It is easy to conceive that great evils to our country and its institutions [would] flow from such a concentration of power in the hands of a few men irresponsible to the people.

Is there no danger to our liberty and independence in a bank that in its nature has so little to bind it to our country? . . . Should the stock of the bank principally pass into the hands of the subjects of a foreign country, and we should unfortunately become involved in a war with that country, what would be our condition? Of the course which would be pursued by a bank almost wholly owned by the subjects of a foreign power, and managed by those whose interests, if not affections, would run in the same direction there can be no doubt. All its operations within would be in aid of the hostile fleets and armies without. Controlling our currency, receiving our public moneys, and holding thousands of our citizens in dependence, it would be more formidable and dangerous than the naval and military power of the enemy. . . .

It is to be regretted that the rich and powerful too often bend the acts of government to their selfish purposes. Distinctions in society will always exist under every just government. Equality of talents, of education, or of wealth can not be produced by human institutions. In the full enjoyment of the gifts of Heaven and the fruits of superior industry, economy, and virtue, every man is equally entitled to protection by law; but when the laws undertake to add to these natural and just advantages artificial distinctions, to grant titles, gratuities, and exclusive privileges, to make the rich richer and the potent more powerful, the humble members of society—the farmers, mechanics, and laborers— who have neither the time nor the means of securing like favors to themselves, have a right to complain of the injustice of their Government. There are no necessary evils in government. Its evils exist only in its abuses. If it would confine itself to equal protection, and, as Heaven does its rains, shower its favors alike on the high and the low, the rich and the poor, it would be an unqualified blessing. In the act before me there seems to be a wide and unnecessary departure from these just principles. . . .

Experience should teach us wisdom. Most of the difficulties our Government now encounters and most of the dangers which impend over our Union have sprung from an abandonment of the legitimate objects of Government by our national legislation, and the adoption of such principles as are embodied in this act. Many of our rich men have not been content with equal protection and equal benefits, but have besought us to make them richer by act of Congress. By attempting to gratify their desires we have in the results of our legislation arrayed section against section, interest against interest, and man against man, in a fearful commotion which threatens to shake the foundations of our Union. It is time to pause in our career to review our principles, and if possible revive that devoted patriotism and spirit of compromise which distinguished the sages of the Revolution and the fathers of our Union. If we can not at once, in justice to interests vested under improvident legislation, make our Government what it ought to be, we can at least take a stand against all new grants of monopolies and exclusive privileges, against any prostitution of our Government to the advancement of the few at the expense of the many, and in favor of compromise and gradual reform in our code of laws and system of political economy. . . .

9

Daniel Webster: A Reply to Jackson's Veto (1832)

Before proceeding to the constitutional question, there are some other topics, treated in the message, which ought to be noticed. . . . Now, sir, the truth is, that the powers conferred on the bank are such, and no other, as are usually conferred on similar institutions. They constitute no monopoly, although some of them are, of necessity, and with propriety, exclusive privileges. . . .

Congress passed the bill, not as a bounty or a favor to the present stockholders, not to comply with any demand of right on their part, but to promote great public interest, for great public objects. Every bank must have some stockholders . . . and if the stockholders, whoever they may be, conduct the affairs of the bank prudently, the expectation is always, of course, that they will make it profitable to themselves, as well as useful to the public. If a bank charter is not to be granted because it may be profitable, either in a small or great degree, to the stockholders, no charter can be granted. The objection lies against all banks. . . .

From the commencement of the Government it has been thought desirable to invite, rather than to repel, the introduction of foreign capital. Our stocks have all been open to foreign subscriptions, and the State banks, in like manner, are free to foreign ownership. Whatever State has created a debt, has been willing that foreigners should become purchasers, and desirous of it. . . .

It is easy to say that there is danger to liberty . . . in a bank open to foreign stockholders. . . . But neither reason nor experience proves any such danger. The foreign stockholder cannot be a director. He has no voice even in the choice of directors. His money is placed entirely in the management of the directors appointed by the President and Senate, and by the American stockholders. So far as there is dependence, or influence, either way, it is to the disadvantage of the foreign stockholder. . . .

But if the President thinks lightly of the authority of Congress, in construing the constitution, he thinks still more lightly of the authority of the Supreme Court. He asserts a right of individual judgment on constitutional questions, which is totally inconsistent with any proper administration of the Government, or any regular execution of the laws. Social disorder, entire uncertainty in regard to individual rights and individual duties, the cessation of legal authority, confusion, the dissolution of free Government—all these are the inevitable consequences of the principles adopted by the message, whenever they shall be carried to their full extent. . . .

Hitherto it has been thought that the final decision of constitutional questions belonged to the supreme judicial tribunal. The very nature of free Government, it has been supposed, enjoins this: and our constitution, moreover, has been understood so to provide, clearly and expressly. . . .

[W]hen a law has been passed by Congress, and approved by the President, it is now no longer in the power, either of the same President or his successors, to say whether the law is constitutional or not. He is not at liberty to disregard it; he is not at liberty to feel or to affect "constitutional scruples," and to sit in judgment himself on the validity of a statute of the Government, and to nullify it if he so chooses. After a law has passed through all the requisite forms; after it has received the requisite legislative sanction and the Executive approval, the question of its constitutionality then becomes a judicial question. . . . In the courts, that question may be raised, argued, and adjudged; it can be adjudged nowhere else. . . .

It is to be remembered, sir, that it is the present law, it is the Act of 1816, it is the present charter of the bank, which the President pronounces to be unconstitutional. It is no bank to be created, it is no law proposed to be passed; which he denounces; it is the law now existing, passed by Congress, approved by President Madison, and sanctioned by a solemn judgment of the Supreme Court which he now declares unconstitutional, and which, of course, so far as it may depend on him, cannot be executed. . . .

If these opinions of the President be maintained, there is an end of all law and all judicial authority. Statutes are but recommendations, judgments no more than opinions. Both are equally destitute of binding force. Such a universal power as is now claimed for him, a power of judging over the laws, and over the decisions of the tribunal, is nothing else but pure despotism. If conceded to him, it makes him, at once, what Louis the Fourteenth proclaimed himself to be, when he said, "I am the State. . . ."

If that which Congress has enacted be not the law of the land, then the reign of law has ceased, and the reign of individual opinion has already begun. . . .

10

John Quincy Adams: State of the Union Message (1825)

Elected in 1824 after a heated and controversial campaign, Adams was burdened with charges of corruption and presided over a deeply divided electorate. Nevertheless, as the sixth president of the United States, John Quincy Adams promoted a vigorous national economy based on international trade and internal improvements. Because of his vast experience in international diplomacy before his move to the White House, Adams maintained generally positive views regarding foreign trade and with his New England Puritan background, he also was receptive to the burgeoning market economy that had begun to influence American society. In the following reading, the president outlines various economic developments that had transpired during his first year in office and expresses optimism for the future.

Fellow Citizens of the Senate and of the House of Representatives:
In taking a general survey of the concerns of our beloved country, with reference to subjects interesting to the common welfare, the first sentiment which impresses itself upon the mind is of gratitude to the Omnipotent Disposer of All Good for the continuance of the signal blessings of His providence, and especially for that health which to an unusual extent has prevailed within our borders, and for that abundance which in the vicissitudes of the seasons has been scattered with profusion over our land. Nor ought we less to ascribe to Him the glory that we are permitted to enjoy the bounties of His hand in peace and tranquillity—in peace with all the other nations of the earth, in tranquillity among our selves. There has, indeed, rarely been a period in the history of civilized man in which the general condition of the Christian nations has been marked so extensively by peace and prosperity. . . .

The policy of the United States in their commercial intercourse with other nations has always been of the most liberal character. In the mutual exchange of their respective productions they have abstained altogether from prohibitions; they have interdicted themselves the power of laying taxes upon exports, and when ever they have favored their own shipping by special preferences or exclusive privileges in their own ports it has been only with a view to countervail similar favors and exclusions granted by the nations with whom we have been engaged in traffic to their own people or shipping, and to the disadvantage of ours. . . .

Among the unequivocal indications of our national prosperity is the flourishing state of our finances. The revenues of the present year, from all their principal sources, will exceed the anticipations of the last. The balance in the Treasury on the first of January last was a little short of $2,000,000, exclusive of $2,500,000, being the moiety of the loan of $5,000,000 authorized by the act of 1824-05-26. The receipts into the Treasury from the first of January to the 30th of September, exclusive of the other moiety of the same loan, are estimated at $16,500,000, and it is expected that those of the current quarter will exceed $5,000,000, forming an aggregate of receipts of nearly $22,000,000, independent of the loan. The expenditures of the year will not exceed that sum more than $2,000,000. By those expenditures nearly $8,000,000 of the principal of the public debt that have been discharged. . . .

The purchasers of public lands are among the most useful of our fellow citizens, and since the system of sales for cash alone has been introduced great indulgence has been justly extended to those who had previously purchased upon credit. The debt which had been contracted under the credit sales had become unwieldy, and its extinction was alike advantageous to the purchaser and to the public. Under the system of sales, matured as it has been by experience, and adapted to the exigencies of the times, the lands will continue as they have become, an abundant source of revenue; and when the pledge of them to the public creditor shall have been redeemed by the entire discharge of the national debt, the swelling tide of wealth with which they replenish the common Treasury may be made to reflow in unfailing streams of improvement from the Atlantic to the Pacific Ocean. . . .

The appropriations made by Congress for public works, as well in the construction of fortifications as for purposes of internal improvement, so far as they have been expended, have been faithfully applied. Their progress has been delayed by the want of suitable officers for superintending them. An increase of both the corps of engineers, military and topographical, was recommended by my predecessor at the last session of Congress. The reasons upon which that recommendation was founded subsist in all their force and have acquired additional urgency since that time. The Military Academy at West Point will furnish from the cadets there officers well qualified for carrying this measure into effect.

The Board of Engineers for Internal Improvement, appointed for carrying into execution the act of Congress of 1824-04-30, "to procure the necessary surveys, plans, and estimates on the subject of roads and canals," have been actively engaged in that service from the close of the last session of Congress. They have completed the surveys necessary for ascertaining the practicability of a canal from the Chesapeake Bay to the Ohio River, and are preparing a full report on that subject, which, when completed, will be laid before you. The same observation is to be made with regard to the two other objects of national importance upon which the Board have been occupied, namely, the accomplishment of a national road from this city to New Orleans, and the practicability of uniting the waters of Lake Memphramagog with Connecticut River and the improvement of the navigation of that river. The surveys have been made and are nearly completed. The report may be expected at an early period during the present session of Congress. . . .

The laws relating to the administration of the Patent Office are deserving of much consideration and perhaps susceptible of some improvement. The grant of power to regulate the action of Congress upon this subject has specified both the end to be obtained and the means by which it is to be effected, "to promote the progress of science and useful arts by securing for limited times to authors and inventors the exclusive right to their respective writings and discoveries." If an honest pride might be indulged in the reflection that on the records of that office are already found inventions the usefulness of which has scarcely been transcended in the annals of human ingenuity, would not its exultation be allayed by the inquiry whether the laws have effectively insured to the inventors the reward destined to them by the Constitution—even a limited term of exclusive right to their discoveries? . . .

11

Henry Clay: A Defense of the American System (1832)

One of the most active politicians of his era, Henry Clay was also an ardent supporter of a vibrant American economy, internally capitalistic but sheltered from foreign competition. Initially opposed to a national bank, Clay eventually embraced the concept along with a plethora of infrastructure improvements and protective economic policies. The following reading is from a series of remarks given by Clay over several days before the House of Representatives imploring for higher tariffs to preserve America's economic liberty.

. . . I have now to perform the more pleasing task of exhibiting an imperfect sketch of the existing state of the unparalleled prosperity of the country. On a general survey, we behold cultivation extended, the arts flourishing, the face of the country improved; our people fully and profitably employed, and the public countenance exhibiting tranquility, contentment and happiness. And if we descend into particulars, we have the agreeable contemplation of a people out of debt, land rising slowly in value, but in a secure and salutary degree; a ready though not extravagant market for all the surplus productions of our industry; innumerable flocks and herds browsing and gamboling on ten thousand hills and plains, covered with rich and verdant grasses; our cities expanded, and whole villages springing up, as it were, by enchantment; our exports and imports increased and increasing; our tonnage, foreign and coastwise, swelling and fully occupied; the rivers of our interior animated by the perpetual thunder and lightning of countless steam-boats; the currency sound and abundant; the public debt of two wars nearly redeemed; and, to crown all, the public treasury overflowing, embarrassing Congress, not to find subjects of taxation, but to select the objects which shall be liberated from the impost. If the term of seven years were to be selected, of the greatest prosperity which this people have enjoyed since the establishment of their present constitution, it would be exactly that period of seven years which immediately followed the passage of the tariff of 1824.

This transformation of the condition of the country from gloom and distress to brightness and prosperity, has been mainly the work of American legislation, fostering American industry, instead of allowing it to be controlled by foreign legislation, cherishing foreign industry. The foes of the American System, in 1824, with great boldness and confidence, predicted, 1st. The ruin of the public revenue, and the creation of a necessity to resort to direct taxation. The gentleman from South Carolina (General Hayne), I believe, thought that the tariff of 1824 would operate a reduction of revenue to the large amount of eight millions of dollars. 2d. The destruction of our navigation. 3d. The desolation of commercial cities. And 4th. The augmentation of the price of objects of consumption, and further decline in that of the articles of our exports. Every prediction which they made has failed—utterly failed. Instead of the ruin of the public revenue, with which they then sought to deter us from the adoption of the American System, we are now threatened with its subversion, by the vast amount of the public revenue produced by that system. . . .

If the system of protection be founded on principles erroneous in theory, pernicious in practice—above all if it be unconstitutional, as is alledged, it ought to be forthwith abolished, and not a vestage of it suffered to remain. But, before we sanction this sweeping denunciation, let us look a little at this system, its magnitude, its ramifications, its duration, and the high authorities which have sustained it. We shall see that its foes will have accomplished comparatively nothing, after having achieved their present aim of breaking down our iron-founderies, our woollen, cotton, and hemp manufactories, and our sugar plantations. The destruction of these would, undoubtedly, lead to the sacrifice of immense capital, the ruin of many thousands of our fellow citizens, and incalculable loss to the whole community. But their prostration would not disfigure, nor produce greater effect upon the *whole* system of protection, in all its branches, than the destruction of the beautiful domes upon the capitol would occasion to the magnificent edifice which they surmount. Why, sir, there is scarcely an interest, scarcely a vocation in society, which is not embraced by the beneficence of this system. . . .

When gentlemen have succeeded in their design of an immediate or gradual destruction of the American System, what is their substitute? Free trade? Free trade! The call for free trade is as unavailing as the cry of a spoiled child, in its nurse's arms, for the moon, or the stars that glitter in the firmament of heaven. It never has existed, it never will exist. Trade implies, at least two parties. To be free, it should be fair, equal and reciprocal. But if we throw our ports wide open to the admission of foreign productions, free of all duty, what ports of any other foreign nation shall we find open to the free admission of our surplus produce? We may break down all barriers to free trade on our part, but the work will not be complete until foreign powers shall have removed theirs. There would be freedom on one side, and restrictions, prohibitions and exclusions on the other.

The bolts, and the bars, and the chains of all other nations will remain undisturbed. It is, indeed, possible, that our industry and commerce would accommodate themselves to this unequal and unjust, state of things; for, such is the flexibility of our nature, that it bends itself to all circumstances. The wretched prisoner incarcerated in a jail, after a long time becomes reconciled to his solitude, and regularly notches down the passing days of his confinement.

Gentlemen deceive themselves. It is not free trade that they are recommending to our acceptance. It is in effect, the British colonial system that we are invited to adopt; and, if their policy prevail, it will lead substantially to the recolonization of these States, under the commercial dominion of Great Britain....

Gentlemen are greatly deceived as to the hold which this system has in the affections of the people of the United States. They represent that it is the policy of New England, and that she is most benefitted by it. If there be any part of this Union which has been most steady, most unanimous, and most determined in its support, it is Pennsylvania. Why is not that powerful State attacked? Why pass her over, and aim the blow at New England? New England came reluctantly into the policy. In 1824 a majority of her delegation was opposed to it. From the largest State of New England there was but a solitary vote in favor of the bill. That enterprising people can readily accommodate their industry to any policy, provided it be *settled*. They supposed this was fixed, and they submitted to the decrees of government. And the progress of public opinion has kept pace with the developments of the benefits of the system. Now, all New England, at least in this house (with the exception of one small still voice) is in favor of the system. In 1824 all Maryland was against it; now the majority is for it. Then, Louisiana, with one exception, was opposed to it; now, without any exception, she is in favor of it. The march of public sentiment is to the South. Virginia will be the next convert; and in less than seven years, if there be no obstacles from political causes, or prejudices industriously instilled, the majority of eastern Virginia will be, as the majority of western Virginia now is, in favor of the American System. North Carolina will follow later, but not less certainly. Eastern Tennessee is now in favor of the system. And finally, its doctrines will pervade the whole Union, and the wonder will be, that they ever should have been opposed....

12

John C. Calhoun: Speech Against the Force Bill (1833)

Passed to ensure that South Carolina would adhere to federal tariff policy, the Force Bill was the culmination of the nullification crisis, which erupted specifically after the passage of the Tariff of 1832. On the brink of open rebellion by South Carolina, which claimed that the tariff was "nullified" within its borders, President Jackson and Congress asserted its right to regulate national commerce and control the flow of goods in and out of the United States and ultimately approved the Force Bill, which provided sweeping authority to the federal government for such purposes. The states' rights position supported by those such as John C. Calhoun of South Carolina and the animosity that resulted in the Force Bill foreshadowed future conflicts over slavery that would emerge over the subsequent decades. Here Calhoun, who had recently resigned as Jackson's vice president to accept a Senate seat representing South Carolina, argues that it is the clear right of a state to disregard legislation that is unconstitutional and encroaches on the economic liberty of its citizens.

. . . The people of Carolina believe that the Union is a union of States, and not of individuals; that it was formed by the States, and that the citizens of the several States were bound to it through the acts of their several States; that each State ratified the Constitution for itself, and that it was only by such ratification of a State that any obligation was imposed upon its citizens. Thus believing, it is the opinion of the people of Carolina that it belongs to the State which has imposed the obligation to declare, in the last resort, the extent of this obligation, as far as her citizens are concerned; and this upon the plain principles which exist in all analogous cases of compact between sovereign bodies. On this principle the people of the State, acting in their sovereign capacity in convention, precisely as they did in the adoption of their own and the Federal Constitution, have declared, by the ordinance, that the acts of Congress which imposed duties under the authority to lay imposts, are acts, not for revenue, as intended by the Constitution, but for protection, and therefore null and void. The ordinance thus enacted by the people of the State themselves, acting as a sovereign community, is as obligatory on the citizens of the State as any portion of the Constitution. In prescribing, then, the oath to obey the ordinance, no more was done than to prescribe an oath to obey the Constitution. . . .

It has been further objected that the State has acted precipitately. What! Precipitately! After making a strenuous resistance for twelve years—by discussion here and in the other House of Congress—by essays in all forms—by resolutions, remonstrances, and protests on the part of her legislature—and, finally, by attempting an appeal to the judicial power of the United States? I say attempting, for they have been prevented from bringing the question fairly before the court, and that by an act of that very majority in Congress who now upbraid them for not making that appeal; of that majority who on a motion of one of the Members in the other House from South Carolina, refused to give to the Act of 1828 its true title—that it was a protective, and not a revenue Act. The State has never, it is true, relied upon that tribunal, the Supreme Court, to vindicate its reserved rights; yet they have always considered it as an auxiliary means of defense, of which they would gladly have availed themselves to test the constitutionality of protection, had they not been deprived of the means of doing so by the act of the majority. . . .

If we take from one side a large portion of the proceeds of its labor and give it to the other, the side from which we take must constantly decay, and that to which we give must prosper and increase. Such is the action of the protective system. It exacts from the South a large portion of the proceeds of its industry, which it bestows upon the other sections in the shape of bounties to manufactures, and appropriations in a thousand forms; pensions, improvement of rivers and harbors, roads and canals, and in every shape that wit or ingenuity can devise. Can we, then, be surprised that the principle of monopoly grows, when it is so amply remunerated at the expense of those who support it? And this is the real reason of the fact which we witness, that all acts for protection pass with small minorities, but soon come to be sustained by great and overwhelming majorities. . . .

Having made these remarks, the great question is now presented, Has Congress the right to pass this bill, which I will next proceed to consider. The decision of this question involves an inquiry into the provisions of the bill. What are they? It puts at the disposal of the President the army and navy, and the entire militia of the country; it enables him, at his pleasure, to subject every man in the United States, not exempt from militia duty, to martial law; to call him from his ordinary occupation to the field, and under the penalty of fine and imprisonment, inflicted by a court-martial, to imbrue his hand in his brother's blood. There is no limitation on the power of the sword;—and that over the purse is equally without restraint; for among the extraordinary features of the bill, it contains no appropriation, which, under existing circumstances, is tantamount to an unlimited appropriation. The President may, under its authority, incur any expenditure, and pledge the national faith to meet it. He may create a new national debt, at the very moment of the termination of the former—a debt of millions, to be paid out of the proceeds of the labor of that section of the country whose dearest constitutional rights this bill prostrates! Thus exhibiting the extraordinary spectacle, that the very section of the country which is urging this measure, and carrying the sword of devastation against us, is, at the same time, incurring a new debt, to be paid by those whose rights are violated; while those who violate late them are to receive the benefits in the shape of bounties and expenditures. . . .

Disguise it as you may, the controversy is one between power and liberty; and I tell the gentlemen who are opposed to me that, as strong as may be the love of power on their side, the love of liberty is still stronger on ours. History furnishes many instances of similar struggles, where the love of liberty has prevailed against power under every disadvantage, and among them few more striking than that of our own Revolution; where, as strong as was the parent country, and feeble as were the colonies, yet, under the impulse of liberty and the blessing of God, they gloriously triumphed in the contest. There are, indeed, many and striking analogies between that and the present controversy. They both originated substantially in the same cause with this difference—in the present case the power of taxation is converted into that of regulating industry; in the other, the power of regulating industry, by the regulations of commerce, was attempted to be converted into the power of taxation. Were I to trace the analogy further, we should find that the perversion of the taxing power, in the one case, has given precisely the same control to the northern section over the industry of the southern section of the Union, which the power to regulate commerce gave to Great Britain over the industry of the colonies in the other, and that the very articles in which the colonies were permitted to have a trade, and those in which the mother country had a monopoly, are almost identically the same as those in which the Southern States are permitted to have a free trade by the Act of 1832, and in which the Northern States have, by the same Act, secured a monopoly. The only difference is in the means. In the former, the colonies were permitted to have a free trade with all countries south of Cape Finisterre, a cape in the northern part of Spain; while north of that, the trade of the colonies was prohibited, except through the mother country, by means of her commercial regulations. If we compare the products of the country north and south of Cape Finisterre, we shall find them almost identical with the list of the protected and unprotected articles contained in the act of last year. Nor does the analogy terminate here. The very arguments resorted to at the commencement of the American Revolution, and the measures adopted, and the motives assigned to bring on that contest (to enforce the law), are almost identically the same. . . .

13

The Bylaws for the Philadelphia and California Enterprise Association (1849)

The discovery of gold in California in 1848 sent thousands west in search of a quick fortune and the American dream. The following document includes the bylaws for an organization founded in Philadelphia comprised of a small group of investors who were pooling their resources to maximize success. Aside from the standard outline for operation, note also the religious overtones of the group, which required its members to observe the Sabbath and avoid drunkenness and gambling.

We, the undersigned, Citizens of the United States, being about to leave our homes for California, for the purpose of mining and digging gold, or engaging in other profitable business in that country; for our mutual benefit and protection, having agreed to unite together and form an association, declare the following to be articles, conditions and objects by which we are to be governed and which we bind ourselves to observe and carry out.

1st. The Association shall be called the Philadelphia and California Enterprise Association.

2nd. The Association shall consist of 21 members, who shall subscribe to these articles, and agree to continue in the association one year or more after their arrival in California.

3d. Each member shall contribute to the funds of the Association the sum of $300—$200 of which shall be applied to the payment of passage from the port of Philadelphia to San Francisco in California; the remaining $100 shall be expended for the purchase of provisions, boat, wagon, tent equipage, mining and other necessary implements for the furtherance of the objects of this expedition.

4th. The Officers of this Association shall consist of a President, Secretary, Treasurer, and a Board of Three Directors.

5th. It shall be the duty of the President to preside at all meetings—sign all orders as directed by the Association and drawn on the Treasurer.

6th. It shall be the duty of the Secretary to keep a just and impartial account of the proceedings and affairs of the Association—to receive all moneys, &c. due the Association, paying them over to the Treasurer, and taking his receipt for the same, and to draw all orders on the Treasurer, as directed by the Association.

7th. It shall be the duty of the Treasurer to take charge of all monies and bullion belonging to the Association, subject to the orders drawn by the Secretary and signed by the President. He shall keep a faithful account of all receipts and disbursements, and present a full report of the same at every monthly meeting.

8th. It shall be the duty of the Board of Directors to carry out the views and resolutions of the Association, to audit all accounts, and to call special meetings, which may be done at the written request of five members of the Association.

9th. The term of office shall be three calendar months, but any officer shall be eligible for re-election.

Sect. 2. The officers shall be elected by ballot, a majority of the votes cast, being necessary to a choice.

Sect. 3. The presiding officer shall appoint the judges of the election.

10th. The first election shall be held on the first Saturday in the month after leaving Philadelphia.

11th. At the regular monthly meetings, a dividend shall be declared 5 per cent. of which shall be paid into the funds of the Association to be merged into Stock, and the balance to be paid to the several members of the association individually.

12th. Any member being charged with defrauding the Association, and his guilt being clearly proved upon an impartial trial, shall forfeit all claim to his share in the Association. The member thus charged shall have at least two weeks notice of the pending trial, and shall be furnished with a written copy of the charge so made.

13th. Any member guilty of Drunkenness, Gambling, or other vice or immorality injurious to the interests of this Association, for the first offence shall be reprimanded by the presiding officer, and for any subsequent one, may be expelled by a vote of two thirds of all the members of this Association at a stated meeting—the Association paying him his proportion of the profits up to the time of his expulsion.

14th. In case of the death of a member of the Association all his goods and effects, with the next succeeding dividend and his share in full—as much so as if he had withdrawn from the Association—shall be remitted as he may have directed—or to his nearest relative.

15th. Nine members shall constitute a quorum for the transaction of business.

16th. Any member wishing to withdraw from the Association 12 months or at any time thereafter from the date of our arrival in California, may do so by giving one months notice to the directors previous to the Quarterly Meeting, when he shall receive from the Association the proportion due him of the profits and stock of the Association.

17th. Any member of the Association being sick, shall receive all necessary attention from the physician and the kind and constant attention of one of the members.
Sect. 2. The member being sick shall have the same benefits of the Association as when in health.

18th. The members of this Association shall observe the Sabbath by refraining from all secular business, except it be a work of necessity.

19th. There shall be a regular monthly meeting held on the first Saturday evening in each month for the purpose of declaring dividends and such other business as may be necessary for the Association.

20th. Any alteration or amendment can be made to this Constitution at any regular meeting after the first, and by a vote of two thirds of all the members.

14

Homestead Act (1862)

Arguably the most important law passed for the promotion of economic liberty in the United States, the Homestead Act made available over 250 million acres of land to individuals willing to live and make improvements on claims of up to 160 acres each for the relatively minimal sum of $18. The act allowed for previously dispossessed and impoverished individuals and families to acquire the means necessary to support themselves and gave millions of Americans greater financial opportunities before homesteading was eliminated in the twentieth century.

SEC. 1. Be it enacted by the Senate and House of Representatives of the United States of America in Congress assembled, That any person who is the head of a family, or who has arrived at the age of twenty-one years, and is a citizen of the United States, or who shall have filed his declaration of intention to become such, as required by the naturalization laws of the United States, and who has never borne arms against the United States Government or given aid and comfort to its enemies, shall, from and after the first January, eighteen hundred and sixty-three, be entitled to enter one quarter section or a less quantity of unappropriated public lands, upon which said person may have filed a preemption claim, or which may at the time the application is made, be subject to preemption at one dollar and twenty-five cents, or less, per acre; or eighty acres or less of such unappropriated lands, at two dollars and fifty cents per acre, to be located in a body, in conformity to the legal subdivisions of the public lands, and after the same shall have been surveyed: Provided, That any person owning and residing on land may, under the provisions of this act, enter other land lying contiguous to his or her said land, which shall not, with the land so already owned and occupied, exceed in the aggregate one hundred and sixty acres.

SEC. 2. And be it further enacted, That the person applying for the benefit of this act shall, upon application to the register of the land office in which he or she is about to make such entry, make affidavit before the said register or receiver that he or she is the head of a family, or is twenty-one years or more of age, or shall have performed service in the army or navy of the United States, and that he has never borne arms against the Government of the United States or is given aid and comfort to its enemies, and that such application is made for his or her exclusive use and benefit, and that said entry is made for the purpose of actual settlement and cultivation, and not either directly or indirectly for the use or benefit of any other person or persons whomsoever; and upon filing the said affidavit with the register or receiver, and on payment of ten dollars, he or she shall thereupon be permitted to enter the quantity of land specified: Provided, however, That no certificate shall be given or patent to issued therefor until the expiration of five years from the date of such entry; and if, at the expiration of such time, or at any time within two years thereafter, the person making such entry; or, if he be dead, his widow; or in case of her death, his heirs or devisee; or in case of a widow making such entry, her heirs or devisee, in case of her death; shall prove by two credible witnesses that he, she, or they have resided upon or cultivated the same for the term of five years immediately succeeding the time of filing the affidavit aforesaid, and shall make affidavit that no part of said land has, been alienated, and that he has borne true allegiance to the Government of the United States; then, in such case, he, she, or they, if at that time a citizen of the United States, shall be entitled to a patent, as in other cases provided for by law: And provided, further, That in case of the death of both father and mother, leaving an infant child, or children, under twenty-one years of age, the right and fee shall enure to the benefit of said infant child or children; and the executor, administrator, or guardian may, at any time within two years after the death of the surviving parent, and in accordance with the laws of the State in which such children for the time being have their domicile, sell said land for the benefit of but for no other purpose; and the purchaser shall acquire the absolute title by the purchase, and be entitled to a patent from the United States, on payment of the office fees and sum of money herein specified.

SEC. 3. And be it further enacted, That the register of the land office shall note all such applications on the tract books and plats of his office, and keep a register of all such entries, and make return thereof to the General Land Office, together with the proof upon which they have been founded.

SEC. 4. And be it further enacted, That no lands acquired under the provisions of this act shall in any event become liable to the satisfaction of any debt or debts contracted prior to the issuing of the patent therefore.

SEC. 5. And be it further enacted, That if, at any time after the filing of the affidavit, as required in the second section of this act, and before the expiration of the five years aforesaid, it shall be proven, after due notice to the settler, to the satisfaction of the register of the land office, that the person having filed such affidavit shall have actually changed his or her residence, or abandoned the said land for more than six months at any time, then and in that event the land so entered shall revert to the government.

SEC. 6. And be it further enacted, That no individual shall be permitted to acquire title to more than one quarter section under the provisions of this act; and that the Commissioner of the General Land Office is hereby required to prepare and issue such rules and regulations, consistent with this act, as shall be necessary and proper to carry its provisions into effect; and that the registers and receivers of the several land offices shall be entitled to receive the same compensation for any lands entered under the provisions of this act that they are now entitled to receive when the same quantity of land is entered with money, one half to be paid by the person making the application at the time of so doing, and the other half on the issue of the certificate by the person to whom it may be issued; but this shall not be construed to enlarge the maximum of compensation now prescribed by law for any register or receiver: Provided, That nothing contained in this act shall be so construed as to impair or interfere in any manner whatever with existing preemption rights: And provided, further, That all persons who may have filed their application for a preemption right prior to the passage of this act, shall be entitled to all privileges of this act: Provided, further, That no person who has served, or may hereafter serve, for a period of not less than fourteen days in the army or navy of the United States, either regular or volunteer, under the laws thereof, during the existence of an actual war, domestic or foreign, shall be deprived of the benefits of this act on account of not having attained the age of twenty-one years.

SEC. 7. And be it further enacted, That the fifth section of the act entitled "An act in addition to an act more effectually to provide for the punishment of certain crimes against the United States, and for other purposes," approved the third of March, in the year eighteen hundred and fifty-seven shall extend to all oaths, affirmations, and affidavits, required or authorized by this act.

SEC. 8. And be it further enacted, That nothing in this act shall be so construed as to prevent any person who has availed him or herself of the benefits of the first section of this act, from paying the minimum price, or the price to which the same may have graduated, for the quantity of land so entered at any time before the expiration of the five years, and obtaining a patent therefore from the government, as in other cases provided by law, on making proof of settlement and cultivation as provided by existing laws granting preemption rights.

15

California Anti-Chinese Immigration Law (1862)

By the 1860s, thousands of Asian Americans, most of them Chinese, had entered the United States and had settled in areas along the West Coast. In response to the perceived economic threats against native white workers, the state of California passed a series of measures in the 1850s and 1860s that limited the ability of Chinese immigrants to obtain gainful employment. As indicated here, most of the provisions in the 1862 law—which was soon declared unconstitutional—related to preserving the economic security of white Californians.

The People of the State of California, represented in Senate and Assembly, do enact as follows:

SECTION 1. There is hereby levied on each person, male and female, of the Mongolian race, of the age of eighteen years and upwards, residing in this State, except such as shall, under laws now existing, or which may hereafter be enacted, take out licenses to work in the mines, or to prosecute some kind of business, a monthly capitation tax of two dollars and fifty cents, which tax shall be known as the Chinese Police Tax; provided, That all Mongolians exclusively engaged in the production and manufacture of the following articles shall be exempt from the provisions of this Act, viz: sugar, rice, coffee, tea. . . .

SECTION 4. The Collector shall collect the Chinese police tax, provided for in this Act, from all person refusing to pay such tax, and sell the same at public auction, by giving notice by proclamation one hour previous to such sale; and shall deliver the property, together with a bill of sale thereof, to the person agreeing to pay, and paying, the highest thereof, which delivery and bill of sale shall transfer to such person a good and sufficient title to the property. And after deducing the tax and necessary expenses incurred by reason of such refusal, seizure, and sale of property, the Collector shall return the surplus of the proceeds of the sale, if any, to the person whose property was sold; provided, That should any person, liable to pay the tax imposed in this Act, in any county in this State, escape into any other County, with the intention to evade the payment of such tax, then, and in that event, it shall be lawful for the Collector, when he shall collect Chinese police taxes, as provided for in this section, shall deliver to each of the persons paying such taxes a police tax receipt, with the blanks properly filled; provided, further, That any Mongolian, or Mongolians, may pay the above named tax to the County Treasurer, who is hereby authorized to receipt for the same in the same manner as the Collector. And any Mongolian, so paying said tax to the Treasurer of the County, if paid monthly, shall be entitled to a reduction of twenty percent of said tax. And if paid in advance for the year next ensuing, such Mongolian, or Mongolians, shall be entitled to a reduction of thirty-three and one third percent on said tax. But in all cases where the County Treasurer receipts for said tax yearly in advance, he shall do it by issuing for each month separately; and any Mongolian who shall exhibit a County Treasurer's receipt, as above provided, to the Collector for the month for which said receipt was given. . . .

SECTION 7. Any person or company who shall hire persons liable to pay the Chinese police tax shall be held responsible for the payment of the tax due from each person so hired; and no employer shall be released from this liability on the ground that the employee in indebted to him (the employer), and the Collector may proceed against any such employer in the same manner as he might against the original party owing the taxes. The Collector shall have power to require any person or company believed to be indebted to, or to have any money, gold dust, or property of any kind, belonging to any person liable for police taxes, or in which such person is interested, in his or their possession, or under his or their control, to answer, under oath, as to such indebtedness, or the possession of such money, gold dust, or other property. In case a party is indebted, or has possession or control of any moneys, gold dust, or other property, as aforesaid, of such person liable for police taxes, he may collect from such party the amount of such taxes, and may require the delivery of such money, gold dust, or other property, as aforesaid; and in all cases the receipt of the Collector to said party shall be a complete bar to any demand made against said party, or his legal representatives, for the amounts of money, gold dust, or property, embraced therein.

SECTION 8. The Collector shall receive for his service, in collecting police taxes, twenty percent of all moneys which he shall collect from persons owing such taxes. All of the residue, after deducting the percentage of the Collector, forty percent shall be paid into the County Treasury, for the use of the State, forty percent into the general County Fund, for the use of the County, and the remaining twenty percent into the School Fund, for the benefit of schools within the County; provided, That in counties where the Tax Collector receives a specific salary, he shall not be required to pay the percentage allowed for collecting the police tax into the County Treasury, but shall be allowed to retain the same for his own use and benefit; provided, That where he shall collect the police tax by Deputy, the percentage shall go to the Deputy . . .

DISCUSSION QUESTIONS FOR CHAPTER 7

1. How does the tone of the first two readings differ regarding life in the colonies? What accounts for the stark differences? Why do many Americans, such as Dickinson, begin criticizing the taxation by the British government despite the fact that the American colonies were taxed relatively little in comparison to other colonial holdings?

2. Why was there such animosity between rural and urban interests at the time of the founding and beyond? Why was Jefferson so adamant about maintaining a rural base for the new nation? Why was Hamilton so insistent on cultivating a vibrant urban, business component within American society?

3. Between Jefferson and Hamilton, who presents a stronger argument relating to the constitutionality of the First National Bank? Why was the issue so controversial? How does the debate surrounding the First National Bank relate to the debate on the Second National Bank? What are the similarities and differences between the two events?

4. How did Americans such as John Quincy Adams and Henry Clay view the evolution of the American economy during the nineteenth century? What seems to be the focal point for both? Do you notice any omissions in their observations about the development of the American economy?

5. How does the Force Bill, in the opinion of Calhoun, deprive South Carolinians of their economic liberty? Why did Americans risk their lives and economic future to travel west, either as gold prospectors or homesteaders? What was the main motivation for California in passing the anti-Chinese immigration laws?

Index

A

Academy of Philadelphia, 93–95
Act of 1816, 192
Adams, Abigail, 12
Adams, John
  discussion question, 31
  on natural aristocracy, 8–10
  on political role of religion, 64–65
Adams, John Quincy, 193–195, 207
Adams, Samuel
  on republican government, 120–121, 144
  on virtue, 35–36
Admissions, Yale regulations (1745), 90–93
African Americans
  education rights, 115
  equality goals, 28–30
  suffrage, 140–144, 145
Agriculture
  currency driven economy vs.
    (Hamilton), 184–185
  Homestead Act, 202–204
  opportunities for settlers, 178–179
  Shays' Rebellion, 181–182
  "yeoman farmer" ideal (Jefferson),
    183–184
Alcohol abuse
  address to Temperance Society
    (Lincoln), 47–49
  evils of (Beecher), 45–46
  women suffering from evils of
    (Anthony), 53–54
Alcott, William A., 50–52
Alien and Sedition Acts, 157–158
Alphabet, New England Primer, 95–96
Ambition, 41
American Crisis, The (Paine), 39–40
American Revolution
  consequences and causes of, 119–120
  hereditary succession of officers
    (Franklin), 5–6
  history of (Warren), 76–79
  perseverance and fortitude in, 39–40
  vice of British government and, 36–38
Anger, 33
Anthony, Susan B., 53–55, 61
Anti-Chinese immigration laws,
  204–206, 207
Anti-Federalists
  aristocratic charges of (Bryan), 127–128
  defense against aristocratic charges,
    128–130
  unlimited government charges of, 148
Aristocracy
  Constitution tending toward (Bryan),
    127–128
  against creating American, 6–7
  defense against charges of (Madison),
    128–130
  natural, 8–9, 31
Armies, in free republics, 126–127
Artificial aristocracy, 8–10
Arts, women's, 105
Autobiography (Franklin), 34–35, 66–67
Avarice, 41, 51

B

Bache, Sarah Franklin, 5–6
Baltimore, 165–166
Baltimore, Barron v., 165–166
Banks, national
  First National Bank of the U.S.,
    185–188
  Second National Bank of the U.S.,
    161–165, 189–193
Baptism, slavery and, 2
Baptist Association of Danbury, 75
Barron v. *Baltimore,* 165–166
Beecher, Catharine, 106, 108–110
Beecher, Lyman, 45–47
Bill for Establishing Religious Freedom, 67
Bill of Rights
  argument against, 155–156

argument for, 152–155
in *Barron* v. *Baltimore,* 165–166
Congress ratifying, 155
discussion questions on, 176–177
Fourteenth Amendment and, 165
Birth. *See also* Hereditary succession
artificial aristocracy by, 8–9
attacking notion of equality at (Calhoun),
14–15
Black Code, 30
Boston Gazette, 35–36
Boucher, Jonathan, 119–120, 144
Britain. *See* Great Britain
Brutus 1 (Yates), 124–127, 151–152
Brutus 2 (Yates), 152–155
Bryan, Samuel, 127–128, 144–145
Buel, David, 132–133, 145
Bureaucracy, salaried, 40–41
Burwell, Nathaniel, 104–105
Business rights, 30

C
Calhoun, John C.
on Force Bill, 197–200, 207
on Oregon Bill, 14–15
California, anti-Chinese immigration law,
204–206
Census, slaves and, 11
Centinel 1 (Bryan), 127–128
Channing, William Ellery, 58–61
Chapman, George, 98–99
Charles the First, 155
Chase, Chief Justice Salmon P., 174–176,
177
Chastity, 35, 52–53
Children. *See also* Education
baptism of slave, 2
eliminating child laborers, 110–111
Penn's letter on virtue to his, 32–34
status of mixed blood, 1
training women to teach, 107,
108–110
Christianity. *See* Religion
Cicero, 43
Citizenship, of negroes, 19–20, 30
Civil rights, 118–119, 120–121
Classical thought, 43–44
Clay, Henry, 195–197, 207
Cleanliness, 33–35
Colored State Convention statement,
28–30
*Commentaries on the Constitution of the
United States* (Story), 79–81
Common Sense (Paine), 4–5
"Compact" theory, 167–171

Compulsory education
Compulsory School Attendance Act,
110–111
discussion question, 116
Harper's Weekly article on, 115
Mann on, 111–113
Morill Act and, 113–115
Webster on, 100–101
Confederacy, 150
Congress, Constitution on, 127
Constitution. *See also* First Amendment;
Limited government
Federalist No. 54 (Madison), 10–11
Fifteenth Amendment, 140–144
Fifth Amendment, 165–166
Massachusetts yeomen opposing, 6–7
national banks and, 185–188
on religion clauses (Story), 79–81
on right to vote, 131–132
slavery sentiment at time of, 17
Tenth Amendment, 75–76, 79–81
Continental Congress, 117–118, 144
Craft, William, 115
Currency-driven economy, 184–185

D
Davis, Justice David, 171–174, 177
Declaration of Causes of Secession (South
Carolina), 167–169
Declaration of Independence
attacking notion of equality (Calhoun),
14–15
on equality (Jefferson), 3–4
equality of negroes (Lincoln), 20
inequality of negroes (Douglas), 19–20
republican government and, 117–118
women's rights (Stanton), 26–28
Declaration of Right, 155
Democracy
comparing republics to, 123–124
in large territories, 124–127
Democracy in America (Tocqueville)
defects of universal suffrage, 136–140
equality of sexes, 23–24
religious freedom, 81–83
virtue of self-interest, 56–58
Despotic governments, 21, 100
Dickinson, John, 179–180, 206
Divorce, 27
Dixon, Senator James, 141–142, 145
Douglas, Stephen
discussion questions, 31
inequality of negroes, 19–20
Kansas-Nebraska Act, 21–23
Lincoln debates, 20

E

Economic liberty, 178–207
    anti-Chinese immigration law, 204–206
    British tax policy (Dickinson), 179–180
    bylaws for enterprise, 200–202
    discussion questions, 206–207
    Force Bill (Calhoun), 197–200
    higher tariffs (Clay), 195–197
    Homestead Act, 202–204
    market economy (Hamilton), 184–185
    national bank (Hamilton), 185–187
    national bank (Jackson), 189–191
    national bank (Jefferson), 187–188
    opportunities for settlers (Thomas),
        178–179
    Second National Bank of the U.S.
        (Webster), 191–193
    Shays' Rebellion (Manning), 181–182
    State of the Union message (Adams),
        193–195
    yeoman farmer ideal (Jefferson),
        183–184
Education, 88–116
    African Americans, 30, 115
    benefits of (Rush), 102–104
    compulsory, 110–111
    discussion questions, 115–116
    ending prostitution with, 55
    female (Beecher), 108–110
    female (Jefferson), 104–105
    female (Stanton), 27
    female (Willard), 105–108
    identifying talent (Jefferson), 96–98
    letter to son at Harvard (Shephard),
        88–90
    Morrill Act democratizing, 113–114
    New England Primer alphabet, 95–96
    promoting virtue (Washington), 98–99
    proposals (Franklin), 93–95
    reforming (Webster), 99–101
    as right of all citizens (Mann), 111–113
    Yale College regulations (1745), 90–93
Elections, 10
Equality
    African American rights, 28–31
    Declaration of Independence
        (Jefferson), 3
    democracy not satisfying, 137–138
    discussion questions, 31
    hereditary succession and (Franklin), 5–6
    hereditary succession and (Paine), 4–5
    natural aristocracy and (J. Adams), 9–10
    natural aristocracy and (Jefferson), 8–9
    opposition to aristocracy (Massachusetts
        yeomen), 6–7

    opposition to republican government
        (Boucher), 119–120
    slavery acts passed, 1–2
    slavery and (Calhoun), 14–15
    slavery and (Douglas), 19–20
    slavery and (Lincoln), 20–23
    slavery and three-fifths clause (Madison),
        10–11
    slavery and (Webster), 15–18
    women's rights (Murray), 12–14
    women's rights (Stanton), 26–28
    women's rights (Tocqueville), 23–25
Europe
    principle of self-interest in, 57
    property ownership in, 135–136
    role of sexes in, 24–25
    universal suffrage in, 137
Ex Parte Milligan
    concurring opinion in (Chase),
        174–176
    opinion of court (Davis), 171–174

F

Faction, 121–123
Family, 34
Farewell addresses
    Lincoln, 84
    Washington, 42–43, 73–74
"The Farmer Refuted" (Hamilton),
    118–119
Federalism
    applying principles of, 161–165
    discussion questions on, 176–177
    limited government and, 150–151
Federalist
    No. 10 (Madison), 121–124
    No. 39 (Madison), 128–130, 150–151
    No. 44 (Madison), 148–150
    No. 52 (Madison), 131–132
    No. 54 (Madison), 10–11
    No. 71 (Hamilton), 130–131
    No. 84 (Hamilton), 155–156
Felony, 2
Fifteenth Amendment
    opposing (Dixon), 141–142
    proposing (Stewart), 140–141
    proposing (Warner), 143–144
    terms of, 140
Fifth Amendment
    military tribunals and, 175
    states rights vs. federal rights and,
        165–166
First Amendment
    commentaries on (Story), 79–81
    discussion question, 87

Jefferson on, 75
Washington on, 72–73
First National Bank of the United States
discussion questions, 206
Hamilton on, 185–187
Jefferson on, 187–188
Flattery, 33, 38
Force Bill, 197–200, 207
Foreign trade, 193–195
Fortitude, Revolutionary War, 39–40
Founding Fathers
discussion questions, 31
on slavery (Douglas), 19–20
on virtue (Franklin), 34
Fourteenth Amendment, 165
Franklin, Benjamin
on dangers of a salaried bureaucracy,
40–41
on education, 93–95
letter to Sarah Franklin Bache, 5–6
on political role of religion, 66–67
on satirizing religion, 65–66
on virtue, 34–35
Freedom
Colored State Convention statement,
28–30
notion of (Calhoun), 15
women's rights (Stanton), 26–28
French language, 105
"Friend of Virtue," 52–53
Friendship, 33
Frugality, 33, 35
Fugitive Slave Act, 115

G

Gender equality, 12–14, 23–25
Gerry, Elbridge, 7
Gold, discovery of, 200–202, 207
Government
despotic, 21, 100
limited. See Limited government
republican. See Republican
government
self-government, 21–23
Great Britain. See also American
Revolution
hereditary succession in, 4–5
levying taxes in America, 179–180
loss of morality, 37–38
mimicking educational practices from,
99–101
Parliamentary power in law-making, 148
religion in, 81
Greece, 16, 77
Gunpowder, 8

H

Hamilton, Alexander
on Bill of Rights, 155–156
on economic liberty, 184–187, 206
on influence of public opinion, 130–131
on limited government, 176
on republican government, 118–119,
144
Harper's Weekly: "An Undoubted Right"
(1874), 115
Harvard College, 88–100, 115
Hebrews, 74
Hereditary succession
discussion questions, 31
dislike for (Adams), 10
in monarchy (Paine), 4–5
Revolutionary War officers and
(Franklin), 5–6
History of the Rise, Progress, and Termination of
the American Revolution (Warren), 76–79
Homestead Act, 202–204
Homesteads, for negroes, 30
House of Representatives
Constitution on, 127–128
defending Constitution on (Madison),
129–130
election process of (Tocqueville),
139–140
voting rights (Madison), 131–132
Humility, 35

I

Immigration laws, anti-Chinese, 204–206
"Immutable principles," 42
Improving Female Education (Willard),
105–108
Inaugural Address, Washington, 42
Industry. See also Manufacturing
Franklin on, 35
Penn on, 33
Intemperance, 45–49
Investors, 200–202

J

Jackson, Andrew, 189–193
Jefferson, Thomas
on economic liberty, 206
on education, 96–98, 104–105, 115–116
on equality, 3–4, 31
on First and Tenth Amendments, 75–76
on national bank, 187–188
on "natural aristocracy," 8–9
on religion, 67, 87
repealing Alien and Sedition Acts, 158
slaves kept by, 19

Jefferson, Thomas (*continued*)
on virtue, 43–44
on "yeoman farmer" ideal, 183–184
John, King, 155
Justice
Colored State Convention on, 30
Franklin on, 35
Penn on, 34

K
Kansas-Nebraska Act, 21–23
Kent, Chancellor James
discussion questions, 145
response to (Buel), 134–136
on right to vote and private property, 132–133
Ku Klux Klan, 115

L
Laboring classes, elevating, 58–61
Land ownership. *See* Property
Langdon, Samuel, 36–38
Liberty. *See also* Economic liberty
Declaration of Independence on, 3
extinguishing slavery to preserve (D. Webster), 15–18
government representing citizens', 117–118
of press, 156
speech against Force Bill, 199–200
winning of (Calhoun), 15
Licentiousness, 52–53
Limited government, 146–177
on Alien and Sedition Acts, 157–158
Barron v. Baltimore (Marshall), 165–166
on Bill of Rights (Hamilton), 155–156
on Bill of Rights (Yates), 152–155
discussion questions, 176–177
on Federalism (Madison), 150–151
on inadequate securing of (Yates), 151–152
Marbury v. Madison (Marshall), 159–161
McCulloch v. Maryland (Marshall), 161–165
on military tribunals (Chase), 174–176
on military tribunals (Davis), 171–174
natural human rights and (Locke), 146–147
on necessity of (Madison), 148–150
"Old Whig" letters on, 147–148
on secession (Lincoln), 169–171
on secession (South Carolina), 167–169
on Virginia Resolutions, 158–159
Lincoln, Abraham
on equality, 31

on Kansas-Nebraska Act, 21–23
military tribunals authorized by, 171–174
on religion, 83–87
on secession, 167–171, 177
on slavery, 19–20
on temperance, 47–49
Loans, national banks, 186–187, 188
Locke, John
on Constitution, 80–81
Jefferson borrowing from, 3
on limited government, 146–147
Luxury, 33, 37–38

M
Madison, James
on Alien and Sedition Acts, 157–158
on aristocratic government, 128–130
on equality, 31
on Federalism, 150–151
on limited government, 148–150, 176–177
on religion, 67–70, 87
on republican government, 121–124, 144–145
on slavery, 17–18
on slavery and three-fifths clause, 10–11
on voting rights, 131–132
Madison, Marbury v., 159–161
Magna Charta, 155
Mann, Horace, 111–113
Manning, William, 181–182
Manufacturing
expanding (Hamilton), 184–185
limiting (Jackson), 189
limiting (Jefferson), 183–184
Marbury v. Madison, 159–161
Marriage
advice to his children (Penn), 32–33
equality of sexes in (Anthony), 55–56
role of women in (Alcott), 50–52
women's rights in (Stanton), 27
Marshall, Chief Justice John
Barron v. Baltimore, 165–166
on limited government, 177
Marbury v. Madison, 159–161
McCulloch v. Maryland, 161–165
Martial law, 173–174
Maryland, 161–165
Maryland, McCulloch v., 161–165
Massachusetts Compulsory School Attendance Act (1836), 110–111
McCulloch v. Maryland, 161–165
Memorial and Remonstrance (Madison), 67–70

Memory, 12–13
Men
  equality of sexes (Murray), 12–14
  equality of sexes (Tocqueville), 23–25
  role of women in marriage (Alcott), 50–52
  women banishing licentious, 52–53
  women's rights (Stanton), 27
Military tribunals, 171–176
Miller, Rev. Samuel, 75–76
Milligan, 171–176
Missouri Compromise, 21
"Model of Christian Charity, A" (Winthrop), 62–64
Moderation, 33–35
Monarchies
  Adams on, 9
  education in, 100
  on hereditary succession, 4–5
Money, 33
Montaigne, 57
Morality, 27–28, 35–36
Morrill Act (1862), 113–114
Mother, honoring of, 32
Murray, Judith Sargent, 12–14

N

National Banks. See Banks, national
"Natural aristocracy"
  Adams on, 9–10
  discussion questions, 31
  Jefferson on, 8–9
Nebraska, 21–23
"necessary and proper" clause, 148–150
New England Primer alphabet, 115
New York State Constitutional Convention (1821), 132–133, 134–136
Nobility. See Hereditary succession
Notes on State of Virginia (Jefferson), 96–98

O

"Old Whig, An" 147–148, 176
On the Education of Youth in America (Webster), 99–101
Orange, Prince of, 155
Order, 35
Oregon Bill, 14–15

P

Paine, Thomas
  on equality, 4–5
  on virtue, 39–40, 61
Patents, 195
Patriot view
  Alexander Hamilton, 118–119

Continental Congress, 117–118
  discussion question, 144
Penal laws, Yale College, 92–93
Penn, William, 32–34
Pennsylvania, 93–95, 178–179
Persecution, 81
Perseverance, 39–40
Petition of Right, 155
Philadelphia and California Enterprise Association bylaws, 200–202
Physical education, 108–109
Politeness, 43–44
"poor man's" haven, 178–179
Poverty, 54–56
Power
  Alien and Sedition Acts violating, 157–158
  Bill of Rights and Fifth Amendment, 165–166
  Bill of Rights arguments, 152–156
  Congressional laws and, 147–148
  Federalism and, 150–151
  federal vs. state, 151–152
  Force Bill opposition, 199–200
  limited government "necessary and proper" clause, 148–149
  limiting scope of government, 146–147
  military tribunals and, 171–174
  secession from Union and, 167–171
  Supreme Court, 159–161
  war giving more governmental, 171–176
President of the United States, 127–128, 129
Press, liberty of, 156
Proclamation of Thanksgiving (Lincoln), 85–86
Property
  Homestead Act, 202–204
  for negroes, 30
  slaves considered as, 10–11
  universal suffrage and (Buel), 134–136
  universal suffrage and (Kent), 132–133
Proposals Relating to the Education of Youth in Pennsylvania (Franklin), 93–95
Prostitution
  banishing licentious men, 52–53
  poverty of women leading to, 54–56
Public servants, 40–41
Public works, 194–195

Q

Quakerism, 32–34, 178–179

R

Randolph, Thomas Jefferson, 43–44
Rape, 25

Reason, equality of sexes, 12–13
Religion, 62–87
  Bill for Establishing Religious Freedom, 70–72
  confining to private sphere (Madison), 67–70
  First Amendment and (Jefferson), 75–76
  First Amendment and (Washington), 72–73
  free government and (Warren), 76–79
  free government and (Washington), 73–74
  God's judgment and (Lincoln), 86–87
  Harvard education and, 88–90
  importance of (Winthrop), 62–64
  morality and (Franklin), 66–67
  moral/political usefulness of (J. Adams), 65–66
  moral/political usefulness of (Lincoln), 83–84
  moral/political usefulness of (Tocqueville), 81–83
  New England Primer alphabet and, 95–96
  politics and (Madison), 67
  satirizing (Franklin), 65–66
  slavery and, 2
  solace of (Lincoln), 84–85
  Tenth Amendment and (Jefferson), 75–76
  Tenth Amendment and (Story), 79–81
  tolerance of minority, 74, 178–179
  virtue and (Langdon), 37–38
  women's rights and (Stanton), 27–28
  Yale College regulations, 91–92
Republican government, 117–145
  arguments against (Boucher), 119–120
  as aristocracy (Bryan), 127–128
  as aristocracy (Madison), 128–130
  controlling deficiencies of (Madison), 121–124
  controlling deficiencies of (Yates), 124–127
  discussion questions, 144–145
  education in (Rush), 102–104
  education in (Webster), 100
  founder's commitment to (Hamilton), 118–119
  political justice requiring, 117–118
  public opinion influence in (Hamilton), 130–131
  sound policy and individual rights in (S. Adams), 120–121
  voting rights and Fifteenth Amendment (Dixon), 141–142
  voting rights and Fifteenth Amendment (Stewart), 140–141
  voting rights and Fifteenth Amendment (Warner), 143–144
  voting rights and property ownership (Buel), 134–136
  voting rights and property ownership (Kent), 132–133
  voting rights (Madison), 131–132
  voting rights (Tocqueville), 136–140
Resolution, 35
Revolutionary War. *See* American Revolution
Rhode Island, 158–159, 176–177
Roman commonwealth, 77–78
Rural interests. *See* Agriculture
Rush, Benjamin, 102–104, 116

S
Salaries, bureaucratic, 40–41
Scholastic exercises
  Academy of Philadelphia, 93–95
  Harvard student recommendations, 88–90
  Yale College regulations, 92
Secession
  discussion questions, 177
  Lincoln argues against, 169–171
  S. Carolina declares causes of, 167–169
Second National Bank of the United States
  Jackson on, 189–191
  McCulloch v. Maryland, 161–165
  Webster on, 191–193
Second Treatise of Civil Government (Locke), 146–147
Self-government, 21–23
Self-interest, 56–58, 61
Senate
  Constitution on, 127–128
  defending Constitution on (Madison), 129–130
  election process of (Tocqueville), 139–140
Seneca Falls Declaration (Stanton), 26–28
Sexes. *See* Men; Women's rights
Shays, Daniel, 181–182
Shays' Rebellion, 181–182
Shephard, Thomas, 88–100
Silence, 33, 35
Sincerity, 33, 35
Six Sermons on Intemperance (Beecher), 45–47
Sixth Amendment, 172–173
Slavery
  discussion questions, 31

evils of (Webster), 15–18
Fifteenth Amendment abolishing, 140–141
history of, 16
on inequality of negroes (Douglas), 19–20
Kansas-Nebraska Act and (Lincoln), 21–23
opposing Douglas (Lincoln), 20
Oregon Bill and (Calhoun), 14–15
S. Carolina secession and, 167–169
three-fifths clause and (Madison), 10–11
Virginia House of Burgesses Acts on, 1–2
Social purity speech, (Anthony), 53–55
Society of Cincinnati, 5–6
South Carolina
    African Americans appeal for equality to, 28–30
    causes of secession in, 167–169
    Force Bill opposition of, 197–200
Stanton, Elizabeth Cady, 26–28
State of the Union message (Adams), 193–195
States
    Bill of Rights and power of, 165–166
    federal power vs., 151–152, 161–165
    Fifteenth Amendment and, 141–144
    Force Bill opposed by, 197–200
    limited government and, 177
    opposing Alien and Sedition Acts, 157–158
    secession from Union, 167–171
    Supreme Court vs. power of, 159–161
Stewart, Senator William, 140–141, 145
Stockholders, national bank, 190–192
Story, Justice Joseph, 79–81, 87
Strength, 13–14
Suggestions Respecting Improvements in Education (Beecher), 108–110
Supreme Court
    discussion questions, 177
    establishing power of, 159–161
    state vs. federal power conflict, 161–165

T

Talent, 8–9
Tariffs. *See* Taxation
Taxation
    argument for higher tariffs (Clay), 179–180
    by British (Dickinson), 179–180
    Chinese police tax, 205–206
    discussion questions, 206
    Force Bill opposition, 197–200
    national banks and, 186, 187–188
    slaves and, 10–11

Temperance
    address to Temperance Society (Lincoln), 47–49
    discussion question, 61
    evils of alcohol abuse (Beecher), 45–46
    virtue of (Franklin), 35
    virtue of (Penn), 33
Tenth Annual Report of the Secretary of the Massachusetts State Board of Education (Mann), 111–113
Thanksgiving, Proclamation of (Lincoln), 85–86
Thomas, Gabriel, 178–179
Thought, clear, 59
three-fifths clause, 10–11
Tocqueville, Alexis de
    on defects of universal suffrage, 136–140, 145
    on democracy's need for religion, 81–83, 87
    on equality of sexes, 23–25
    on self-interest as virtue, 56–58, 61
Tories, 119–120, 144
Townshend Acts, 180
Trade
    foreign, 193–195
    free, 196–197
Trials, military tribunals, 171–176

U

Universities, and Morrill Act, 113–115
University of Pennsylvania, 93–95
Urban interests. *See* Manufacturing

V

Vice, governmental, 36–38
Victorian culture
    on education of women, 53–56
    on qualities of virtuous women, 50–52
    on women banishing licentious men, 52–53
View of the Causes and Consequences of the American Revolution, A (Boucher), 119–120
Virginia
    agriculture vs. manufacturing in (Jefferson), 183–184
    education notes to (Jefferson), 96–98
    House of Burgesses on slavery, 1–2
Virginia Resolutions (Madison), 157–159, 176–177
Virtue, 32–61
    discussion questions, 61
    education and (Washington), 99
    education and (Webster), 101

Virtue (*continued*)
intemperance and (Beecher), 45–47
intemperance and (Lincoln), 47–49
laboring classes and (Channing), 58–61
morality and (S. Adams), 35–36
natural aristocracy and, 8–9
productive citizens and (Franklin), 34–35
promoting (Penn), 32–34
public servant salaries and (Franklin), 40–41
religion and (Langdon), 36–38
republican (Jefferson), 43–44
republican (Washington), 42–43
Revolutionary War and (Paine), 39–40
women's rights and (Alcott), 50–52
women's rights and (Anthony), 53–56
women's rights and ("Friend of Virtue"), 52–53
Yale College regulations on, 91–92
Voting rights
African Americans and, 30
Constitution provision for (Madison), 131–132
defect of universal suffrage (Tocqueville), 136–140
discussion questions, 145
Fifteenth Amendment and (Dixon), 141–142
Fifteenth Amendment and (Stewart), 140–141
Fifteenth Amendment and (Warner), 143–144
property qualifications and (Buel), 134–136
property qualifications and (Kent), 132–133
women's rights (Stanton), 27–28
women's rights (Tocqueville), 56

W

War. *See also* American Revolution
constitutionality of military tribunals, 174–176
discussion questions, 177
national banks and, 186
unconstitutionality of military tribunals, 171–174

Warner, Senator Willard, 143–144, 145
Warren, Mercy Otis, 76–79, 87
Washington, George
on education, 98–99
Massachusetts opposing Constitution and, 6–7
on religion, 73–74, 87
on virtue, 42–43, 61
Washington Temperance Society address, 47–49
Wealth
addressing laborers on (Channing), 59–60
artificial aristocracy and (Adams), 8–9
dangers of a salaried bureaucracy (Franklin), 41
virtue and (Langdon), 37–38
women's rights for (Stanton), 27
Webster, Daniel, 15–18, 191–193
Webster, Noah, 99–101, 116, 120–121
Willard, Emma, 105–108
William and Mary College, 96–97
Winthrop, John, 62–64, 87
Women's rights
banishing licentious men, 52–53
education (Anthony), 53–56
education (Beecher), 108–110
education (discussion question), 116
education (Jefferson), 104–105
education (Rush), 103–104
education (Willard), 105–108
equality of sexes (discussion question), 31
equality of sexes (Murray), 12–14
role in marriage (Alcott), 50–52
Seneca Falls Declaration (Stanton), 26–28
Tocqueville on, 23–25
on virtue, 61

Y

Yale College regulations (1745), 90–93, 115
Yates, Robert
on Bill of Rights, 152–155
on limited government, 151–152, 176
on republican government, 124–127, 144
Yeoman farmer ideal, 183–184
Young Wife, The (Alcott), 50–52